BOOMERANG CHAVEZ

BOOMERANG CHAVEZ

The Fraud That Led to Venezuela's Collapse

Emili J. Blasco

Boomerang Chávez. The Fraud That Led to Venezuela's Collapse
First edition, June 2016
© Emili J. Blasco

Original Spanish edition:
Bumerán Chávez. Los fraudes que llevaron al colapso de Venezuela

Translation:
Alexandre Muns
Design of cover and back cover:
Daniela Santamarina
Layout and production:
Angel Luis Fernández Conde
Portrait on back cover:
David Salas

ISBN-13: 978-1533585639
ISBN-10: 1533585636

Washington D.C.

With collaboration of:
Venezuelan American Leadership Council (VALC)

To the incredulous.
At one point or another
we were all unbelievers.

CONTENTS

Ten Chapters of a Deception

I f anything we are discussing is leaked, you will be responsible; you are the only person here". As he uttered these words, Hugo Chávez peered into his assistant's eyes. Leamsy Salazar did not blink. "Of course, *mi comandante*," he replied with a firm voice. Chávez dismissed the matter with a "I hope that will be the case." He knew his young assistant had seen and heard too much, but he was certain that he would understand the warning. Summoned to serve in the Venezuelan president's inner circle shortly after graduating from the Naval Academy, by then Salazar began to realize that the chavista revolution was a great fraud. More years would need to go by—he would hear and see more things—before Salazar was fully convinced. In the end, caught in the middle of internal disputes, he decided to reveal what he knew, and he did so from the place from which he could cause the most harm.

It was Easter 2007 (maybe Easter 2006, Salazar cannot specify) when the junior officer witnessed how Chávez personally negotiated with the leaders of the Revolutionary Armed Forces of Colombia () the purchase of drug shipments and the delivery of weapons and other military equipment from the Venezuelan armed forces with which the FARC could combat the legitimate government in Bogota.

Chávez retreated during the holy days to an estate in Barinas, a Venezuelan state not far from the border with Colombia, accompanied by Rafael Ramírez, Energy minister and president of Petróleos

9

de Venezuela (PDVSA), and Ramón Rodríguez Chacín, former Interior minister and owner of the estate. Ramírez ran the money laundering system through the national oil company; Rodríguez Chacín, who was constantly in touch with the , took care of picking up the guerrilla leaders (the senior commanders: Iván Márquez, Rodrigo Granda, and Rafael Reyes) and returning them to their base, as they did not lodge in the estate. He undertook these trips behind the wheel of a SUV without any escort.

During the first two days, the three Venezuelan leaders and the three Colombian insurgents talked between 8 pm and 4 am. During one of the sessions, Iván Márquez's wife joined the discussion since she also led a guerrilla unit. On the third day, a one-to-one meeting between Chávez and Raúl Reyes took place and lasted until 5:30 am. Leamsy Salazar was ordered to stay away from this meeting. Chávez kept him in his field of vision in case he needed his services, but the assistant was not within hearing distance. During the two prior days, however, Salazar had moved around freely between the attendees, serving water and coffee and monitoring the personal telephones, which they had set aside. He was the only one outside the conspiratorial circle who was permitted to enter and leave the room. He was therefore able to hear many of the orders that Chávez gave:

–"Rafael, buy from the any merchandise they produce, any crops and cattle. Pay them an initial installment of $500 million. We are going to break Uribe's back, to screw him!"

Salazar recalls how Chávez's reference to the president of Colombia, Alvaro Uribe, his neighbor and adversary, was expressed with special delight. It was clear that, in the presence of the assistant, the *comandante* avoided being explicit and all attendees spoke with inferences. What crops did the grow or how many heads of cattle grazed to warrant the payment of such a high sum of money? In fact, they only delivered a few cows, branded with a long mark in the stomach. Salazar knew about this procedure since during his enrolment he had served on the border and had come across the cattle, which were put under the knife in order to insert shipments of cocaine into the diverse cavities of the stomach that a ruminant has; after sowing them up, the animals could be transported without raising any suspicions.

–"Rafael, reach an agreement with *El Pollo*. Given that we are purchasing Russian weapons and dismantling some of our weaponry, we can supply part of it to the ."

As the dealings undertaken with *El Pollo* (*The Chicken*)— General Hugo Carvajal, who headed the Directorate of Military Intelligence (DIM)—were delayed, Chávez himself frequently called him through an encrypted network to relay his orders. The president also used a separate telephone through which he contacted the guerrilla leader Iván Márquez when he was not present.

–"Has everything been delivered? How much is still needed? Supply anything that our comrades ask for," he would tell Carvajal.

The shipments delivered to the included large quantities of Venezuelan uniforms, military boots, computers, photocopy machines, and scanners, among other equipment. They were also supplied with abundant medical products. In fact, General Carvajal was in charge of coordinating the medical assistance at the FARC camps on both sides of the border between Venezuela and Colombia. The doctors were taken to a certain location, from whence they were picked up by guerrillas and driven to their operational camps. Part of Carvajal's activity, as well as the tight bond between the chavista leadership and the FARC, was revealed on March 1, 2008, after an attack by the Colombian armed forces flattened a camp led by the guerrilla commander Raúl Reyes and provided access to his computer. Compromising emails and pictures proved the ties between Chavismo and the FARC. "I am loaded," remarked at the time María Gabriela, Chávez's favorite daughter, who had greeted the guests and had had pictures taken with them during the Barinas meetings. "I assure you that the Colombians saw those pictures. I don't know why they have not made them public," he told Salazar referring to the Colombian authorities.

Leamsy (Ismael spelled backwards) was born in Caracas in 1974. In 1998 he graduated from the Naval Academy and underwent a year of special training in a Marine Infantry battalion at the Punto Fijo naval base. While serving at the post, on a particular day he was urgently ordered to the general command. The country's new president, Hugo Chávez, wanted to select the top graduates of the most recent classes from each branch of the military to make up his honor guard: young military officers who would serve as his personal assistants and guarantors of his safety. Salazar, who was twenty-five years old at the time, was chosen. He served Chávez for a couple of years until the events of 2002 that overthrew him from the presidency for a few days. While Chávez retook power, Salazar was caught on camera waving the Venezuelan flag from the top of the Palacio de Miraflores, the presidential palace—an action that the president later publicly praised.

Devoted to special operations, in 2006 Salazar took part in a military exercise witnessed by the president. His skill and courage—he parachuted from a helicopter onto Lake Maracaibo to install an explosive—caught Chávez's attention. When Chávez shook Salazar's hand and congratulated him, he recognized him and asked the minister of defense to assign him again to the Miraflores Palace as head of the security detail during trips, in addition to serving as an assistant. After Chávez's death, Salazar was chosen by Diosdado Cabello, the president of the National Assembly and Chavismo's deputy leader, to perform the same tasks.

Besides incriminating Chávez in the organization of a narco-state, Salazar's testimony in the United States singled out Cabello as the leading operative of the drug trade and the regime's illegal business transactions. During his service for his new boss, he witnessed operations that ultimately convinced him about the criminal nature of the chavista leadership.

On a Friday in 2013, at about 10 pm, Cabello instructed Salazar to organize a speedy trip to the Paraguaná Peninsula, a salient that projects into the Caribbean and is Venezuela's northernmost territory. Lansford José Castillo, Cabello's closest advisor, was also on the flight. After the Falcon aircraft landed in Punto Fijo, the three got into an awaiting car and the chavista leader got behind the wheel. Two security vehicles accompanied them. During the drive, Cabello spoke several times on the phone with General Hugo Carvajal, director of military intelligence, but he did so warily and through short conversations.

–"*Chicken*, what's up? Hold on, I am on my way there."

It was apparent that the president of the National Assembly did not want Salazar to hear him. The young bodyguard thought that the conversation dealt with a national security matter. But as time went by, his puzzlement increased. When they reached Piedras Negras—they had driven across the peninsula from west to east and were getting on the coastal road towards Cape San Román—, Cabello told Salazar to instruct the security personnel in the other two cars to stop there. Cabello and his assistants drove on to the cape, on the northernmost point. On the other side of the sea, fifteen miles away, the lights of the Dutch island of Aruba were visible. It was already midnight. Several men on the beach with head masks and equipped with shotguns allowed the vehicle to proceed. The car stopped after spotting four powerful speedboats. *The Chicken* was next to them. Cabello got off the car and gave the final go-ahead.

–"Are the *hallacas* ready? Get the speedboats going, one after the other."

It was obvious that the cargo was not *hallacas*, which is a traditional Venezuelan dish (flour dough filled with corn flour stuffed with stew and wrapped in a rectangular shape in plantain leaves), but this was the term they used during the operations to refer to the drug packages in order to deceive. The speedboats and their cargo of several tones of cocaine set sail immediately, commanded by operators with night vision equipment. The men on the beach did not apparently belong to the military as their uniforms had no emblems; they appeared to have been deployed by a drug mafia, with which—there was no doubt—the highest echelons of state power were coordinating.

On the drive back to the airport, Cabello tried to confuse Salazar, who was drawing his own conclusions. "Now we are really going to screw the opposition leaders!" he burst out, suggesting that the drug shipment was being carried out in order to uncover it officially and blame it on the political opposition. Although he tried to pretend on several occasions, at other times Cabello added more alarming facts about his illegal business dealings. At a particular point in time, he told the passenger seated next to him:

–"Castillo, look, this week be alert because *The Chicken* is going to send cash in one of those trucks. It should stop at Tareck's place, and he should keep his share. Then the truck should proceed to the office. You must be there to greet it."

Five days later a truck from the National Integrated Service of the Customs and Tax Management (SENIAT) arrived at Fuerte Tiuna, Caracas' biggest military installation, where Cabello had a house converted into office, apart from the one he had in the National Assembly. According to the instructions that had been relayed, the convoy should have earlier stopped by the office of Tareck el Aissami, governor of Aragua and former Interior and Justice minister. The president of the SENIAT at the time was José David Cabello, Diosdado's brother. As we shall explain later, both brothers were deeply involved in the chavista corruption.

Leamsy Salazar was putting on new clothes in order to go home after finishing his work when the unloading of the truck's cargo began. He saw the back doors open and the interior of the vehicle filled with suitcases, all of which were alike and were locked. He mustered the courage to investigate and ascertained that one of the suitcases had been carried to one of the house's rooms and been opened. It contained stacks of one hundred dollar bills. Although they were wrapped in plastic film, they smelled like new bills. The money was to be inserted into a large safe measuring ten feet by thirteen and five feet deep. It appeared to be cash for daily use. In fact, Cabello instructed that everything be paid in cash. When they did not do so, according to Salazar's testimony, they were services paid by the SENIAT, such as the cost of hotels and all of the travel and security logistics.

Despite the large size of the safe in Cabello's office, it could not store all of the stacks of bills that filled the suitcases which had arrived. Moreover, Salazar recalled having seen on at least two other occasions the arrival of a truck from the customs and tax agency, whose real cargo he had not imagined at the time. Where was the rest of the money going? It did not take him long to find out the answer.

Diosdado Cabello likes to go hunting. In one of these excursions, Leamsy Salazar witnessed something strange. It happened on a farm that extends between Barinas and Apure states. At nightfall the group of four people started walking through the countryside, lighting their way by flashlight. After a while, Cabello ordered Salazar to stay behind, while he, his brother José David, and his direct assistant, Lansford Castillo, kept walking. After few hundred yards, the three men stopped. The flashlights were suddenly turned off. A few minutes later, the flashlights beamed again and Cabello shouted from a distance that they were going on a hunt.

After they disappeared, Salazar made his way to the spot where Cabello, his brother, and Castillo had earlier stopped and stood. He rummaged the ground by beaming his flashlight and discovered a large hatch. After he opened it, it led him to a ladder that descended to an underground area. He found a switch near the entrance and turned it on. Before him lay a large bunker, about thirty-three feet in length and sixteen feet in width. Piles of cash were stacked up from wall to wall. Salazar told one of his colleagues in the security team about his discovery and he replied that he had found two additional bunkers owned by Cabello, which also had electrical lighting and a dehumidifier. One was located in the state of Monagas and the other in Ciudad Bolívar. "I saw big mounds of cash there," confided Salazar's colleague, stunned by the money caches. When his colleague was later unfairly charged of committing several crimes, Salazar realized that he had to flee as the situation was taking a turn for the worse.

In the first half of 2014 he had a run-in with Cabello. He was accused of having stolen $120,000 from a safe. When the bodyguard presented graphic evidence that the theft had been the work of a Cabello's lover (the soap opera actress Gigi Zanchetta), the boss reacted lividly, as offended that the affair was being attributed to him, suspended Salazar without pay and mandated that he attend a course of no interest to him. Fearing a bigger reprisal—and probably as an act of revenge—in the fall 2014 Captain Salazar reached out to the United States' Drug Enforcement Administration (DEA), with whom he met on a trip to the Bahamas. In preparation of his escape, he married Captain Anabel Linares, a high-ranking official in the Ministry of Finance, on Margarita Island. When the couple left Venezuela their absence did not raise any suspicion, as they were going on their honeymoon. But as the days went by, alarms were raised. The pilot of the private plane that had taken them to the Dominican Republic was violently interrogated until Cabello extracted the data he needed about the flight. Salazar's plan was to flee to Colombia and await a visa to enter the United States. But in order to avoid a possible extradition, he traveled with his wife to Madrid, where they arrived shortly before Christmas.

I met him a few days later, on January 6, 2015, the festivity of the Epiphany. I was not able to eat the renowned *roscón*, a dessert which in Spain crowns the midday meal on this special holiday, since the meeting took place at lunch time. I did not know where he was lodging until I took a cab and had to provide an address. We met at a bar. Leamsy Salazar looked around nervously to ensure that he was not being overheard. He told me everything I have already put down in writing, as well as other disclosures I will reveal later on. On January

26 he arrived in Washington, D.C., and in March he testified in the case brought by the U.S. Attorney's Office of the Southern District of New York against Diosdado Cabello: the indictment of Cabello as the manager of the drug trafficking and corruption empire built by Hugo Chávez and endorsed by Nicolás Maduro was presumably already a fact, although it still required the final go ahead from the White House. If politically approved, it would probably remain secret for some time.

These first pages are like the stairs that lead to the mysterious bunker in the remote estate located in the plains of Venezuela. The reader has opened the hatch and begun to walk down the ladder's steps. We have just turned the light on and what we see is unforgivable.

BOOMERANG CHAVEZ

Introduction

They lifted their helmets and furiously struck them against the head and body of the detainee. Wounded by pellets shot at point-blank range, the young man was lying on the floor and pinned down by three national guards. They were beating him up with the rifle butts and the helmets of their anti-riot gear. Close to losing consciousness, Willie David only heard the repetition of a sentence: who is your president?

Nicolás Maduro's legitimacy as president was the focal point of the massive protests that rocked Venezuela in February 2014, less than a year after the burial of Hugo Chávez. Hundreds of thousands of Venezuelans took then to the streets. Popular rejection of the chavista regime prompted a strong vote of protest against the government in the parliamentary elections held in December 2015. The population's discontent with Maduro's presidency was a result of the scarcity of food and medicine, the long lines in stores, the rolling power outages, the unbearable insecurity—Caracas had already been branded the world's most dangerous city—and a runaway inflation that each year was beating its own world record.

Whether it was verbally expressed or not, whether it was present in banners and political demands, the underlying matter was the illegitimacy of the chavista institutional framework. With an adulterated democracy, Chavismo's only recourse was to impose the president by employing force: on the streets, by helmet and rifle butt blows; in the political realm, by abusing a submissive judicial system to over- turn the legislative branch's actions when the opposition gained con- trol of the National Assembly.

It was not an unbridled reaction by an incompetent Maduro, una- ble to bring to fruition the project which he inherited from Chávez. Venezuela's political authoritarianism and economic collapse simply reflected Chavismo's ripening (*maduración* in Spanish)—a blooming or full epiphany of a process set in motion by Chávez. It was the consequence of the policies and strategies carried out by the founder of the Bolivarian Republic. It was the boomerang, which on its return shattered the glass into which Chávez had stared: those that hailed him as the savior of the poor could clearly see how it was precisely the lower class that most endured the shortage of basic goods and medicines, the lines at stores, the insecurity... That was certainly a mirror, because Chavismo was a set of frauds from its outset.

It must be acknowledged that Hugo Chávez at first well per- ceived the satiety that prevailed in Venezuela in the last two decades of the 20th century because of the traditional political parties' inabil- ity to address the population's worries and their recurring corruption. He won the 1998 presidential elections because he was able to excite the popular masses—more than half of the population, in a country of thirty million inhabitants—with the prospect of a new beginning they would lead.

Chávez can take credit for executing at the beginning of his pres- idency what would turn out to be the most important decision during his time in office: securing within the Organization of Petroleum Exporting Countries a policy that resulted in a substantial increase in the price of the barrel of oil and, hence, an enormous rise in the reve- nue derived from the sale of crude oil, which is Venezuela's main source of wealth. The higher oil price was also caused by interna- tional events such as the war in Iraq or the embargo on Iran. But the trigger for the rise in oil prices was a confluence of interests between Caracas and Riyadh. In the middle of 2014, however, Saudi Arabia's position shifted and Venezuela began to suffer the effects of the dramatic drop of oil value in the markets. The chavista revolution rode the wave of higher crude prices, and their plunge seemed to indicate its death warrant, apparently validating the theory that in Venezuela major political and social changes are aligned with the cycles of international oil prices.

During the Chávez era, the price of oil rose from a low of $10.5 a barrel in 1998 to $103.4 in 2012. During the fourteen years that the Bolivarian leader was in power, Venezuela produced oil worth a $1.1 trillion. With such generous revenues, the Venezuelan budget was equally lavish in funding social policies. According to government statistics, it financed social policies to the tune of $500 billion, almost half of the oil revenue. The budget surplus also bolstered a foreign policy which shaped the region and shows Chávez's strategic intelligence: funding for allied countries in the continent and the sale of oil at discounted rates for the countries in the Caribbean.

But the management of such a great amount of revenue also engendered a scale of corruption unprecedented in the country's history, and turned Venezuela into the ideal place to launder money from drug trafficking. The government fostered both narco-trafficking and money laundering—two important elements of the chavista fraud.

* * *

This book addresses the great deceit of Chavismo. Heralded in many parts of the world as the supreme benefactor of the disenfranchised, Hugo Chávez will not go down in history as a leader who reduced poverty in Venezuela: the majority of countries in the continent achieved substantial progress during the same time period, some with greater success, such as Peru, Brazil, Chile, and Uruguay. In light of the public funding spent in Venezuela, greater and more sustained progress in the fight against poverty would be expected. The uniqueness of Chávez's legacy, which will be described in history manuals, is twofold: having developed an authoritarianism (a system whereby his presidential authority prevailed without the checks and balances nor accountability essential to a democracy) capable of ensuring re-election at the ballot box and, above all, having turned over control of the country to the leaders of another one.

The book first describes the fraud in the relationship with Cuba. Leaving aside the Venezuelan people, few realize the extreme interference exerted by Havana in the internal affairs of Venezuela, not resulting from a subtle and hostile intrusion concealed from the government in Caracas, but rather at its behest. With Chávez, Cubans became the managers of the issuance of identity documents and passports, as well as of the commercial registry and public notaries; they became as well co-director of ports and controllers of security, supervisors of the armed forces and counterintelligence activities... Maduro himself was promoted by the Cubans as successor.

Such developments are unthinkable in any other country in the world. In Venezuela it became a reality because much was done behind the population's back: the government covered up the number of Cubans in the country and their activities, and democratic shortcomings prevented the opposition from holding the government accountable. As a witness documents, Chávez once ordered the removal from the national accounts of $5 billion owed by Cuba: the Bolivarian leader decided on his own to present a gift to Cuba with the population's money and without their knowledge. Venezuelans were also unaware of the real subsidies Venezuela bestowed on Cuba; the shipment of 100,000 barrels of oil per day to Cuba was in the public domain, but there was no way to audit the payment of the castrista regime, which was not financial, but rather through the provision of services by doctors, nurses, sports coaches, and other *advisors* dispatched by Cuba.

Chávez came to depend so much on Fidel and Raúl Castro that he put his own life in their hands. When he was diagnosed with cancer in 2011, the Venezuelan president chose the secretiveness which Cuba offered. Although his illness was irreversible, he could have received better treatment in another country. This would have extended his life and, with the necessary convalescence, would have eased the agony he endured for months. Chávez preferred to cling to power and put up a farce regarding supposed medical recoveries. The entire effort was aimed at staying alive until the presidential elections of October 2012, so that another victory would ensure Chavismo would remain in power for another six years, even if a successor would serve out the presidential mandate. Chávez made it to the finish line hiding from voters his frail health, which restricted his appearances, and lying about the outlook for another term, which would be stillborn.

The sham of the last weeks of his life was improper for the transparency a democracy requires, and were unworthy for the citizens of Venezuela. The government plagiarized Chávez's signature on appointments when he became disabled, and ridiculed the sincere feelings of thousands of Venezuelans when it paraded the coffin through the streets of Caracas without his body inside. There was not even a public death certificate, signed by a doctor, which would attest to the cause, time and place of his death.

Chávez had reached out to Cuba to seek advice from Fidel Castro on how to remain in power. From Havana sprang the idea of the social *missions*, thirty aid programs for the poor, whose condition would be improved while simultaneously enhancing Chavez's political power. They were managed without the involvement of the corresponding sectorial ministries, and with financing withheld from parliamentary scrutiny. As assistance their nature was more charity than an attempt to foster structural changes. Chávez ensured that the number of people signed up for the missions and that of public employees jointly reached at least half of the electoral roll: Chavismo's message was always aimed at that half of Venezuela, pitting it against the other half in order to stoke class resentment. With a methodical mobilization, and government resources, the regime ensured that those whose names appeared on the lists of public benefits would be forced to vote for the government. This technique was known as *ventajismo*, which included practices such as abuse of the assisted vote, threats of dismissal, and denying the opposition access to the electoral roll.

But this was only part of the electoral skullduggery. As is revealed in the book, in the presidential elections of 2012, Chávez's last ones, and those of 2013, with Maduro as candidate, Chavismo activists were in charge of running the voting machines and the voter identification devices at the poll stations, in cahoots with the National Electoral Council (CNE). This enabled the deployment of a parallel IT system alongside that of the CNE, which provided the regime information about the voting trends during election day, so that it could react with last-minute mobilizations or with the fraudulent activation of voting machines. This parallel system was coordinated by Cuba. Two senior Chavismo leaders have admitted privately that hundreds of thousands of votes for Maduro were falsified; meaning that the opposition leader, Henrique Capriles, won the elections.

The validity of these revelations about the electoral fraud are not undercut by the opposition's landslide victory in the 2015 parliamentary elections. Fraud had its limits, and it could be overcome with a massive vote against Chavismo. Moreover, the system designed to rig elections was more efficient when only one electoral district was at play, as was the case in presidential elections or a referendum.

The extraordinary oil revenues financed a Bolivarian revolution that went on a spending splurge: household appliances and housing for loyal social sectors, condoning Cuba's debt, assisting regimes with a similar ideology, purchasing weaponry from Russia that turned Venezuela into the biggest importer of arms in all of Latin America... Petróleos de Venezuela S.A. (PDVSA), which had been a public company not managed by the government, was subsumed into the governmental structure of command and embarked on operations beyond oil, such as construction and food processing and distribution. When he needed them for his policies, Chávez was able to obtain funds from PDVSA, in an official manner through the issuance of bonds by the company, or under the table, such as the first $4 billion of a loan from China in return for oil, which Chávez kept to use as he saw fit, beyond the official registry, as the minister that had to turn over the money confirmed. With so many off balance sheet operations, PDVSA's accounts began to falter.

The economic malaise that Venezuela would later undergo was caused by this plucking of the goose that laid golden eggs. Eager to spend the revenue collected by the public coffers, Chávez did not push PDVSA to reinvest in the oil fields, a key requirement in the sector as wells decline with time and always need maintenance. The production thus declined: from 3.3 million barrels per day in 1998 to 2.3 million in 2013. While oil prices rose, revenue continued to increase, but when the price of oil stagnated in 2013 and began to drop in 2014, PDVSA and the government entered a dangerous situation. To maintain the clientelist structure he had built up, Chávez resorted to loans in exchange for future production of oil. He was mortgaging Venezuelans' future through loans whose liabilities have grown as the price of oil has continued its downward trend.

The rise of the price of oil by a factor of ten in very few years generated an increase of capital for the government that fostered corruption on an unprecedented level. Easy money obtained illegally—commissions, bribes, seizure of assets—made many chavista officials wealthy. In very few years, those with connections rose from humble origins to become multimillionaires. A prime example is Rafael Ramírez, president of PDVSA for ten years and a key figure in the misappropriation of funds and money laundering. The wealth that Chávez amassed for his children is estimated to be hundreds of millions of dollars. It was corruption on a monumental scale that spawned a huge stash of cash, which grew exponentially through financial operations that took advantage of the vagaries of an exchange-rate system controlled by the government. While they denounced U.S. imperialism, the new rich of Venezuela went on a shopping spree to purchase private jets, mansions, and luxury goods in the United States.

The economic corruption went hand in hand with judicial misconduct. Judges and lawyers had to obey political orders dictated by the Attorney General's Office and the Supreme Tribunal of Justice (TSJ). Both institutions interfered in many cases, with Chavez's personal intervention, to convict innocent persons and acquit guilty ones, as described by the magistrate Eladio Aponte, president of the Criminal Court of the TSJ, who fled Venezuela in 2012. Any constitutional violation, such as appointing Maduro as acting president after Chávez's death, had the blessing of the TSJ.

The mobilization of capital on an unprecedented scale and practically no oversight enabled money laundering. Chávez turned his country into a drug trafficking hub. Venezuela became the exit point for 90 percent of Colombian drugs shipped to the United States and Europe. He conceived it as part of his Bolivarian project—a way of supporting Colombia's guerrilla movements against the government of Bogota, that was opposed to Chávez's regional leadership—and as a means to launch an *asymmetric war* against Washington. According to testimony provided by witnesses protected by U.S. law enforcement authorities, the Venezuelan president was periodically informed about the main drug shipments through Venezuelan territory in operations often directed by senior military commanders. Maduro also partook in this activity, and Diosdado Cabello, the regime's second most powerful figure, became completely involved.

There are many indications that the U.S. Drug Enforcement Administration has launched investigations against more than thirty Venezuelans and federal prosecutors are likely to bring charges against leading public officials. The public disclosure of such prosecutions may be delayed due to operational circumstances or political considerations, but the scope of drug trafficking merit labeling Venezuela as a narco-state. The decision to turn Venezuela into a transit point for Colombian drugs increased crime and hooked the more vulnerable population groups on drugs.

The fraud that Chávez committed against his own citizens also encompassed other domains, such as security. Chávez welcomed Hezbollah into Venezuela: he expedited the issuance of visas and false passports to members of the terrorist group and provided a safe haven for some of its cells. In 2007, he arranged for Maduro, then Foreign Affairs minister, to meet in Damascus with the leader of the aforementioned Shia Lebanese militia, Hassan Nasrallah. The main activity undertaken by Islamic extremism in Venezuela, agreed upon with the government, was money laundering and drug trafficking. Although some training camps were set up, no terrorist operations were carried out. Nevertheless, there are indications that Hezbollah cells made their way north to Central America and they might have crossed the border into the United States, while radical Iranian agents drew up plans to launch terrorist attacks against U.S. targets.

The special relationship with Iran was shrouded in deceit. The purpose of many agreements signed between Chávez and Iranian President Mahmoud Ahmadinejad was to simulate activities that justified capital flows, thereby enabling Tehran to evade international sanctions imposed to curb its nuclear program. As part of his support for the ayatollahs, Chávez allowed Iran to conduct speculative currency operations that committed fraud against the Venezuelan Central Bank.

The relationship with Iran enabled Chávez to access certain technologies, but especially cranked up his confrontation with the United States. Gaining international stature by verbally attacking Washington cost Venezuela money. During his entire presidency, Chávez financed lobbies and public relations agencies in the United States, and provided cheap oil to the districts of certain politicians in order to improve his government's image in the U.S. and to try to build up support in Congress. But his verbose diatribes ruined his public relations work: it was an onerous weaving and unweaving. This became somewhat of a schizophrenic situation, as Venezuela garnered the lion's share of its foreign currency by regularly exporting oil to the United States, which shored up Venezuela's economy.

Chávez forged a foreign policy with two dimensions: anti-American propaganda and the exertion of influence in Latin America through the provision of economic assistance (the ALBA alliance) and the sale of oil with generous financing terms (Petrocaribe). In addition to the reduction in revenue brought about by the oil diplomacy, the worst consequence for Venezuelans was the opportunity granted to the benefiting countries to repay in goods. This led the government to arrange for imports that harmed Venezuela's productive sector, which was already constrained by nationalizations, as well as price and exchange-rate controls. In order to increase its stature among neighboring countries, Chavismo engaged in a inverted neocolonialism: instead of fostering national industries, it increased the import of goods.

All of these policies were part of the boomerang thrown by Hugo Chávez, whose consequence—the returning flying stick—would be a serious and unsustainable economic, social, and institutional crisis. The gifts to Cuba, Iran, and other countries; the electoral nature of part of public spending; the abuse committed against PDVSA, and corruption emptied public coffers, leaving them without sufficient international reserves to meet the need for increasing imports. In 2012 imports exceeded exports: a trade deficit in a country with enormous energy wealth! And the plummeting of the oil price was yet to come.

Fostering street gangs as a locknut of the revolution, the ties with terrorist groups, and the sponsorship of drug trafficking led to an increase in crime and drug consumption which especially battered the weakest classes, already impacted by inflation and product shortages. Cuba's interference in Venezuela's sovereignty, the deceit surrounding Chávez's inability to seek re-election due to his terminal illness, the manipulation of the elections, and the politicization of justice led to a dead end.

The negative effects of his mismanagement of Venezuela turned against Chávez when he was on his way out and fully impacted Maduro. The successor was confronted by an oil price that first stopped surging and then plunged, overturning all of the parameters that had buttressed the Bolivarian revolution.

* * *

After more than forty deaths, eight hundred wounded and three thousand arrests, Human Rights Watch released a report in May 2014 about the street protests of that time in Venezuela. This international organization expressed surprise at its findings. In Latin America, anti-government demonstrations were not unusual, nor was the excessive force employed by some of the security forces. But when these events had occurred, democratic presidents had condemned them and had taken measures to punish some of those responsible for the harsh crackdowns. The Venezuelan government's attitude was very different: it denied the assaults, which it blamed on the opposition—which it called "murderous", without providing any evidence—, it honored the police corps most involved in the repression, and fostered civilian armed groups to pursue their use of violence.

The Human Rights Watch report, the source of the tale of police violence endured by the young Willie David that started this introduction, concluded that the human rights abuses were not isolated cases, but rather were a "systemic practice". It admitted that in some cases the demonstrators had attacked the police, but found that a majority of the excessive violence had been employed by security forces. The illegitimate use of force included "violently beating persons who were unarmed; shooting firearms, pellet and tear-gas in an indiscriminate way against the crowds, and deliberately firing bird shot at close range against persons that were unarmed, and in some cases, when they were already in custody". After the "arbitrary arrests", many suffered physical and psychological abuse, and there were some cases of torture. Moreover, there was a constant violation of due process, with the "complicit assistance" of judges and prosecutors. The member of the opposition Leopoldo López was arrested without evidence, as well as the mayors Antonio Ledezma and Daniel Ceballos. They were on the top of a list of about eighty political prisoners.

The authoritarian nature of the Venezuelan regime was uncovered, but it should not have come as a surprise. Chavismo had an anti-democratic core. It could have made a significant contribution to freedom in Venezuela, as a left-wing party that was the depository of the aspirations of thousands of citizens that had traditionally been cast aside, but instead its objective was the imposition of a revolution. There was ample proof to back this up: the institutional glorification of the original attempted coup d'état by Chávez, marked yearly with parades; the obligation that radio and television stations broadcast live Chávez's speeches—longer or shorter, sometimes daily and lasting several hours—, as a part of the gag applied to a disappearing freedom of the press, or the permanent verbal harassment of the opposition, in an effort to taint it as an enemy against which a permanent state of war was needed. The objective was to reach the Cuban *nirvana*: continuity in power through a social control; with electoral manipulation if necessary, and if it was not enough, by replacing nominal democracy with a *Communal State.*

However, when the electoral fraud committed by Chavismo was insufficient to carry the legislative elections of December 2015, the regime did not summon the will to stage a coup in the face of the opposition victory, which would have required the armed forces' involvement. Without becoming a full-fledged dictatorship and suppressing the electoral results, Chavismo deepened its authoritarianism by discarding the work of a National Assembly with an opposition majority.

The outlook for Venezuela is bleak. The country could avoid its near *default* by simply liberalizing the exploitation of the Orinoco Oil Belt, one of the biggest oil reserves in the world, whose difficult extraction requires the technologies of the most advanced multinationals. But such a development would need to be added to a process whereby the main tenets of chavista orthodoxy would be overturned, and Chavismo advocates revolution, not democracy. The thawing between Cuba and the United States, should it usher in economic development in the island, will allow Havana to diminish its reliance on subsidies from Caracas. But Castrismo can always resort to Venezuela's government—especially now when at home it must tone down its criticism of the United States—to hurl rhetorical salvos and bring together the left in Latin America. Even if economic difficulties stifle the economic management by the government of Venezuela, it might be able to stay on its feet, avoid default and allot resources to soothe the popular masses, already used to hardship.

Maduro, for the time being, has been able to stave off a social uprising and a military coup, which could come from the ranks of Chavismo. But his position is by no means secure. In the absence of other clear legal means, the opposition resorted to a recall referendum. If Maduro were to be voted out of the presidency before the beginning of 2017, new elections should be held. If it would happen later, his hand-picked successor would finish out his term in 2019, which would lengthen Chavismo's hold on power in Venezuela to twenty years.

* * *

Boomerang Chávez was written in Washington, D.C. As correspondent of the newspaper *ABC* in the capital of the United States, I was able to access confidential reports about the evolution of Hugo Chávez's health, which gave way to a series of scoops with great international coverage. This opened the door to other sources and contacts as well as new documents. Washington is a hub for the transmission of information and for political and diplomatic activity that involves actors from all of the countries in the continent.

The most substantive accounts in this book are by persons that at first worked at the core of chavista power and who at the end of the Chávez era, as discontent spread within the regime and internal rivalries were declared, fled the country and accepted the protection of the United States in return for testimony to prosecute higher ranking officials. There are also accounts by chavista leaders who reached out to U.S. authorities but preferred to not burn their bridges, at least for the time being. In some cases their names are mentioned, and in others their request to remain anonymous is honored. Other disclosures are from documents provided by high-ranking civil servants who worked in Venezuelan government and from a leak in the Frente Francisco de Miranda, the organizer from Cuba of the electoral fraud. The information is supplemented by interviews with Venezuelans who reside in the United States and Venezuela, and by the contributions of experts from think-tanks. A trip to Chávez and Maduro's motherland was unanimously advised against due to personal threats. We trust that the country will find its way to national understanding and a democratic renaissance.

Washington, D.C., June 2016

1

THE CARIBBEAN FAUST

Cuba's Interference

[He sold out his motherland in order to extend his life, and he wound up losing both. At first, Hugo Chávez approached Cuba due to the elixir of eternal power on offer from the Caribbean Mephistopheles. In the end, he sacrificed his soul to avoid a death which he would anyway suffer. His fate was akin to that of Faust, whose deal with the devil led to a lonely and bitter death. And Venezuela, in any case, had to endure bitterness.]

H elp me, help me!" Hugo Chávez pleaded to Fidel and Raúl Castro persistently during the last months of his life. "I do not want to die; please, do not let me die!" The head of the presidential guard, José Ornella, saw this plea on Chávez's face in his deathbed, shortly before he lost consciousness. "He could not talk, but he said it with his lips," the general explained to the press on March 5, 2013, as the country mourned the passing of the leader of the Bolivarian revolution. "He suffered a lot. Those of us who were by his side witnessed the suffering inflicted on him by the disease. Somebody will write the story someday."

General Ornella's remarks to the media were an admission that the government of Venezuela had not revealed certain facts about Chávez's illness. More importantly, they also appeared to subtly suggest a hidden grudge, a political agenda that had unnecessarily prolonged Chávez's suffering, against the wishes of those who held him in high esteem. The promise, made as the leader's body lay in state, that the true tale would be revealed someday sounded like a warning. Similarly, the refusal by Chávez's eldest daughters, Rosa Virginia and María Gabriela, to vacate La Casona, the mansion for the president's family, so Nicolás Maduro and his family could move in might amount to blackmail. What did they know that allowed them to belittle Maduro in such a blatant fashion?

Someday the entire story will be told, when those that have sworn secrecy finally speak out. Although many details are unknown currently, the embarrassing truth is sufficiently revealing. Chávez used Castro's help to extend his time in power to such an extent that, as his death neared, he appointed the Cuban regime as executor of the Bolivarian revolution he had undertaken. Distrustful of his entourage, Chávez in life relied greatly on Cuba as an advisor, spymaster, and enforcer of the revolution within Venezuela. His dependence on Cuba was such that near his death he could only envision maintaining Cuban control over Venezuela in order to guarantee the survival of his political legacy. But Chávez's passing also entailed the disappearance of someone who could act as a check on Cuban power in Venezuela. His illness was a catalyst of the final transition, in which Chávez himself and his legacy remained at the hands of the Cuban regime. Maduro was then thrust into power, and later propped up, by Havana.

The most extraordinary feature of chavista Venezuela may precisely be the voluntary obedience to a smaller and poorer country located almost nine hundred miles away. There have been many revolutions, charismatic dictators, popular movements, and repressions throughout history, especially in that of Latin America. But Chavismo will go down in history books due to its unique subjection to a foreign power.

The visionary of the Venezuelan plains first turned to Fidel Castro mesmerized by his historical aura. As a result of his brief ouster from power in 2002, Chávez reached out to Castro as an alternative to Venezuela's traditional political and military system, and one which would help him vanquish it. The Castro regime furnished Chávez with cunning for his periodic electoral challenges. Cuba did not hold elections, so it could deploy its political craftiness to serve other regimes. In the end, Chávez regarded Fidel as the only figure who could simultaneously play the role of mentor and doctor, and who could be entrusted with secrets, without concern over power grabs. What stuns is not so much that Chávez sought counsel in Havana on so many occasions, but rather that Castro was able to play so many different roles.

Carlos Alberto Montaner, a Cuban intellectual who was able to emigrate in 1960 precisely by seeking political asylum at the Venezuelan Embassy, describes the Cuban-Venezuelan relationship "as an unnatural servitude." "How can a small, unproductive and impoverished Caribbean island, mired in a rusty Soviet past consigned to the dustbin of history, control a much bigger, more modern, richer, more populated, and more educated nation without having previously conquered it?" Montaner reflected on this paradox in an op-ed column a year after Chávez's death. According to Montaner, Chávez submitted himself to the Cuban regime in exchange for what it could provide: "a vision, a method, and a mission, but, above all, intelligence reports about politicians, journalists, and military officers. They detected or inflated alleged disloyalties, and they revealed them to Chávez. Information was power. Cuba assembled and handed over all of the information it collected, highlighting threats to Chávez so he would remain eternally grateful."

We keep asking ourselves the same question. How could Venezuela, a country with a Gross Domestic Product (GDP) of almost $400 billion, wind up so dependent on Cuba, whose GDP is only $60 billion? Andrés Oppenheimer, a journalist originally from Argentina who, like Montaner, resides in Miami, offers three causes to explain "this first case in history when a country subsidizes another one and is dominated by the latter," as he pointed out in one of his contributions to the media. In first place, the psychological-emotional cause: when Chávez first met Castro the Venezuelan was forty years old, had two unsuccessful coup attempts behind him and had been discharged from the armed forces. And suddenly the great mentor of the Latin American revolutions was there, standing, ready to receive him, putting him on a pedestal. Since their first encounter, Castro became for the restless Venezuelan "a father figure, a political guru, and a personal advisor." In second place, there is the security cause: Castro was able to instill in Chávez a paranoid fear of suffering an attack from his inner circle; Chávez therefore surrounded himself with Cuban bodyguards and entrusted counterintelligence duties to Cuban officers. Finally, the political reason: Castro furnished the political manual on how to cling to power, conjuring up a permanent *state of war* that justified Chávez taking on absolute powers. "Cuba manipulated the government of Venezuela as no country has meddled in the internal affairs of another in the region's recent memory."

The great paradox was summarized very well as a tale by Moisés Naím, a global analyst based in Washington and former editor of *Foreign Policy*. He is probably the most respected Venezuelan voice in Latin America. Naím surprisingly began one of his TV shows with an animated cartoon and the text that follows below, which he read out in his unmistakable diction:

> "Once upon a time, there was a small island ruled by an ageing dictator. It was a very poor island. Over the years, the dictator had decimated all factories, harvests, and any important remaining economic activity. Nobody trusted him. Nobody wanted to lend him money, and his people endured ever increasing hardship. The lack of progress and opportunity overwhelmed the island's population. There was a big and powerful country located near this small island. The old dictator, who was very cunning, invited its president and made him an offer. If he turned over some of his country's wealth, he would teach him how to stay in power forever. The president of the bigger country liked

the deal and began to provide generous assistance to the small island; in exchange, the dictator sent his advisors. But these advisors gradually became very influential and took over power in the bigger country. They gave orders instead of advice, and thereby the cagey tyrant not only took advantage of the neighboring country's wealth, but also managed to run it. And the powerful country became impoverished, just like the island."

The Psychologist Fidel Castro

Since the triumph of the Cuban revolution, Fidel Castro set his sights on Venezuela's oil. Both countries emerged from dictatorships almost simultaneously. Marcos Pérez Jiménez was overthrown on December 23, 1958, in Caracas. The new Venezuelan Patriotic Junta rushed to supply weapons to the guerrillas battling Fulgencio Batista in Cuba. Four days after the proclamation of the victory of the Cuban revolution on January 1, 1959, Venezuela became the first country to officially recognize the new order in Havana. Two weeks later, acknowledging this gesture, Fidel traveled to Venezuela and spent five days in the country in his first foreign foray as Cuba's leader.

Chavismo always heralded Castro's 1959 trip as prophetic. Summoning the historical figure of Caracas-born Simón Bolívar, who in the 19th century liberated a great part of South America from the Spanish Crown, Castro proclaimed that Venezuela should be a "leading country in the union of the peoples of America." Given the lifeline that Venezuelan oil provided to Castro after the downfall of the Soviet Union, another remark made by Fidel during the 1959 trip proved very prescient. "Entering Caracas was more moving for me than doing so in Havana, because here I have received everything from those who have received nothing for me," told Castro.

The bearded leader of revolutionary Cuba met during his 1959 trip with Venezuelan President-elect Rómulo Betancourt, founder of the political party Democratic Action (AD). During the encounter, Castro urged him to extend a loan to Cuba for the purchase of Venezuelan oil. Betancourt's refusal and the ensuing split between the democratic socialism of AD and Cuban communism would soon bring about significant consequences.

Cuba fostered a guerrilla movement in Venezuela, the first country it sought to extend its revolution to. In fact, Che Guevara made swift plans to move to and take up arms in Venezuela. Only because difficulties arose with regard to his Venezuela mission did Che decide to travel to and fight the regimes in Congo and Bolivia. The first overt guerrilla campaign in Venezuela took place in 1963. In 1966-67 Castro supervised the preparation of two naval landings of guerrilla forces in Venezuela. Details of both operations are narrated in *La invasión de Cuba a Venezuela* (2007) [The Invasion of Venezuela by Cuba]. The book underlines Fidel's enduring obsession with his project to expand the revolution to South America. Despite the fact that Castro sided with President Carlos Andrés Pérez when Chávez staged his 1992 military coup, the Cuban dictator quickly acknowledged the young Venezuelan military officer's aptitude and his potential contribution to his longstanding aspirations. They first met when Chávez traveled to Cuba in 1994 after being released from prison. "Chávez was a kind of clay in the hands of a craftsman like Fidel, a master goldsmith," wrote Héctor Pérez Marcano, one of the authors of the aforementioned book. Marcano was a member of the Cuban guerrilla force sent to Venezuela, but later renounced Castrismo.

With the passage of time, the chavista government unveiled a plaque in the fishing village of Machurucuto to honor the guerrillas from Cuba who forty years earlier had landed in Venezuela to spread communism. As they had been defeated by the Venezuelan armed forces, they had always been denounced as invaders. Now they were turned into heroes. "The Cuban communist regime has finally achieved its goal of invading oil-rich Venezuela, on this occasion without having to fire a single shot," concluded *The Economist*, whose writer visited Machurucuto.

The first and crucial meeting between Chávez and Fidel Castro took place on December 14, 1994. The experienced Cuban leader had sized up the former officer's personality before he set foot on the island. The initial plan called for Chávez to travel to Cuba with Luis Miquilena, a veteran Venezuelan politician with longstanding and strong ties to the Cuban regime. Upon learning that Castro would not be able to meet with them during their planned visit, Miquilena chose not to travel and arranged for Chávez to hold meetings with lower-level Cuban officials. When Chávez's plane landed in Cuba, Fidel was there to greet him. The old leader shrewdly surmised that the ego card would work best with Chávez. He would employ it often and in many ways.

Fidel Castro deduced that Chávez had emotional complexes. Opening the account in such a manner is not intended to personally discredit Chávez; Oppenheimer's aforementioned quote described the Chavez-Fidel relationship specially in a psychological-emotional context. Born in the town of Sabaneta, in the state of Barinas, on July 28, 1954, Chávez was the second of six brothers. The fact that he grew up at his grandmother's house and therefore separated from his siblings spawned anxiety in him about his mother's affection and the true paternity of his father. Both of his parents were teachers from humble backgrounds. Chávez married twice, first with a young lady from Sabaneta, Nancy Colmenares, with whom he had three children (Rosa Virginia, María Gabriela, and Hugo Rafael) and, on his way to the presidency, with the journalist Marisabel Rodríguez, with whom he had a daughter (Rosinés). Chávez separated from his second wife in 2003. He remained single for the rest of his life and had no stable long-term relationships, although he did have sexual relations with numerous women.

"Chávez was a sick man. On a particular day, he would choose one, and the next day he would fancy a different woman. On certain nights, he would tell me: 'tell her to come,' despite the fact that it was well beyond 1 am. There was a list. If one was not available, another one was called and we sent someone to pick her up from her house." This is a recollection by someone who was in Chávez's inner circle and who often had to deal with the president's pressing personal needs. The person also discloses that Fidel Castro, who was well aware of Chávez's weakness for attractive women, arranged for him to meet with the top model Naomi Campbell in Cuba. As a surprise on one of Chavez's birthdays, the Cuban leader had the British model of Jamaican descent flown to Havana on a private plane from Petróleos de Venezuela (PDVSA). "It was a way to feed his ego, to show him that he could obtain great trophies. A few months later she flew to Caracas to see Chávez." Campbell posed for the cameras at the entrance of Miraflores Palace, in October 2007, as she was in Venezuela officially as a good-will ambassador for a humanitarian cause.

Chávez's promiscuity, according to the witness, bore the hallmark of an insecure personality, and it extended to the wives of several generals. "He offered money to the wives, promoted their husbands, or granted them positions that enabled them to easily earn $10 million or $20 million." In such a way Chávez sought to display his superiority over his generals, whom he blackmailed with the prospect of their wives' betrayal going public. He also held sway over them by entangling them in his corrupt dealings. Chávez also had relationships with beauty queens and several female ministers. It serves no purpose to disclose their names, some are already in the public domain.

Some women distanced themselves when they realized they were part of a harem. Others accepted the situation and believed they were Chávez's true love. This was the case with Nidia Fajardo, a stewardess on his first presidential flights, who in 2008 gave birth to a girl, Sara Manuela; her persistence prolonged the relationship. In 2005, Chávez had fathered another girl, Génesis María, with his housekeeper, Bexhi Lissette Segura. Both girls received silent acknowledgment from Chávez: he paid child support but did not grant them the same legal recognition as his children from his marriages. A year after his death, the girls were admitted by the family as part of Chávez's offspring.

Castro also took advantage of the Venezuelan leader's bipolar disorder. "He would swing from euphoria to sadness, splitting his personality and undergoing episodes with a loss of touch with reality. He would swing between these two poles, with a greater tendency towards euphoria, hyperactivity, and mania" as one of his first doctors, Salvador Navarrete, described to the press. The wily Cuban dictator treated Chávez as if he were a reincarnation of Simón Bolívar.

Rise and Consolidation of Chavismo

By the first time Hugo Chávez shook Fidel Castro's hand, he had already distinguished himself among his comrades-in-arms. He had forged close friendships with many fellow officers after graduating from the Military Academy in 1975, with which he maintained close links in the ensuing years. In 1982, he founded the Bolivarian Revolutionary Movement 200. The following year, the bicentennial of Simón Bolívar's death, he connived with fellow officers to bring about a new republic in Venezuela. The group hastened its machinations after the *Caracazo* of February 27, 1989, the bloody suppression of widespread protests prompted by the economic measures adopted by the recently elected president of Venezuela, Carlos Andrés Pérez.

On February 4, 1992, Chávez staged a military coup with three other lieutenant coronels. Although the plot was successful in most military districts, Chávez was unable to take over Caracas. As Chávez urged his followers to lay down their arms in a televised address, he conveyed to the country that he was retreating "for the time being." This expression later became a cornerstone of chavista ideology, along with the Fourth of February coup itself. A few months thereafter, on November 27, 1992, a second coup was attempted. One of its main objectives was Chávez's release from the San Francisco de Yare prison where he had been confined. But this plot also failed.

Rafael Caldera, who was elected president in 1994, freed Chávez from prison but banned him from returning to the military. Chávez therefore focused on attaining power through political means. He was well aware of the social discontent and the corruption engendered by decades of a pact known as *Punto Fijo* whereby the social democrats of Democratic Action (AD) and the Christian democrats of COPEI took turns running Venezuela. This partitocracy had resulted in alternating presidencies by the center-right Rafael Caldera (1969-1974 and 1994-1999) and the center-left Carlos Andrés Pérez (1974-1979 and 1989-1993). Disenchanted with both AD and COPEI, many Venezuelans demanded a real and accountable democracy with a strong commitment to social justice. Chávez transformed his MRB 200 group into a political party, Movement Fifth Republic (MVR), and contested the 1998 presidential elections. He romped to victory with 56.5 percent of the vote.

Shortly before being sworn into office as president of Venezuela in February 1999, Chávez traveled to Cuba for another encounter with Fidel. He was accompanied on the flight back to Caracas by the Colombian Nobel laureate Gabriel García Márquez. After landing in Caracas, García Márquez would later write, "he [Chávez] sped off surrounded by his bodyguards and longtime friends, I shuddered with the thought that I had traveled and held pleasant conversations with two men who were polar opposites. One whom inveterate luck was offering a opportunity to save his country. The other, an illusionist who could go down in history as just another tyrant."

Chávez's main electoral promise was to do away with the old political 98system. Stretching the Venezuelan constitutional order, in 1999 Chávez called a referendum to put an end to the Fourth Republic and hold elections to a constituent assembly. The new Constitution was approved in late 1999 at the ballot box. New regional, legislative, and presidential elections were held in July 2000, reaffirming Chávez's power. "Some believe that Fidel Castro is guiding this revolution. We hold Fidel in high esteem, but Bolívar is the real leader of the revolution," thundered Chávez in a passage of his speech at his second swearing-in ceremony. Chávez had acted in an autonomous way, but events which would soon unfold would increase his dependence on Havana.

The new Constitution awarded greater powers to the presidency, whose term was lengthened to six years. Other articles of the Constitution decreased the checks and balances between the separate powers. For example, it did away with the two-chambered Congress and replaced it with a one-chamber National Assembly. These changes fanned protests by political opposition and businessmen, the latter led by the business association Fedecámaras (Federation of Chambers and Associations of Commerce and Production of Venezuela). A general strike called on April 9, 2002, extended the protests. Two days later, a large crowd assembled in downtown Caracas and marched to Miraflores Palace. Chávez's sympathizers confronted the protesters. Nineteen people were killed in the ensuing violence, prompting the Military High Command to force Chávez's resignation, which was announced on the morning of April 12.

Pedro Carmona, the chairman of Fedecámaras, was sworn in as acting president. This violated what the Constitution set out in the case of a resignation by the head of state. Carmona issued decrees dissolving most elected bodies and had to confront street protests by chavista supporters, who demanded that the vice president (the position was then held by Diosdado Cabello) be appointed acting president until Chávez could resume his presidency. Loyal military officers freed their leader and Chávez took again office on April 14, alleging that he had never tendered a written resignation. The Supreme Tribunal of Justice settled the matter by declaring that a power vacuum had occurred, whereas Chavismo henceforth always referred to the events as a coup d'état. In any case, Carmona's appointment had clearly violated the Constitution.

The tug of war between Chávez and the opposition continued in the ensuing years. The opposition was emboldened by its perceived weakness of the regime. Chávez, on the other hand, was determined to subdue those that attempted to slow down the implementation of his political and economic measures. A majority of the employees of the state-owned oil company Petróleos de Venezuela Sociedad Anónima (PDVSA) staged a tough strike between December 2002 and February 2003. Then the opposition started collecting signatures for a recall referendum, something allowed by the Constitution, to oust Chávez. It was not only the conservative opposition, sometimes too strident in tone, that railed against the president, but also some sectors of the moderate left grew disenchanted with Chávez's authoritarian tricks.

Faced with this hostility, Chávez strengthened his ties to Cuba. In October 2000, during a visit by Fidel Castro to Caracas, the two countries had signed a ten-year comprehensive cooperation agreement, which would later be extended for another decade. After the 2002 coup, Chávez brought Cuban agents into his security detail and entrusted Cuban officials with military counterintelligence, specifically the task of eavesdropping on military barracks to detect any mutinous saber-rattling.

Between the end of 2003 and the beginning of 2004, following Havana's forceful advice, Chávez launched the so-called Bolivarian Missions: approximately thirty programs that tended to the needs of the population with fewer resources (more than half of the electorate) and that greatly enhanced governmental sway over low-income Venezuelans. Chávez delayed the recall referendum against him long enough to have the missions in place. When the referendum was held in August 2004, 59.1 percent of the voters decided against the president's removal. The blow to the opposition's morale resulted in most opposition parties boycotting the legislative elections that were held in December 2005. As a consequence, the new National Assembly was completely dominated by Chávez's allies. This greatly facilitated the task of appointing Chávez loyalists to all of the institutions elected by the National Assembly, such as the Supreme Tribunal of Justice and the National Electoral Council (CNE).

The next step dictated by Cuba's advisors was the design of a highly precise electoral mobilization and the coordination of a computer system which, in cahoots with the CNE, enabled the commission of fraud in Venezuela's automated elections. Chávez first employed this system in the presidential elections of 2006, which he won with 62.8 percent of the vote. This electoral engineering would increase its efficiency in subsequent elections. In May 2007, the government barely lost a referendum on constitutional reform which banned term limits for the presidency. But the government did pull out a victory in a second referendum on the same matter in February

2009. Chávez's political party was rebranded as the United Socialist Party of Venezuela (PSUV) and adopted the color red—*rojo, rojito* (redder than red or very red)—as its emblem. During one of Chávez's frequent visits to Havana, Fidel stated that Venezuela and Cuba were "two countries, one nation." Chávez added "with only one flag," and Castro concluded: "We are *Venecubans.*"

Cuban Advisors, Agents, and Spies

A former high-ranking civil servant who was posted at Miraflores Palace witnessed first hand how Cuban officials took on growing powers within the Venezuelan command structure. He recalls the freedom of movement enjoyed by the agents sent from Havana for Chávez's security, very similar to those maintained under Maduro, who inherited the retinue of bodyguards of Cuban training and undisputed loyalty.

According to this witness, in order to enter the Miraflores compound there were four kinds of identification badges. All of them displayed a hologram with the national coat of arms, as well as a stripe of a different color to indicate the restricted movements. The badge with a yellow stripe only allowed access to the administrative area of the Palacio Blanco, a building contiguous to Miraflores and connected to it by an underground passage. The one with a blue stripe permitted access to the directorates-general and the offices of the deputy ministers in both the Blanco and Miraflores palaces. The ministers and vice presidents, with a red-striped ID, could move around the entire compound with the exception of the areas reserved for the president. Finally, a special badge with all three colors (white, blue and red) was needed for the area used by the head of state. It was granted only to the head of the Military Household and to members of Chávez's security team, among them Cuban agents. Not even the minister of the President's Office was allowed into the area unless he was summoned by Chávez. In fact, the Cubans ordered that the minister be removed from the presidential palace altogether in order to further isolate Chávez.

Approximately ten Cuban officials were posted at Miraflores. Most of them resided there permanently, although they rotated on a quarterly basis. They made up the innermost security circle, in charge of the president's security and care. The innkeeper, cook, and medical team were all Cuban. One of the members of the team was assigned the mission of accompanying Chávez and carrying an emergency medical suitcase. The suitcase was stacked with painkillers, syringes, a resuscitation device, and a cardiac defibrillator, as well as small firearms which the president could resort to in self-defense should his bodyguards not be able to fully repel an attack against him.

Communication with Cuba was telephonic and electronic. But there were also weekly dispatches of commands dictated from the top. Every Monday afternoon an envelope arrived at the airport of Maiquetía on board a Cubana de Aviación airplane. A deputy minister was in charge of personally retrieving the envelope and taking it to the minister of the President's Office, who handed it to Chávez. The content of these communications is unknown, but judging by the ritual procedure followed it must have been a secret postal dispatch from the Cuban presidency.

The Cuban advisory function was small-scale at first. Fidel Castro sent a dozen communists to Venezuela in 1997 to assist with the electoral campaign that Chávez was launching. In 1999, during the first year of his presidency, sixteen hundred Cubans were flown to Venezuela in the context of an international relief campaign that assisted those stricken by devastating mudslides in the state of Vargas. The signing of the Comprehensive Cooperation Agreement in 2000 paved the way for the permanent presence of a bigger Cuban force in Venezuela. The agreement led to the signing of more than 150 accords between Cuba and Venezuela "in order to guarantee the well-being of the people" of both countries, according to the institutional propaganda.

The agreements encompassed a wide range of sectors: healthcare, education, culture, sports, energy efficiency, mining, information technology, telecommunications, agriculture, and political training of civil servants. The objective of this commonwealth was "the economic complementarity" of both countries. The first specific agreement was a medical covenant, signed in November 2001. It led to the arrival in Venezuela of six thousand Cuban doctors and paramedics and enabled one of the best-known Bolivarian missions—that of Barrio Adentro (Inside the Neighborhood). The mission had a grass-roots approach. The doctors and other medical personnel would live in the neighborhoods where the clinics were located. This brought medicine closer to peoples' homes, although the Venezuelan government could have achieved the same objective by expanding its network of public hospitals. The political gain derived from this mission was that the medical centers served to control the communities.

Uberto Mario has been featured on several television channels as a former agent of the Cuban intelligence service (as well known as G2) in Venezuela. In these television appearances, he has explained that one of his tasks was to "look after" the Cuban doctors. "I needed to know what they were up to," should any entertain the thought of hanging the medical robes and disappearing. That is the reason the medical personnel had to turn in their passports after arriving in Venezuela. The Barrio Adentro program, with some variations, was present in several countries. Such scattering of Cuban medical personnel was susceptible to dissidence. By the end of the Chávez era, more than three thousand Cuban medical personnel sent to other countries had fled to Florida, where the association Solidarity Without Borders helped them to join the U.S. labor market. In 2014 alone seven hundred Cuban medical personnel defected, most of them from Venezuela. Uberto Mario's cover was as a journalist, the correspondent in Venezuela of Radio Rebelde, a radio station founded by Che Guevara in Sierra Maestra, the Cuban mountain range. The former G2 agent also points to Venezuela National Radio and YVKE Mundial, both public Venezuelan radio stations, as a nest of Cuban spies. G2's main venue in Caracas was the office of the delegation of Prensa Latina, Cuba's news agency.

Another important media outlet for the Cubans was the program *La Hojilla* (The Razor Blade), broadcast on the public channel Venezolana de Televisión (VTV). Conducted by the PSUV activist Mario Silva, the nightly news program became a highly-rated show during the Chávez era as it broadcast propaganda about him and Chávez himself employed it to transmit messages. For many chavista leaders the show was a source of advice and inspiration. Judging by a tape released by the opposition in May 2013, after Chávez's death, Silva was a common confidant of the Cuban hierarchy. "Yesterday we held an intelligence meeting with two Cuban comrades, two officers, in Fuerte Tiuna," Silva would recount in the tapes secretively recorded. Silva criticized in them the leadership of his party. As a result of the controversy, Silva was banished from the media and VTV shut down (it returned to the airwaves in 2015).

Silva's contact was Lieutenant Colonel Adamis Palacio, with whom the TV host spoke as if the Cubans should have the last word regarding Venezuela's affairs. Palacio was in Caracas stationed in the Military Household of the president, and served as the head of counterintelligence. In addition to teaching courses to Venezuelan officers on counterintelligence and other matters, he also served at the Maiquetía airport. His cover for this post was as representative of the airline Cubana de Aviación in Venezuela. In fact he was in charge of security for ramp number four, which usually provides access to the Venezuelan presidential plane. His mission there involved controlling the arrival and departure of Venezuelan and Cuban officials. During his stays in Cuba he was a member of Raúl Castro's presidential guard.

An Army under Watch

During last year of Chavez's life forty-five thousand Cubans were officially registered in Venezuela as providers of services. Roughly thirty thousand of them were doctors and medical personnel. Most were probably members of the so-called Committees for the Defense of the Revolution (CDR) of Cuba. The head of the CDRs boasted in 2007 that thirty thousand Cubans under his command were serving in Venezuela. But the overall number of Cubans in Venezuela was probably much higher. In addition to the Cubans who publicly worked as sports trainers, teachers, social workers, or consultants for the public sector (tasks specifically mentioned in the cooperation treaty between the two countries) there were other Cubans who operated in a clandestine manner, for example as military and intelligence officers. General Antonio Rivero was an enthusiastic early supporter of Chavismo who was later ostracized precisely for questioning Cuban interference in the armed forces of Venezuela. Rivero reckoned that in 2012 roughly 100,000 Cubans were stationed in Venezuela. In media appearances Rivero estimated that there were four thousand Cuban intelligence officers and personnel.

Rivero was in Chávez's inner circle at first. His mission during the second attempted coup of 1992 was to free Chávez from the Yare prison. He did not achieve his objective, but nonetheless assisted Chávez when he was temporarily forced to resign in 2002. General Rivero took part in the operation to restore Chávez to power by returning him to the Miraflores Palace and ensured that the president had donned Rivero's bulletproof vest before he acknowledged and thanked his cheering supporters from the balcony of the palace. But the relationship between Chávez and Rivero soured thereafter as the president moved to further tighten ties with Cuba. Years after he was removed from a command position, Rivero left the Venezuelan armed forces in 2010. He was placed under arrest and later managed to travel to the United States.

The adoption by the Venezuelan armed forces (the National Armed Force, FAN) of the Cuban military model took place in 2007. That was the year when military barracks around Venezuela took up the slogan "Fatherland, Socialism, or Death," which officers had to repeat, thus violating the political neutrality that had traditionally been demanded of them and which is a cornerstone of a democratic political system. The Bolivarian National Militia was also created in 2007 as a civilian corps with military training and weapons. The Militia had its own joint chief of staff, which was made up of military officers who reported directly to the leadership of the FAN. By 2014 the Militia boasted close to one million members with varying degrees of training and engagement, while the regular Venezuelan armed forces numbered 200,000. The justification for a mobilization on such a massive scale was that the country needed to maintain a "popular continued struggle" to face the U.S. imperialist challenge.

Rivero tracked the Cuban military build-up in Venezuela. He estimated that five hundred Cuban uniformed military officers served as strategic and operational advisors, as well as assisting in intelligence, engineering, communications, and weaponry tasks. A Cuban general who had permanent and direct access to the Venezuelan Defense minister's office was in command of this Cuban personnel. Between two hundred and three hundred were stationed in Fuerte Tina, a big military base in Caracas where the Ministry of Defense is located. Colonel Cecilio Díaz was deployed in Fuerte Tiuna before he deserted and fled to the United States in 2014. He revealed that the Cuban Occupation Army, as the Venezuelan opposition called it, was forty thousand strong, most of which were scattered around the country and disguised as Venezuelan officers. The deployment of the Cuban troops would be directed by the so-called Cooperation and Liaison Group of the Cuban Revolutionary Armed Forces, which would be headed by generals Herminio Hernández Rodríguez, Fran Yánez, and Leopoldo Cintia Fría.

Rivero displayed to the Venezuelan newspaper *El Universal* a picture which portraited Leonardo Andollo Valdés, chief of staff of the Cuban armed forces, in a meeting with Venezuelan officers where strategic matters were allegedly discussed. The picture showed a map of Venezuela below the caption "Operational Chart" which displayed apparently classified information as it included units of the western region and the security system deployed to deal with neighboring Colombia.

El Nuevo Herald of Miami, a leading U.S. Spanish-language newspaper, also added denunciations from an anonymous Venezuelan military officer, whose identity was not been revealed to protect him. He highlighted the submission to the Cuban military establishment. He mentioned the summit of the Community of Latin American and Caribbean States (CELAC) held in Caracas in December

2011. In the run-up to the summit, Venezuelan officials prepared security rings to protect the attendees. The Cuban agent employed in the Military Counterintelligence Directorate General, known as Coronel Alcides, dismantled the security apparatus which his Venezuelan counterparts had designed. "No, this is not right," Alcides told them. "Before we knew it, the first three security rings were Cuban," as the aforementioned Venezuelan official disclosed to the journalist Antonio María Delgado. "The Cubans made the decisions within the Directorate General for Military Counterintelligence. A lot of attention is paid to the suggestions and comments they make. And they are the ones who manage the plans and shape the way the Directorate General deals with opposition groups and students." The Venezuelan official also described the mandatory training courses that many Venezuelan military officers, especially in counterintelligence, had to attend in Cuba. "They are ideological training courses, where they teach you that your overriding priority is to protect the life of the commander-in-chief of the revolution, followed by the Constitution and lastly the people."

Given these precedents, Cuba was also involved in the organization of the violent crackdown that the government of President Nicolás Maduro unleashed against the massive demonstrations that broke out in February 2014. Sources referenced by the newspaper *El Nuevo Herald* alleged that a Cuban team of twenty officers and high-level civil servants settled into the Miraflores Palace in order to organize the crackdown, especially the coordination between the security forces and the armed civil groups. This task was undertaken formally through the Venezuelan Revolutionary Secretariat, which coordinated all of the civil groups or *collectives* and was penetrated by Cuban officials. The Cuban team working out of the Miraflores Palace was also entrusted with the task of reinforcing the security controls in the presidential compound to prevent a repeat of the events of 2002, when a large demonstration that marched on the palace led to the temporary ouster of Chávez. Not surprisingly, some demonstrators attested that they had detected Cuban accents among the security officials.

"The Cubans are here to stay; the union between Cuba and Venezuela cannot be reversed," Vice President Jorge Arreaza asserted during the 2014 clashes. Arreaza, who was married to Chávez's eldest daughter Rosa Virginia, was promoted to vice president when the Bolivarian leader passed away. Arreaza went on to proclaim that "to raise flags against the Cuban revolution and to raise voices against the Cuban presence in Venezuela is an insult." With these direct remarks, Arreaza was addressing the unpopularity of Cuba's interference among many sectors of the Venezuelan population. The castrista revolution, the vice president averred, was "the reference, the light, the sun" of the Bolivarian revolution, and showed "the path we must follow."

The trail blazed by the Cuban revolution required that Venezuela undergo a transformation into a *Communal State*, a project already launched by Chávez with Fidel Castro's advice but whose implementation had been slow. It amounted to the model of Soviets for the Caribbean. Assemblies of citizens would become communal councils, and several of them would become a commune, whose representational and governance bodies would be chosen through different kinds of indirect elections. According to this scheme, the government would maintain a direct relationship with the communes, bypassing the structure of state governments and municipalities, where the opposition held some power. The plan also called for the creation of the Communal Militia, a neighborhood guard modeled on the Cuban Committees for the Defense of the Revolution. This thorough transformation was crucial to ensure Chavismo's future given the uncertainty over how long it could continue to manipulate presidential elections—an alternative for the moment when the regime would have to disavow elections that produced undesired results.

Since the risk of losing power at the ballot box had heretofore been very low, the creation of the communes had not been a priority. Social unrest forced Maduro into accelerating the transition towards a communal state. In 2014, the National Assembly adopted laws to foster the communes, transferring to them control over certain services and responsibilities, as well as funding, which had previously been run by the municipalities. The plan called for a gradual elimination of the powers of the governors and mayors in order to replace the state structure with the new one. In order to speed up the transition, Maduro appointed the former Foreign Affairs Minister Elías Juana, who had been trained by the Cubans, to head the Ministry of the Communes. But the government's financial hardship stymied the administrative and state overhaul. After losing the majority in the National Assembly in December 2015, the government launched a Communal Parliament in order to bypass the legal one, but it was convened only once.

Cuba's Big Business

Given the Cuban influence in Venezuela, a naive question springs to mind: how much has Cuba paid to the government of Venezuela over the past years in order to run the country? The answer is as surprising as the situation itself: it was Venezuela that was doing the paying. The South American country was providing each year approximately 100,000 barrels of oil and derivatives daily. At a market price of $100 per barrel on average during the boom years, it amounted to $3.7 billion per year. In stark contrast to Venezuelan crude delivered to other allies, Cuba was neither required to pay anything at the time of delivery nor complete the purchase at some future point in time. Cuba paid for all of the oil with the provision of the aforementioned services: doctors, sports trainers, military advisors... Cuba consumed part of the crude oil, but sold most of it to other countries, thus turning the sale of oil into its main source of hard currency.

According to the government-run web *Cubainformación*, the agreements between the two countries "involve bilateral exchanges which include the steady supply of Venezuelan oil to Cuba. In addition, Cuba undertakes the enormous effort to deploy more than forty thousand professionals in the educational, health, sports, agriculture and culture programs that the government of Venezuela could not have executed without Cuban cooperation. This arrangement obviously defies classical free-market rules."

The scheme's true defiance of market rules was highlighted by the absence of any transparency. There were no public documents that specified the value of the services provided by Cuba, depriving the opposition of any means to investigate the amounts and value of the exchanges. If we divide the market price for the oil given to Cuba annually among the forty-five thousand Cubans officially stationed in Venezuela in the framework of the agreements, each would earn a yearly salary of $82,000. A very high salary which none of them received. The NGO Solidarity Without Borders projects that Venezuela was paying between $1,500 and $4,000 monthly for every Cuban, although in reality they were paid less than $100. The government of Cuba kept the rest.

Due to the lack of public accountability, it is impossible to know the total value of the subsidies that Cuba received from Venezuela. In addition to the provision of social services, the agreements envisaged trade deals and concessional loans for the castrista regime which were never audited. Such loans financed many projects in Cuba in sectors such as rail infrastructure, development of tourism, and energy. Various analysts estimated that in 2013, at the end of Chavez's presidency, Venezuelan subsidies amounted to almost $13 billion, which was 21 percent of Cuban GDP.

The total absence of accountability and audits also hinder the task of assessing the debt that Cuba owed to Venezuela. Any estimate has to factor in items deleted in the public accounting logs, as the one disclosed by Rafael Isea, who was named Finance minister in 2008. Isea, who will be introduced in more detail in the next chapter, recounts the conversation in which he confronted Chávez over the Cuban debts:

–"Mr. President, Cuba owes us $5 billion.
–Delete it from the debts, Rafael.
–How? It is in our accounting logs!
–I am telling you to delete it, and that it not be registered in our accounting."

Chávez spent money which belonged to all Venezuelans. Despite the fact that poorer Venezuelans would have objected to largesse lavished on the Castros with public money, the president lashed against the upper class. "The bourgeoisie cannot stand that we talk about Cuba. We are going to talk about Cuba left right and center! Long live Cuba! Long live Cuba! Long live Cuba!" This was a method that Chávez employed to hide something: publicize it, preferably in the form of excoriations against his opponents, to try to pretend that there was nothing to hide.

With the "Long Live Cuba" slogan the Venezuelan president greeted Ramiro Valdés in February 2010 upon his arrival in Caracas. A historical leader of the Cuban revolution, Valdés was heading a commission that had to resolve the electricity production crisis that Venezuelans were enduring. The decrease in hydroelectric capacity was partly caused by a drought. But the structural problem was the lack of investment in the maintenance and upgrade of the electricity network. Blackouts were occurring frequently. The government simply did not invest in the network and wound up having to cut supplies to the population. But Cuba did not have expertise in hydro-electricity, and Valdés was also not an expert on the matter. The opposition always suspected that there was a different reason for Valdés' presence in Venezuela. He had founded the feared G2 and served twice as Interior minister. At the time of his arrival in Caracas, he was IT and Communications minister. The digital era turned the connection between modern equipment into a realm where the state's repressive apparatus needed to be extended to. At the time, a project had been launched that would lay an underwater fiber optic cable between Cuba and Venezuela.

Ramiro Valdés was in charge of the control of the identity cards and passports of all Venezuelans, a technological procedure which had been turned over to Cuba. A few years earlier, Venezuela had commissioned the Cuban company Albet with the task of implementing a program of "transformation and modernization" of the identification, migration, and foreign aliens' registration system. Albet was linked to the University of Computer Sciences, which was under

Valdés' supervision. According to one of the documents in the contract that I was able to obtain, the Cuban officials handled millions of blank cards to produce identity and passports documents. The process' lack of transparency spawned doubts about the destination of the cards. The possibility that they would be used to create fictitious electoral rolls could not be ruled out, as the opposition alleged on numerous occasions. Valdés left Caracas without having resolved the electricity shortages, but in the following presidential elections the computer connectivity between Cuba and Venezuela proved to be very important. The computer systems employed in Miraflores Palace and in the government departments were also Cuban, as well as those for social programs, police services and the state-owned oil company PDVSA.

In addition to managing the Administrative System of Identification, Migration, and Foreign Aliens (SAIME), which gave Cuba access to the database containing Venezuelans' personal information, the Cubans also took over the Autonomous Service of Records and Notaries (SAREN), which included civil, merchant, and property records. The Cubans could thus acquire knowledge about goods and transactions. Moreover, Cubans served as co-directors of the ports, were present at airports and at immigration and customs control points, and were in charge of different sectors of the Venezuelan state apparatus. Among the latter were the cases of Bárbara Castillo, member of the Communist Party of Cuba, who exercised great authority over the management of food resources in Venezuela, whose distribution during periods of shortages amounted to an ideological tool. Rosa Campo Alegre supervised the drafting of the syllabus for the National Police University, and therefore influenced the indoctrination of the security officers.

Cuba also played a role in the indoctrination of Venezuelan schoolchildren. In 2013 more than twenty million textbooks were printed for Venezuela's school system. Many of them included socialist content, which some associations of parents and teachers denounced. One of the books reminded that a Cuban breast-fed Simón Bolívar, the Liberator of the 19th century. "As his mother had health problems, she was unable to breast-feed her son. The boy was first breast-fed by a Cuban creole and friend of the mother, and later by the black Hipólita, a family slave. Simón Bolívar treated both with great love during his entire life." The historical tradition gives all prominence to the Venezuelan wet nurse, *la negra* Hipólita, but Cuba was determined to elevate itself to the status of the Liberator's godmother in order to win the hearts of the new generations, lest they later question Venezuela's uncommon obedience.

Militarization and Collectives

After Cuba, Venezuela has been the most militarized country in the Americas over the past years. It should probably be counted as one of the formal democracies with the greatest involvement by the military in public life. Hugo Chávez promoted twelve hundred members of the military to civil service positions. Many of them maintained their uniforms and remained in the armed forces, while others had to retire from active duty to submit to elections as candidates for positions in the civil administration.

Nicolás Maduro relied even more on the military. During his first year in power, he backed the promotion of more than four hundred generals and admirals, and he also appointed a similar number of members of the military to high-level positions in the civil service. Nine months into Maduro's presidency, one-fourth of his ministers were military officers or had military training—among them those in charge of the departments of Economy, Industry, Electric Energy, and Defense, as well as half of the state governors. Many deputy ministers, ambassadors, consuls, and managers of state-owned companies also had military backgrounds. With the promotion of Diosdado Cabello, who had retired from the military, to the rank of captain, the National Assembly was also headed by an active-duty officer—or the like. The "civil-military alliance" that defined the Bolivarian republic called for the creation of military staffs for civilian purposes, such as the military staff for health and the one for economy.

The presence of so many military officials in civil-service positions copied the Cuban model whereby the armed forces identified
with the revolution. Chávez had to make the transition to this model
in a more gradual way. "Despite the 1992 coup and Chávez's role in
it, the prevailing attitude among the armed forces of Venezuela was
one of respect towards the elected authorities," asserts Harold Trinkunas, director of the Latin American Initiative at the Brookings
Institution, one of the leading U.S. think-tanks. Born in Venezuela,
he is the author of studies on the role of the armed forces in Latin
America. Trinkunas explains that, although the military always
sought to wield some power, and to maintain and intervene in certain
political crises, most Venezuelan officers traditionally respected the
elected president of the country. "The president was the commander-
in-chief, a premise that was not questioned. This allowed Chávez to
gradually implement changes without the military perceiving that he
was striving to break with the old order."

As someone with a military background, Chávez's appointment
of his former comrades-in-arms to serve in his government did not
ruffle any feathers. The population became accustomed to more military officers dealing with civilian matters. The military barracks also
benefited at first from a greater presidential sensitivity towards their
problems. Higher salaries and better equipment satisfied many in the
armed forces, while others took advantage of the great possibilities to
earn illegal revenue generated by corruption.

Chávez gradually ostracized the high-ranking officers hostile to
him or who had more respect for the separation of powers, and then
created an alternative encircling structure. He first blatantly promoted the officers who took part in the 1992 coup. He then created the
rank of technical officials, promoting to technical lieutenant or captain long-serving lower-ranking officers. This measure created a
group of officers who owed their jobs to Chávez. In this process of
developing military structures unrelated to the traditional establishment, the next step was the creation of the Bolivarian Militia: a corps
of almost a million armed individuals, most of them civilians, commanded by officers outside of the traditional hierarchy. The National

Armed Force acronym (FAN) was lengthened to include the adjective Bolivarian (FANB) and had to formally endorse the governing party's ideology.

Chávez nonetheless could not resort to all of the military in pursuit of his revolution. As opposed to Cuba, where the dictatorship ensures that the armed forces obey the dictator's every wish, in Venezuela some of the military officers could refuse to carry out certain orders. In his quest to emulate Cuba, Chávez had to address two issues that were substantially different between Venezuela and Cuba: the holding of elections and the fact that weapons were in the hands of a corps where dissidence could arise. Designing an electoral system that guaranteed that control of the country would not be lost at the ballot box partly resolved the first issue. But the second was harder to deal with. If Chavismo resorted to electoral fraud, it faced a double challenge: how to neutralize any military reaction that sought to uphold the popular will, and how to guarantee the obedience of a military that used violence against popular protests. Solving this problem required the chavista infiltration of the National Guard, a component of the FAN which routinely operated as a security force; the creation of the Militia; and the strategic promotion of the so-called collectives: violent street gangs, often armed, which the government could use as shock units.

"Chavismo placed several roadblocks to limit the action of the armed forces," Trinkunas explains, "so that if the military at any point decided to revolt, they would have to surmount a whole range of obstacles. Moreover, the armed forces have no tradition of repression. The military learned the hard way during the *Caracazo* of 1989 that cracking down had serious political, judicial, and personal consequences." The repression against the mass demonstrations that broke out in February 2014 was carried out by the National Guard and by the collectives.

In its report on the riots, the NGO Human Rights Watch (HRW) concluded that there had been cooperation between the security forces, including the National Police and state police, and violent civilians. According to Human Rights Watch, the policemen ignored, acquiesced in and even abetted the attacks carried out by chavista supporters. On the basis of interviews with witnesses, HRW discerned a *modus operandi*: when the armed gangs arrived at a location, the police neither tried to disarm them nor protect the peaceful anti-chavista demonstrators. Instead, the police retreated and hence enabled the violent groups to carry out attacks. "We found convincing evidence that uniformed members of the security forces and armed chavista groups assaulted the demonstrators in a coordinated way." HRW concluded that the human rights abuses committed during the crackdown were not isolated cases or instances of excessive use of force by undisciplined agents, but rather a "systematic pattern."

Arming the thuggish groups was one of Chávez's most antisocial policies because it contributed to an increase in violence around the country and particularly because it affected the inhabitants of poorer neighborhoods. In the poor districts, which unlike better residential areas had no private security, families had to get used to locking themselves in their homes after sunset. The book *Estado delincuente* (2013) [Criminal State] by Carlos Tablante and Marcos Tarre explains that a factor that contributed to the spread of crime was the "governmental tolerance and even complacency with regard to the existence of unofficial armed groups such as the Bolivarian Forces of Liberation (FLB), or the collectives La Piedrita, Carapaica and others, which use their political activity as a cover for control of local drug markets, weapons, and extortion."

During the chavista era crime rates skyrocketed and Venezuela became one of the countries with the highest homicide rate in the world. When Chávez reached power there were ten homicides per 100,000 inhabitants, a rate which had held steady during the preceding decades. By 2013, the rate was seventy-nine homicides per 100,000 inhabitants, according to the non-governmental organization Venezuelan Observatory of Violence, which tallied 24,763 murders in 2013 as opposed to only 4,550 in 1998. The number of people illegally carrying weapons rose from 769 in 2000 to 4,765 in 2010. The number of hijackings jumped from 264 during the decade before

Chávez's rise to power to 3,416 during Chávez's first ten years as president. In 2016 Caracas was rated the most violent city in the world, and two other Venezuelan cities (Maturín and Valencia) ranked among the top seven. This violence resulted in a massive overcrowding of the jail population. Venezuela's prison population grew to three times the jails' maximum capacity.

Russia in a *Ménage à Trois*

Increased crime was the spark that ignited a wave of protests that swept across Venezuela in 2014. An attempted rape against a student at the University of Los Andes, in the city of San Cristóbal in Táchira state, prompted demonstrations by students in February 2014. The arrest of some student leaders in turn led to more protests which were joined by other social sectors in different parts of the country. The overwhelming outcry by Venezuelans was unlucky because it took place as even more worrying events were happening elsewhere. At the time, the mass media and the main diplomatic avenues of the international community were focused on events unfolding in Maidan square in Kiev, not in Altamira square in Caracas.

The United States and the European Union focused their diplomatic efforts on Ukraine and lost interest in Venezuela. But Russian President Vladimir Putin was closely monitoring events in Venezuela. As protests raged in Caracas and other towns, the Russian intelligence ship Viktor Leonov docked at La Guaira port, the closest to Caracas, on February 21 together with the tugboat Nikolai Chiker, with an apparent cargo of anti-riot gear and weapons on board. The ships were later sighted in Havana, but their stop in Venezuela went unnoticed. A few days earlier, Russian Defense Minister Sergei Shoigu announced plans to install new military bases in eight countries, three of them in Latin America: Cuba, Venezuela, and Nicaragua. These plans were probably wishful thinking considering the economic difficulties Russia was facing and the geographic priorities in its near abroad. But they were nonetheless revealing of the thinking in the Kremlin. Putin visited Cuba in July 2014 and signed an agreement condoning $32 billion in debt, which left only 10 percent outstanding.

Putin's objective was to rebuild a Russian empire and recover spheres of influence lost as a result of the break-up of the Soviet Union. The Russian president was making his most audacious moves in Ukraine, but previously, in his earlier term as president and then prime minister, Putin had been making bold moves on the global chessboard. And one of them was strengthening ties with Venezuela, in a *ménage à trois* with Cuba. After the downfall of the Soviet Union in 1991, Venezuela took over from the Soviet Union the role of bankrolling the Castro regime. As Russia made its *comeback*, Moscow continued to have a platform next to Florida which could unsettle the United States. The Russian president owed this to Chávez and Maduro.

The relationship between Russia and Venezuela relied heavily on trade in weapons. Amid appeals to peace in the world, Chavismo turned Venezuela into the first importer of weapons in all of the Americas, only surpassed by the United States, as the reports of the Stockholm International Peace Research Institute (SIPRI), specialized in recording worldwide trade in weapons, reflect. Between 2009 and 2013, 66 percent of the weapons imported into Venezuela came from Russia. Interviewed experts reckon the arms supplied by Russia to the chavista government until 2013 cost about $13 billion. The weapons purchased by Venezuela included two hundred T-72 and T-90 tanks, twenty-four Sukhoi fighter-bombers, 100,000 Kalashnikov AK-103 assault rifles (the revamped version of the AK-47), forty MI-17 helicopters, the S-300 anti-aircraft missile system, and surface-to-air S-125 Pechora 2M missiles.

Venezuela also bought between five thousand and ten thousand Russian iglas, a man-portable missile with a four-mile firing range. Their fate in the case of Venezuela's institutional collapse worried U.S. authorities greatly. The iglas, as well as the 120,000 rifles for the Militia and the 400,000 anti-personnel mines bought to Cuba (the island sold them because it wanted to get rid off these old weapons), could wind up in rogue hands.

The transactions with Russia started in earnest after a Chávez visit to Moscow in 2005, during which Putin offered the Venezuelan president what appeared to be a pre-arranged bribe. "Chávez, there is the suitcase with $20 million that you ordered for the negotiations on the rifles," Putin brazenly told Chávez, according to a later public disclosure by Raúl Baduel, the commanding general of the Venezuelan Army at the time.

Most of the purchases of Russian weapons were deals structured as loans guaranteed by the sale of Venezuelan oil. PDVSA and a consortium of Russian companies, including Rosneft and Gazprom, signed an agreement to work in the Orinoco Belt. The two Russian energy behemoths had already other interests in the Venezuelan oil fields. When Nicolás Maduro made his first trip to Russia as president, in July 2013, Putin estimated that his country's investment in Venezuela stood at $21 billion. These ties also complemented the close alliance that Chávez had developed with Belarus, Russia's ally and fellow member of the Eurasian Economic Union.

But later appeals for help from Maduro to Putin were not as successful. As the price of oil plummeted after June 2014, the Kremlin's maintenance of Russian international expansionism became more expensive. If Moscow had to prioritize, the Caribbean was far from its borders. Besides, in this three-party game—Russia, Cuba, and Venezuela—the Cubans would take a particular path with the normalization of relations announced by Barack Obama and Raúl Castro on November 17, 2014.

Plan of a Coup and Maduro's *Resignation*

Maduro's government not only had no inside knowledge of the thaw between the United States and Cuba; it was also tricked. Two days before the public announcement, the Cuban ambassador in Caracas, Rogelio Polanco, showed up at the office of Venezuelan Finance Minister Rodolfo Marco Torres, demanding payment of $3.2 billion in debt, mostly related to works in Cuba financed by Venezuela and whose payment was in arrears. The following conversation ensued, according to someone present in the minister's office:

> Polanco: "I am coming to get paid following an order by my commander, Raúl Castro."
> Torres: "I cannot withdraw the entire amount you are requesting in dollars. I can pay you whatever you ask for in bolivars. Otherwise I have to take up the matter with the president, as he knows what is in the coffers."
> Polanco: "Fine. Then pay me half in dollars."
> Torres: "I cannot do that."
> Polanco: "Five hundred million."
> Torres: "No."
> Polanco: "I am going to send a briefing to Havana. Chávez committed to paying these amounts."
> Torres: "Do not screw us! We have given you $80 billion in the past ten years!"

When the Cuban ambassador gave up and left, the Finance minister expressed his astonishment. "The Cubans' desperation to be paid fully is strange; we made a payment to them recently," Torres remarked to his assistants. "They are out of touch with the reality in Venezuela," he concluded, referring to the lack of hard currency in the Venezuelan government's coffers. This situation was concealed from the population of Venezuela, but Cuba should have been fully aware of Venezuela's plight. Out of touch? Two days later the Cubans showed that they knew what they were doing and that the Venezuelan officials were the ones in disarray. Havana had rushed to received the payments promised by Venezuela because the diplomatic overture to the United States could chill Cuba's relations with Venezuela.

In the secret conversations held for over a year in Canada and the Vatican between White House officials (Benjamin Rhodes and Ricardo Zuñiga) and a small Cuban delegation, the situation in Venezuela was on the agenda, according to sources privy to the talks.

Washington sought Havana's acceptance that the rapprochement would not break down if the United States would press on Diosdado Cabello, the president of the National Assembly, in order to crackdown on Venezuelan drug trafficking. Shunting Cabello aside was also in the interest of Cuba, as he was never a friend of the Castros. Moreover, Cuba wanted to ensure that Cabello could not take over the leadership of Chavismo should they decide to seek a replacement for Maduro. Although the Cubans also benefited from the drug trafficking, curtailing the so-called *cartel de los Soles* (cartel of the Suns) made life difficult for the pro-Cabello wing of the armed forces. In return for this understanding with Washington, Cuba reserved the right to continue interfering in Venezuela's affairs without this hurting the new relations with the Americans.

Once set this framework the U.S. justice system stepped up its process to possibly indict Cabello, while in Venezuela plans for an internal coup against Maduro were accelerated with Cuban acquiescence, although in low key mode so as to not upset the United States. The most senior official involved in the coup was Admiral Diego Molero, a former Defense minister and in good standing with Cuba. D-Day for the coup was February 27, 2015, according to one of the officers involved. A day earlier, only some hours before leaving the presidency of Uruguay, José Mujica surprised many by warning that "the problem we face is a coup d'état in Venezuela by left-wing military officers, and in such a scenario the defense of democracy would crumble." The plan was certainly to replace Maduro without holding elections, ostracizing the opposition, and alleging that the economic crisis was the most pressing issue. When Mujica spoke (he had obviously been tipped off about the plan) the order to stage the coup had already been revoked.

Exactly a year later, during the first weeks of 2016, Maduro's future was again in Cuba's hands. Venezuela's dire economic situation was unsustainable. It was increasingly difficult for Maduro to deal with the National Assembly, which in January convened with an opposition majority. Maduro reached out to Castro and discussed a possible resignation, according to information gathered by U.S. government agencies and which was shared with some members of the U.S. Senate. During Pope Francis' visit to Havana in February 2016, Castro pointed out to Vatican Secretary of State Pietro Parolin that Cuban did not meddle in Venezuela's internal affairs, as Cardinal Parolin later privately reported to several people. Parolin, who had served as apostolic nuncio to Venezuela between 2009 and 2013, interpreted Castro's remarks as a desire to keep up appearances.

It may very well be the case that Maduro and Castro's conversation about the former's resignation was conducted in hypothetical terms and sought to lay the groundwork for a gradual succession rather than an immediate replacement. In his subsequent cabinet reshuffle, Maduro promoted young activists who had risen up the ranks from the Frente Francisco de Miranda, an organization whose members were indoctrinated by Havana and were firmly aligned with the Cuban revolution. The new generation's leader, Héctor Rodríguez, was appointed head of the chavista parliamentary group in the National Assembly.

While Maduro was relying on this new breed of chavistas, part of the chavista old guard was maneuvering to force the president's resignation. In the name of the 4-F movement (the military officers that took part in Chavez's coup of February 4, 1992), former Interior Minister Miguel Rodríguez Torres tried to persuade Venezuela's military leadership about a change at the top. General Rodríguez Torres was for nine years director of the civil intelligence service of Venezuela, first called Directorate of Intelligence and Prevention Services (DISIP) and later renamed as Bolivarian National Intelligence Service (SEBIN).

But the absence of massive street protests over the lack of food and medicines and over the regime's obstruction of laws approved by the opposition in the National Assembly provided Maduro some temporary breathing room. If Maduro could complete his fourth year as president—until January 10, 2017—, his vice president could complete the six-year term, without elections. Cuba's leadership calculation was just as ruthless with regard to Maduro's future as it had been when it managed Chávez's succession.

2

PAIN IN THE KNEE
Illness and Death of a Titan

Hugo Chávez could not recall when he had started to feel pain. For some months he had experienced discomfort while walking, but he did not think much of it. Doctors would later determine that he had neglected his health for at least a year and a half, a precious period of time that was wasted and which severely diminished his chances of survival. "During my life I committed one of the fatal mistakes, as the philosopher would state; I neglected my health and was very reluctant to submit to regular check-ups and medical treatments," the leader confessed when he was diagnosed with cancer. But this admission of guilt did not change his behavior. The Venezuelan president stuck to his rejection to undergo a regular and exhaustive medical treatment, thus shortening his life. If someone ever wants to measure the price that a person will pay to stay in power, Chávez's immense suffering is a powerful example. Those who were with him near the end can attest to the unbearable pain suffered by the messiah of Bolivarianismo.

In the early stages of Chávez's illness, as in other momentous aspects of his presidency, Fidel Castro played a decisive role. As a father figure, he urged the Venezuelan president to undergo a thorough medical examination. Castro in this way was cunningly placing himself at the helm of the medical process. Castro had known for some time about Chávez's ailments because the medical doctors at the Miraflores Palace were Cuban. Fidel had advised Chávez to be examined by the Spanish doctor José Luis García Sabrido, the head of the surgery department at Madrid's prestigious Gregorio Marañón hospital, as Fidel himself had been his patient. García Sabrido might have traveled to Caracas around January 2011. It is possible that the Venezuelan president already displayed symptoms of a prostrate related affliction at the time. There was some discussion about a more thorough examination and possibly a treatment, but Chávez did not heed the advice. When the pain in his left knee began to hobble him severely at the beginning of May, he had to pay attention to it. Fidel was there again, arranging for a check-up and surgery in Cuba. Castro was the first to know that Chávez had cancer, and was also the one to tell him.

The pain in the knee was revealed to the public for the first time on May 9, 2011. Chávez disclosed it as a way of justifying the cancellation of a trip to Brazil, Ecuador, and Cuba. "Yesterday I was in pain as I reviewed the distribution of housing units in Baruta. I rested last night and prepared for the trip. This morning, when I went for a walk, I run before boarding the plane, which was departing at eleven. I took a blow to my knee and fluid is leaking from it." The blow to the knee sounded like an excuse to cover up a more serious health problem. Chávez almost admitted as much when he added: "I have an old injury in my knee which was never serious, but in the past few months I have been feeling more intense pain in my knee, which moved up to my left calf."

When he recovered enough, Chávez undertook the trip he had canceled and visited Brazil and Ecuador, and on June 8 he arrived in Cuba, where he met with Fidel. "He interrogated me almost as if he were a doctor; I confessed almost as if I were a patient," the Venezuelan president recounted a few days later. Chávez explained that, after a full medical evaluation urged by Castro, a "strange formation in the pelvic area" had been detected, and immediate surgery was carried out. In a press release on June 10, Nicolás Maduro, who was Foreign Affairs minister at the time, announced that Chávez had undergone emergency surgery in Havana after a "pelvic abscess" had been discovered. The draining of the lump revealed the presence of cancer cells and thus of a more serious abscessed tumor, which required more "serious surgery" to "fully remove it," as Chávez himself described on June 30 after his recovery. "Fidel himself, the towering giant, broke the bad news about the cancerous tumor to me," Chávez disclosed in a broadcast to the Venezuelan people from Cuba, which he begun with quotes from Simón Bolívar and Ecclesiastes, a book of the Bible.

Cuba now moved to completely call the shots in Venezuela. The Cuban infiltration over the past years in the structures of the Venezuelan state had been remarkable. Now Havana was taking over full command. Chávez had been able to check the Cuban interference with other influences, distributing some power but ensuring that he had the final say. But with his illness, his absence prevented him from performing this balancing act, and his medical treatment in Cuba meant that Havana would be making the decisions. As the cancer spread, only the Castros and the Venezuelan leaders whom they authorized had access to Chávez. Havana took over the succession process and ensured that it would maintain control in the new post-Chávez era.

Under the Castros' direct supervision, Cuban doctors from the Center for Medical Surgery Research (CIMEQ) of Havana managed the technical aspect of the illness. The lack of experienced oncologists on the island prompted the assistance of specialists from other countries during the entire treatment. Cuban surgeons carried out the first operation, when the diagnosis was still hazy. When the cancer was confirmed, professors A. Mikhailov and F. Abramov secretly traveled from Moscow to Cuba to perform the second operation. Russian specialists then traveled to Havana and Caracas for the first chemotherapy sessions, which were directed by a Cuban-Russian group that remained in Havana. A small team of doctors from Cuba and Russia were also sent to the small Venezuelan island of La Orchila, located eighty-seven miles from Caracas. In addition to a military base, the island also housed a presidential palace which in October 2011 became a retreat where Chávez could undergo treatment and tests on weekends. The island had the advantage of avoiding the public scrutiny of Caracas and not requiring flights to Havana. The Constitution called for the National Assembly to approve the president's medical absences from Venezuela, so the short trip to La Orchila helped to cover up Chávez's nonappearances from the Miraflores Palace.

The Cuban medical team was assisted during the process by the Spanish doctor García Sabrido. Brazilian doctors also weighed in with their opinions. Two of them, doctors Paulo Hoff and Yana Novis, examined the Bolivarian leader when he traveled to Brazil in July 2012. At least two German and one American doctors also joined the team towards the end of the treatment. Chávez also briefly resorted to a Brazilian shaman recommended by President Dilma Rousseff. Several media identified him as João Teixeira de Faria, also known as João de Deus.

Chávez even considered visiting experts in Chinese alternative medicine. Venezuelan doctors were involved in the treatment to a much lesser degree than would have been expected given the president's nationality. But Chávez harbored suspicions about his non-Cuban entourage and wanted to avoid leaks.

"In Venezuela Chávez does not trust anybody except the Cubans," observed the Venezuelan doctor Salvador Navarrete, who had been the president's personal physician. The Mexican publication *Milenio* interviewed doctor Navarrete in October 2011. Navarrete was the first doctor to publicly express skepticism about Chávez's survival chances. He had been posted at Miraflores Palace, alongside two colleagues, in the period before the Venezuelan president was briefly ousted from power in 2002. After those events, "Chávez discarded his Venezuelan doctors and completely relied on the Cuban ones," Navarrete disclosed to the journalist Víctor Flores García. Navarrete had continued to treat other members of the Chávez family, and was thus privy to the president's real condition. The doctor paid a price for divulging information to the press. The security services hounded him in order to send a signal to other potential leakers of sensitive information, forcing Navarrete and his family to leave Venezuela and move to Spain.

Leaks and Diagnosis

Breaking exclusive news is very tempting for journalists, but not only for them: sometimes persons who have confidential information experience the same irresistible desire to share what they know. This was the case with a source of the well-known Venezuelan journalist Nelson Bocaranda, who told him that Chávez had been diagnosed with cancer. Bocaranda broke the news in his blog *runrun.es* on June 25, 2011, five days before Chávez's public admission of his disease. "I received another angry outburst of insults and threats from followers of the revolution," as he later described the intense aggressive twitter traffic from chavista supporters that his breaking news spawned.

Twitter messages were the main source of news in a country where the regime's grip on the traditional media was very strong. Another source of tweets furnished a lot of information about Chávez's evolving illness. Rafael Marquina, a Venezuelan doctor who resides and practices medicine in Florida, also began to receive information from Cuba due to several unforeseen circumstances. Marquina is a good communicator when it comes to making complicated medical situations understandable for the general public. Marquina spent months disclosing details about Chávez's illness in television studios and on radio stations (obviously outside of Venezuela) which most of the chavista leadership was not aware of. They cursed him and called him a necrophilic, but they followed his interviews and messages on the internet: his Twitter account on some important occasions was able to transmit medical updates from Havana almost in real time.

Not exactly coincidentally, as I was in Washington searching for sources with inside information about Chávez's Venezuela, I was able to access accurate information about the illness. One source led to another, and when enough trust had been established, I had access to special reports drafted from medical information managed by people who were in charge of treating the president of Venezuela. Washington is a place where intelligence of diverse origin and destination travels through, and I was lucky to be in a position to gather the flow of confidential information about the health of someone—Chávez—who had been a thorn in the side for those in charge of U.S. foreign policy for many years.

When I managed to get my hands on these intelligence reports, several had already been drafted, as they had been compiled beginning on July 1, 2011, the day after Chávez disclosed that he suffered from cancer. It was difficult to verify the information with other sources given the unique nature of the situation. I spent quite a bit of time confirming the chain of transmission of information and ascertaining whether public events confirmed the reports. Such authentication was possible given the dates of the medical treatment or tests which the reports announced in advance, and which turned out to be accurate. Moreover, the report chronicled Chávez's absences and departures from Caracas to seek medical tests and therapies. The dates of the trips coincided with a lack of public appearances in the capital by the Venezuelan president.

On January 23, 2012, I published the first article in my newspaper about the situation, titled "Chávez Has Only a Year to Live Unless He Accepts Extensive Medical Treatment." The article summarized what the reports had described by then, and included the assessment that if the Venezuelan leader was still alive by the time of the presidential elections, foreseen for the end of 2012, his health would be so poor that he would be unable to discharge his official responsibilities. The events that unfolded proved that these predictions had been accurate.

It was not necessary to wait until the final outcome to corroborate that reality confirmed the intelligence reports. If the first article had already disclosed the appearance of a new tumor, a report I received a few days later, dated February 6, indicated that the tumor had grown in size and that doctors recommended surgery. Two weeks later, on February 21, Chávez admitted it: he announced that the tests had detected the presence of a lesion in the same place and that he would travel to Cuba to undergo surgery again. This sequence—I would receive a disclosure that would be followed by an official confirmation later—continued to repeat itself.

There was another notorious news item that took place at the end of 2012. The sources assured that the sarcoma had grown in size and that a team of Russian specialists flown in from Moscow were ready to carry out another operation. The news about these plans, which I disclosed on November 28 in the newspaper, appeared to be rebuffed on December 7, when Chávez made a public appearance in Caracas after returning from Cuba, and he seemed to have partially recovered. On the next day, however, he publicly announced the recurrence of his illness, and that he was traveling to Cuba to undergo a surgery which he might not survive. The reliability of the sources had been proven again.

Chávez's illness was at first diagnosed as a prostrate cancer which had spread to the colon and to his bones. A few months later the explanation changed. The Venezuelan president was described then as suffering from an aggressive cancer in the pelvic area, which could be a consequence of the prostrate ailment, or which could also be, according to some experts, the source of the cancer itself. Eventually the specific description was that of a rhabdomyosarcoma. It had originated in the soft parts of the pelvic area, with a possible initial lesion in the psoas muscle, which is located in the retroperitoneal zone of the abdomen.

Doctor Marquina believes that at first doctors were confused due to the lack of sufficient reactives in Cuba to determine the nature of the cancerous cells. In any case, the tumor spread to all the pelvic area of the body. In addition to the prostrate, whose cancerous cells were removed in the first hospitalization in Havana, the cancer gradually spread to parts of the colon, intestine, bladder, peritoneum, marrow, and bone structure, such as the lower spine. In the end, the cancer also affected the lungs, severely aggravating the patients' already serious respiratory problems that were ultimately the cause of his death.

Steroids to Tell Lies

The publication of the details of Hugo Chávez's medical condition was continuously assailed by chavistas as morbidity which encroached on the privacy of the head of state. In a regime with accountability, the media would have refrained from digging into the leader's physical condition because there would have been official communiqués providing basic information which citizens were entitled to know. Chávez, however, fooled his people about his health and ran for office while covering up his inability to campaign and to serve as president. Turning his back on his own people, he awarded the country to the Cubans to try to purchase a survival which he failed to achieve. Given these circumstances, the decent way for the media to act was to reveal the scale and nature of the fraud that was taking place.

During the months of illness, Chávez tried to hide his ailment with all kinds of excuses. The fear that his physical condition would prevent him from surviving until the elections prompted Chavismo to slightly move up the date of the elections. The National Electoral Council (CNE) announced in September 2011 that the elections, which had not yet been called, would take place on October 7, 2012. The elections were thus moved up by two months, as December was the traditional month when they were held. The CNE did not provide a reason for this historical exception.

The chavista leadership performed another dirty trick when Venezuela called a plenary meeting of the Community of Latin American and Caribbean States (CELAC), planned for December 2011, and which would take place in a military compound, an anomaly for this kind of international summits. Calling for the meeting to take place in Fuerte Tiuna allowed Chávez to rest and receive medical treatment in between meetings. The regime opted for not cancelling the summit lest Venezuela's close allies in the Bolivarian Alliance for the Peoples of Our America (ALBA) believe their benefactor was no longer able to support them.

The physical effort necessary for the CELAC summit forced the cancellation a few days later of a trip to Argentina and Brazil, alleging that the president needed to address the emergency nature of floods caused by heavy storms in Venezuela. Calling off the trip stoked more rumors about the president's worsening health. Chávez countered this perception by making a surprise trip to Montevideo to attend the Mercosur summit. His presence allowed him to personally seek the endorsement of Venezuela's candidacy for membership in Mercosur. After his return, Chávez fainted for seven minutes on December 21 due to the stress of the trip and his general weakness. The presidential entourage hid the increase in frequency of such losses of consciousness, but they were described in detail in the reports I was receiving.

The consumption of steroids allowed Chávez to pretend that his condition had stabilized, but the abuse of stimulants had negative side effects. On February 12, 2012, Chávez remained standing presiding the military march that marked the twentieth anniversary of his 1992 failed coup. That evening he collapsed at the Miraflores Palace, and he did not recover until one hour and a half later. He was secretly taken to La Orchila Island in order to be under medical supervision for several days. Upon his return to his Caracas residence, Chávez fainted again, prompting his doctors to take him again to La Orchila in order to treat an internal hemorrhage. "The medical team believes that the recurrence in the illness is partially caused by the uncontrolled use of steroids and other substances in order to remain active," another report summarized. In order to keep up appearances, there were false official press releases regarding the president's absences, who on some occasions spent more time in Cuba than the government announced.

Pretending to be cancer-free, Chávez launched the electoral campaign for the presidential elections by registering his candidacy on June 11, 2012, in an event where he avoided strenuous physical movements. He was transported during a mass event, at which he refrained from physical efforts: he was driven in an open top bus, where his hands held on to the railing, as would occur in future events. On that evening, Chávez nevertheless suffered extreme fatigue, dizziness, vomits, and blurred vision. Chávez resorted to the use of morphine (also fentanyl, a sedative which is one hundred times more powerful) to allay the extreme pain and, occasionally, to cocaine to overcome his apathy. These substances allowed Chávez to struggle through the following months. Most of his followers opted to think that their leader had recovered, but any independent observer could discern that the formerly hyperactive Chávez was not able to campaign on a daily basis and only appeared briefly at the end of rallies. He fainted several times at his residence after some electoral events. It was an enormous uphill climb, but Chávez made it to October 7.

Cuba and Russia Bicker over the Jewels

Cuba congratulated Hugo Chávez on his electoral victory on October 7, 2012, several hours before the closure of many polling places. The rush, as we shall describe later, was consistent with the secret management of the electoral process carried out from Cuba. It also revealed a Cuban eagerness to celebrate an objective which had been very difficult to attain: that Chávez survive until polling day. Moving up the elections by two months proved to be decisive. By December 16, when the presidential elections should have been held alongside the gubernatorial ones, Chávez was bed-ridden in a hospital from which he would not emerge.

For the Castros, it was more important that the Venezuelan president make it to October 7 than their Bolivarian brother's real health. Such was the conclusion derived from the discussions within his medical team relayed by the intelligence reports. The reports also revealed rifts between the Cuban doctors, who displayed a short-term interest, and the Russian specialists, who were not focusing on the day-to-day political agenda. Both groups nonetheless followed their respective countries' geopolitical strategies: Cuba firmly held on to its ability to influence Chávez and did not accept that he would escape their control; Russia questioned the quality of the medical care the Venezuelan president was receiving in Havana and pressed for him to be flown to Moscow for treatment. This would have transferred from one capital to another the weight of managing the post-Chávez era.

There was obviously much more at stake for Cuba than for Russia. Havana played its hand very well, taking advantage of the Venezuelan president's reluctance to be too far from his country, fearing that his exercise of a power that he never wanted to share or delegate would be constrained. Moscow guaranteed better health facilities, but in Havana Fidel knew how to keep up Chávez's spirits. During this transitional stage, the octogenarian Fidel committed himself to winning over Chávez's complete trust, while his brother Raúl, not prone to such sentimentalism, focused on how to engineer the succession in Venezuela.

Immediately after the cancer was detected Russian President Dimitri Medvedev contacted Chávez to offer the most advanced Russian medicine and his own presidential plane to fly him to Moscow. President Dilma Rousseff of Brazil assured Chávez confidentiality should he choose to seek treatment in the Syrian-Lebanese Hospital of Sao Paulo, which had proven itself so effective in curing the laryngeal cancer of former President Luiz Inácio Lula and the lymphatic cancer that Rousseff herself suffered. Amid this jockeying, the Russians insisted that CIMEQ in Havana did not fulfill the conditions required to treat Chávez's complex cancer. The Russians suggested that, if the Venezuelan president did not want to abandon the region, he should at least go to Brazil. But Cuba put up a stiff fight and refused to lose influence over Chávez in such special circumstances. A possible trip to the Russian capital, which could be explained to the population as the tangible result of an official visit which had been announced months earlier, remained on the presidential agenda until late November 2011. Chávez called off such a trip at the last moment, and continued to turn it down each time the Kremlin brought it up.

The clash between Cuba and its previous benefactor—Russia—over the terms of Chávez's *will* before his death was grotesque. The Bolivarian leader feared that assets controlled by the Venezuelan government beyond its borders would be frozen or taken over by other countries or the international community. This had happened during the demise of Libyan President Muammar Gaddafi and, to a lesser extent, Syrian President Bashar al-Assad. Chávez hence proceeded to move these assets. The possibility of losing the elections if he did not make it to polling day, and the possibility of having to resort to unconstitutional means to cling to power, aroused the fear that the European Union and the United States could impose sanctions and seize Venezuelan assets around the world.

The Libyan precedent was especially worrying, as the international coalition to confront Gaddafi turned over to the rebels the control of assets the country held abroad. The same could occur in Venezuela and benefit the opposition. It was thus imperative to relocate Venezuelan assets and place them in banks and financial institutions which were beyond the grasp of the U.S. Treasury and the European Union. In accordance with this plan, gold and hard currency reserves, many of which were deposited in English banks, were transferred to Cuba, Russia, China, and Brazil, according to a former high-ranking official at the Venezuelan Finance Ministry. This move also guaranteed that certain supplies would continue to flow, such as those provided by the Russian defense industry. As long as it held custody of Venezuela's gold, Russia would not cut off its weapons deliveries to Caracas, even in the event that Chávez's successor did not have the funds to pay for them.

Cuba and Russia disagreed slightly in their interests for the post-Chávez era. The Cubans had been able to transform the bilateral link *Venecuba* into *Cubazuela* as a result of Chávez's illness. They wanted to make sure that after the passing of the Bolivarian leader, Cuban-Venezuelan ties, although still strong, would not revert to any scenario under which Havana did not exert the most influence. For the Russians, the priority was not that Chávez's successor followed Moscow's orders, which had not occurred earlier, but rather to maintain the preferential trade advantages that had been attained. Moscow worried that a new government might not extend the terms of contracts which allowed Russian companies to operate and exploit Venezuela's oil wells. The Kremlin also feared that, under a new regime in Venezuela, its military might seek to purchase weapons from the United States instead of continuing to rely on Russian deliveries. The man in charge of defending Russian interests during Chavez's illness was Igor Sechin, deputy primer minister under Putin and former strongman at the state-owned oil company Rosneft, to which he later returned.

These different strategic approaches resulted in disagreements between the two countries' respective medical teams that treated Chávez. Both teams also had to content with a particularly difficult patient. "He is becoming more prickly, he looses his cool and sees conspiracies everywhere," the intelligence reports asserted. They also included statements such as the following: "his behavior is erratic with regard to the treatment that he should submit himself to," and "the doctors complain that Chávez ignores their instructions all of the time." He rejected medical treatments and tests, and at times stubbornly claimed against all proof that he had overcome cancer. He rebuked analytical results and angrily charged his physicians with "cowardice and an inability to believe in his recovery." Beyond a common effort to handle the patient's lack of cooperation, the medical teams from Russia and Cuba displayed different priorities.

A special confrontation—"a heated and prolonged debate"—took place as a result of Chávez's first relapse, at the beginning of 2012. The Russians pressed for immediate surgery that would extract the malignant tumor and extend the president's life. The Cubans preferred a smaller operation that enabled him to continue to campaign. Chávez chose the latter approach. "The president completely rejects surgery and asserts that the priority is to win the elections, not his health, and is willing to sacrifice his life to achieve the political objective." After performing only a surgical biopsy, as the weeks went by the doctors determined that Chávez could survive until October 7. Unanimity was therefore reached in applying short-term relief so the candidate could engage in some activity on the electoral trail, thereby postponing a more invasive therapy. There was deceit surrounding these therapeutic measures and their effects. "The Cuban government is not completely honest with Chávez about his illness, preferring to paint an excessively rosy picture about the results of the treatment, which boosts Chávez's morale." A bigger deceit was to come.

"He Fell Apart Emotionally"

On the night of October 7, 2012, the Venezuelan National Electoral Council proclaimed Hugo Chávez's victory in the presidential elections. On the following day, the president summoned Rafael Isea. "Come here on the 10th," he asked him. During their meeting at Miraflores Palace, Chávez informed him that, in the gubernatorial elections two months later, Isea should not run for re-election as governor of the state of Aragua. This position was reserved for Tareck el Aissami, who was minister of Interior and had taken Maduro's side. "I need you with me," he told Isea, offering a form of vague comfort he could not deliver on. "He knew he was dying, but I accepted, as I had no other choice. The president was crestfallen; he was even embarrassed when he told me that," Isea recalls, convinced that Chávez was doing nothing other than executing the course that Havana had charted.

Rafael Isea had seen a father figure in Chávez and he was almost like a brother to his daughters, as he had been by the Bolivarian leader's side since an early age. Isea was only twenty-three years old when he took part in the coup of February 4, 1992, that the future president led in Caracas. Born in Maracay (Aragua state) and the second of five siblings from a very humble family, Isea graduated from the Military Academy in 1989. That was the year of the *Caracazo*, a big popular protest which President-elect Carlos Andrés Pérez put down in a bloody manner. Disenchanted with the political system, Isea joined the Bolivarian Revolutionary Movement 200 (MBR-200) which Chávez founded. Chávez's seductive leadership style from the outset and his popularity among his comrades-in-arms and younger officers, as well as the poverty of Isea's family prompt-ed the latter to partake in the 1992 coup. "My family would tell me, aren't you going to do something to fix this system? One could not simply sit by and do nothing," says Isea as justification for the un-constitutional 1992 coup.

When Chávez was released from Yare prison in 1994, Isea served as his assistant until the electoral victory of December 1998. He was given the post of advisor in the Ministry of Planning and Develop-ment, and a year later was promoted to the position of executive as-sistant to the president. Chávez fostered his economic training by appointing him in 2001 as Venezuela's representative at the Inter-American Development Bank (IDB) in Washington. In 2006, he was named deputy minister of Finance and president of the Economic and Social Development Bank (BANDES), and in 2008 became Finance minister. From these high-level positions, Isea witnessed and was a player in the financial misdeeds carried out by Chavismo.

For the early chavistas, the president's cancer was a double blow. They felt pain as the man they adored fell apart physically and emo-tionally. Moreover, Chávez's illness brought about the relegation of his old guard and its replacement in the presidential entourage by officials close to Cuba. "His illness was our biggest misfortune. Chá-vez had pursued ties with the Cubans, but he had managed to keep them at bay. When his illness struck, he placed all of his faith in them to find a cure, and the Cubans took over political control of him," Isea explains.

Isea recalls that when Chávez suffered his first relapse in Febru-ary 2012, "he fell apart emotionally." "He was very afraid to die. He cried and became depressed." The chemotherapy sessions were ex-cruciating and he writhed in pain. "The Cubans began to execute the transition process months in advance. We assume that, at that time, they told Maduro, 'you are the chosen one,' and placed officials loyal to Cuba in key positions. In the end, Chávez no longer made the de-cisions." In Havana, several names had been considered as potential successors to Chávez. None of the candidates had strong leadership skills, something which guaranteed their meekness. Years earlier, the

Cubans had intensively trained Elías Jaua. When the cancer was diagnosed, they considered a Cuban-like succession, with Adán Chávez, the president's older brother, former minister and governor of Barinas. In the end the Cubans chose Maduro, who, as would be revealed later, had been trained in Cuba in the late 1980s and had since maintained ties with the island's rulers.

After the presidential elections of October 2012, Maduro spent time in Cuba with the ailing president and was often at his side. Meanwhile, in Caracas, Elías Jaua, at the time vice president and later Foreign Affairs minister, was in charge of making key appointments. Chavista governors, ministers, and the rest of the presidential entourage were deprived of the encrypted telephones with access to the head of state.

Facing an emergency surgery that he had put off many times, Chávez briefly returned to Caracas on December 7, 2012. Knowing that he might not survive the operation, he arranged his succession. On the following day, in a television broadcast to the country and seated at a table in Miraflores Palace between Maduro and Diosdado Cabello, president of the National Assembly, Chávez appointed the former as his successor should he not survive the surgery he was about to undergo.

Isea could see him that day. "The last time I saw him was on December 8. He looked emaciated, but he also appeared stronger. His daughter María Gabriela spoke to a Cuban doctor, who told her, 'advise your father that he not submit to surgery, that he pass away in peace,' but the Cubans insisted on surgery. They managed the process of his expiration. In order to master his legacy, they had to wind him down in a controlled fashion."

The chavista snake complete the process of shedding its skin during the funeral feasts of March 2013. According to Isea, the historical loyalists to Chavez were not allowed access to Maduro, who was serving as acting president and was surrounded by a ring of Cuban agents. "On that day it was obvious for all to see who was now in power: in the first row stood Maduro, Jaua, and El Aissami." Maduro addressed Isea with disdain—"you are going to Chile"—clearly vanishing him from the chavista universe. Chávez's *godson* did not accept the appointment of ambassador to Chile. Instead of heading south, he wound up going north. In September 2013, under pressure from charges of corruption leveled at him by El Aissami, who had taken his position in the governance of Aragua state, Isea arrived in the United States to reveal the regime's secrets.

Isea's dramatic account has moved our story forward. Let us now go back in time to the October 2012 presidential elections, so that we can describe in more detail what transpired in the crucial months that followed.

The Goodbye without a Picture

A few days after the elections of October 7, 2012, Hugo Chávez suffered a relapse. The end of his physical efforts to appear in campaign events and the end of the consumption of an abundance of substances which enabled him to perform these activities left him bedridden for a few days. Months of neglect in the treatment of the cancer took their toll. Instead of dealing with it efficiently, the illness had been overlooked so Chávez could continue to campaign. The confidential reports I accessed asserted that on November 24 Chávez's health took a turn for the worse. He was unable to get up from bed and complained about an acute pain in his midsection. The night of the 25th he lost consciousness twice. On the 26th he vomited blood and refused to eat. On the 26th he was secretly whisked off to Havana in a Cuban Air Force plane. He arrived at the island in critical condition.

On that same day, an official communiqué announced that the approval of the National Assembly had been sought so the president could travel to Cuba in order to receive hyperbaric oxygen therapy. It may be that Chávez underwent a few sessions with this technology. Although it is not designed to fight cancer, it can be employed to soothe skin wounds caused by chemotherapy. But the press release withheld the recurrence of the tumor. On November 28 a group of oncologists, surgeons, and a biologist from Moscow were expected in Havana, where they arrived in a specially equipped Russian governmental airplane. The Venezuelan government was covering up all of these developments. On the 29th, Nicolás Maduro, promoted to vice president, proclaimed from Cuba that his boss was "very well." And that is the way things appeared on the evening of December 7 as Chávez walked down the stairs from the plane that brought him from Cuba. It seemed that he came to Caracas to stay, but in reality this was a visit to announce that he was leaving, possibly forever.

The acknowledgment of his real condition happened the following day, in the aforementioned television broadcast which he delivered seated between Maduro and Cabello. "You know, my dear friends, Venezuelans, that it is not my style on a Saturday night, and much less at 9:30 pm, to take to the airwaves... but forced by circumstances beyond my control I address you, the Venezuelan people." It took Chávez fourteen minutes before he broke the news: "due to certain symptoms we decided with the medical team to undertake a new exhaustive test. Unfortunately, the test uncovered yet again malignant cells in the same affected area... and it has been decided that it is absolutely necessary and unavoidable for me to undergo surgery again in the next few days. The doctors have even recommended that the surgery be conducted yesterday or this weekend at the latest." He explained that he had requested first to travel to Caracas for this farewell, "making an extra effort, indeed, because the pain is considerable." "God willing, as in previous occasions, we will prevail. I have complete faith in a positive outcome, and since some time ago, I cling to Christ," he proclaimed, holding a crucifix in his hand.

He then announced his political will, underlining the seriousness of the situation, lest his courageous words be perceived as another medical twist. "If something should happen that prevents me from serving as president of the republic, be it to serve out the few days left in this term [a month] and especially to serve the new term to which I was elected by a great majority of you, Nicolás Maduro no only should serve out the remainder of this term, but it is my firm, absolute, irrevocable, and total belief that under such a scenario, which would under the Constitution force presidential elections to be called, you should elect Nicolás Maduro as president of the republic."

Dressed in a white and blue track suit with sneakers, Chávez said farewell during the night of December 9 to his political advisors. He held a meeting as well with his military officers, broadcast on television. It was his last speech, in which he summoned the outside enemy—imperialism—as a means to continue to rally his supporters. "The revolution is in your hands," he proclaimed, leaving the armed forces as the guarantors of the Bolivarian socialist order. "Fatherland, socialism, or death!," the military officers repeated. Later, on ramp number four of the Maiquetía airport, he bid farewell by shaking the hands of the leaders who had come for a final goodbye. After walking up the steps to the plane, before boarding it, he turned around and shouted: "Long live the fatherland!"

This was a powerful image which Chavismo was unable to employ later. It could also not comfort itself with a lyricism as in the registry of the illness and decease and in the death certificate of Simón Bolívar. The contrast between the two leaders is strikingly clear in the first pages of *El gran engaño* (2014) [The Great Deceit], by Pablo Medina. After the aforementioned documents about Bolívar, printed at the beginning of the book, there are blank pages regarding the passing away of Hugo Chávez: there is no official date of death—it does not exist in the registry—and therefore Chávez as a historical figure fades away. Without a dated elegy a legend cannot be settled.

The images of Chávez in his farewell lost value when weeks later the government released pictures of a sick Chávez with his daughters. The fact that these latest published pictures were not printed on billboards or hand out as a memento for his funeral suggests that they were fake. The regime lost its audacity when it came to creating a graphic myth based on the alleged deceit, and at the same time it could not do so—officially they were not the last pictures—with the inspiring image of Chávez waving goodbye from the entrance of the airplane, when his watch showed that it was already the early morning of Monday, December 10. The following day he lied down on a stretcher to enter the emergency room and he never got up again.

New Years' Eve Vigil

Hugo Chávez's surgery at CIMEQ in Havana on December 11, 2012, the fourth operation he submitted himself to, was especially long. It took nearly seven hours. It was carried out by a team of Russian doctors from the Presidential Medical Center and the Oncological Institute of Moscow, who were assisted by Cuban colleagues and the rest of the international medical team. The surgery's main mission was to remove cancerous tissue from Chávez's body. The doctors extracted part of the small intestine and worked on the tumors in two vertebrae. For the Florida-based doctor Marquina, only the performance of back surgery explained the length and urgency of the operation. According to this version, the tumor's growth was constraining the lumbar region and threatened to paralyze Chávez completely. In any case, the doctors worked on most of the organs located in the pelvic area. A biopsy undertaken during the surgery revealed the presence of cancerous cells in Chávez's abdomen and bladder. Probably a colostomy was carried out before, in order to substitute the anal evacuation. After the seven-hour surgery, the patient's midsection had been torn apart, and was strapped together by a mesh after the muscles in his abdomen had been removed. Some sources indicated that when the operation was being carried out, an artery was accidentally pierced, leading to a great loss of blood and lengthening the already complex surgery.

At the end of such a difficult day, the government of Venezuela announced that the president had survived the surgery. It otherwise did not provide any information other than the approximate length of the operation. A later press release indicated that complications had arisen during surgery, such as bleeding, and that the recovery would be slow. Henceforth most of the medical struggle focused on Chávez's respiratory problems, which were caused by an infection. A tracheotomy was performed on December 19. Additional patient's problems were retention of liquids in the lungs and renal failure. The antibiotics had not been effective for several days. The Venezuelan president's health deteriorated even further at the end of the year.

On December 31 there were rumors that Chávez had passed away. Some sources with information from the Colombian intelligence agency assured that the Venezuelan president's death had been registered by one of the doctors and by Cilia Flores, solicitor general of Venezuela and Maduro's wife. In Washington, the State Department was also aware of the possible death, although in its diplomatic contacts did not disclose the source of the news nor whether it was credible. In a confidential dispatch, the United States shared this information with the government of Spain, although it stated that it was only a rumor that had not been confirmed. There was talk of the life-support systems being plugged off at 5:10 am, and that Chávez had passed away at approximately 11 am.

"Yesterday's news account was accurate," wrote in an email the following morning Mario Silva, anchor of *La Hojilla*, one of the chavista TV programs with the highest ratings, where I was lambasted on several times for publishing information about Chávez's health. "He was about to pass away but the doctors revived him. It was an extremely complicated respiratory ailment," Silva proceeded to explain. Silva's communications were hacked and published later by the press.

It was an intensive New Year's Eve. As journalist I could not let down my guard, thereby risking that a colleague would get the final scoop first. I could not rely on my usual sources because the confidential reports about Chávez's health always reached me after a few days. On the other hand, if Chávez had finally passed away, one would expect that the government of Venezuela would announce it. The absence of an official communiqué, however, could be interpreted as a desire to wait until the following day, January 1, so the death would coincide with the anniversary of the Cuban revolution's triumph. At my newspaper we ran the story with the title "Chávez, in an Induced Coma." That is how we made it into the New Year. Personally, I was unable to join the celebrations of that night.

Afterwards some would assert that by New Year's Eve, or maybe since December 29, Chávez was clinically dead. Doctor Marquina believes that the Venezuelan president suffered a brain stroke. Others were convinced that Chávez passed away on December 31. Leamsy Salazar shared this view. As head of the president's security, he was in Cuba and was in very close touch during those days with Chávez's family members. "The last day I saw him alive was December 23. He was completely sedated. On or around the 29th of December, several foreign doctors signed a certificate whereby they could not be held responsible for the Cuban doctors' actions and withdrew from the medical team. On December 31, Chávez's health took another turn for the worse. A nurse who was very close to one of our bodyguards told us afterwards that he died on New Year's Eve. Henceforth we were all in a state of mourning; family members wept. We were sent back to Venezuela on January 3. They did not allow Chavez's father or mother to see their son. The Cubans kept Chávez's parents in the dark, but Adán [Chávez] was aware of what was going on," Salazar recalls. The Cubans assigned psychologists to treat Chávez's daughters so that, despite their internal grief, they would accept the obligation of not breaking down emotionally in public. In light of these facts, Salazar is convinced that Chávez died then, but he never had complete evidence. A situation of brain death, artificially maintaining the patient alive, could have caused the same grief among the family.

The scene for deceit was set. As all other access to Chávez was cut off, the Castros controlled all news updates regarding the Venezuelan president's health. I continued to receive reports, but looking back it is not easy to determine whether from this time onwards they were still accurate or the Cubans were making up all of the information my sources garnered. Officials in Havana did everything possible to avoid any leak: they would decide the time of Chávez's passing, and his death, or at least its announcement, could not happen before Maduro was entrenched in power.

The first political deadline was January 10, the date when Chávez was due to be sworn into office for the new term he had officially won at the polls three months earlier. As it ascertained that the chavista leader was not recovering, the Supreme Tribunal of Justice, loyal to Chavismo, violated the law and extended the terms of the president and the members of the government. This guaranteed Maduro's continuity as vice president and strengthened him with a view to a second violation of the constitutional order. When the passing of Chávez would be announced, Maduro would be in a position to brush aside Diosdado Cabello as provisional head of state, as the Constitution established that the president of the National Assembly was to take charge of the country until elections could be held. The Cubans feared that Cabello, whom they had vetoed as the successor, would take advantage of the power vacuum to reach the presidency despite Chávez's last will about Maduro.

Cabello's aspirations were buttressed by Maduro's possible birth in the Colombian city of Cúcuta, which if true would disqualify him from becoming president (besides, the law required to be only Venezuelan; in May 2016 the Supreme Tribunal of Justice hinted a change to accept simultaneous nationalities). Actually, Maduro's birth certificate had never been shown. But should Cabello dare to launch a challenge for the presidency, it would be neutralized by the Cuban threat to publicize the reports about his drug trafficking.

The government's lies were outrageous. On Christmas Day, Maduro told the country on national television that their president had been walking and performing physical exercises, when in fact Chávez never got back on his feet after the surgery, as his successor would unintentionally admit later on. On another occasion, a few days later, when Chávez was more dead than alive, Maduro asserted that he had spent five hours discussing matters of state with the president. Government leaders claimed that they continued to talk with Chávez. After I published details about Chávez's inability to speak, they finally stopped such nonsensical talk. But since they were used to deceit, they never felt any embarrassment, even when they were trying to fool the international community.

Maduro read out a letter in Chile on January 28 supposedly written by Chávez and addressed to the leaders of the Community of

Latin American and Caribbean States (CELAC). Standard practice would have been to send a recorded video or audio message with a greeting. But Chávez was not capable of doing that. He was also not able to dictate or write the ten-page speech that Maduro produced. Chávez's alleged signature on the speech was so neat and firm that the delegations of many countries had no choice but to assume that it was a copy. It was also suspected that a copy of Chávez's signature had been employed to appoint Elías Jaua as Foreign Affairs minister on January 15. "The letter is ready. I finished it," said the message that one of Maduro's advisors sent him along with the speech read out in Chile. The document, which one of my sources accessed, bore a copied signature.

Given the blatant forging of Chávez's signature, Diosdado Cabello feared that Chávez had already died and that the Cuban conspiracy was already ruling Venezuela, trying to make time in order to better settle Maduro in power. Three days after the farce at the CELAC summit in Chile, Cabello traveled on January 31 to Cuba to find out whether Chávez was indeed still alive. It is not known whether the Cubans allowed him into the hospital room, but after his return from Havana word spread among Cabello's advisors that the president was still alive.

Hectic Valentine's Day

Other people describe a Hugo Chávez who was still alive and still had some ability to communicate. Nidia Fajardo Briceño, the former stewardess with whom Chávez had had a romantic relationship, asserts that on February 14, St Valentine's Day, she visited the patient at CIMEQ. I afterwards had a conversation with Nidia through a third person, who kept one ear on each phone. The person repeated my questions to Nidia and conveyed her answers. I reached out to Nidia because it was in her interest to force the Chávez family to acknowledge little Sara Manuela, the result of the relationship between the president and Nidia, as Chávez's daughter. The details she provided about the girl were confirmed by several pictures, which showed Chávez and Nidia with Sara Manuela, and by the girl's birth certificate. I published these documents with the cooperation of Braulio Jatar, the director of the Venezuelan online publication *Reporte Confidencial*. This contributed to the Chávez family's decision to formally accept Sara Manuela.

Nidia's version of events depicts a president who had great difficulty communicating, with a tracheotomy that greatly hindered his speech, but who was conscious enough to recognize her. Nidia recounts that, as it was Valentine's Day, she persistently reminded of their long relationship and her wish to marry him. She claims that Chavez promised to marry her the next day. Should this be true, it can only be construed as an attempt to delay the fulfilling of the promise. A wedding was not feasible. Nidia explains that she slept outside of his room and that the day after she was not given the chance to remind him of the promise. She relates that on February 15 she discerned a lot of movements in Chávez's room and that she was banned from seeing the president.

The conversation with Nidia, as I explained, was held through another person. It is conceivable that the questions and answers were not conveyed accurately. It is also possible that she made up the story, dreaming up the episode of Valentine's Day as a way to prove her claim to be Chávez's true love. The dates she mentioned, however, coincide with those provided by another source.

Someone in a very senior position in the chavista leadership, who had worked very closely with Chávez for many years, but now was ostracized from the authorized Venezuelan group whom the Castros welcomed in Cuba, asserts that he had direct information about the illness through two people who attended the patient. This was no easy feat, as there were longtime Chávez aides who had been pushed aside by the Cubans. Personal assistants who supposedly were able to carry on their tasks with Chávez informed this leader that on February 15 Chávez fell into a coma from which he did not recover. This source takes it for granted that on the following day most of the international medical team left Cuba. This source firmly believes that he passed away on February 17, the day before the government of

Venezuela announced the patient's transfer to the Military Hospital Doctor Carlos Arvelo in Caracas.

An exchange on the night of February 17 between Maduro and Roy Chaderton, Venezuela's ambassador to the Organization of American States who at the time was in Cuba as an OAS observer of the negotiations that the government of Colombia was holding on the island with the FARC guerrillas, lends credence to the fact that something could have happened on that day. "Not only were the soldiers in tears. We too, Chávez's longtime civilian aides, are weeping tears of grief at this time," Chaderton expressed in the dispatch, which was obtained by one of my informants. "I am one of these civilians," Maduro countered. This exchange nonetheless does not prove that the actual death occurred on the 17th. These comments could be consistent as well with the decision to fly the patient, whose death was supposedly imminent, to Venezuela.

The official who supports the view that Chávez died on February 17 bases his assumption on the fact that after this date nobody conveyed having seen Chávez and that in the reserved area at Doctor Carlos Arvelo Hospital there was no sign of medical activity. The official asserts that the president's dead body was flown in a medical airplane to the Venezuelan capital with an oxygen mask and catheters, to pretend that he was still alive, and transferred by Cuban intelligence officials disguised as male nurses. A team appointed by Diosdado Cabello would have been in charge of the logistics of the arrival at Maiquetía airport in the early morning of February 18. The arrival was arranged without participation of airport officials, with many lights turned off and without the presence of security guards.

Leamsy Salazar, Chávez's head of security, was at Maiquetía on the 18th. He saw the corpse and concluded that it was the president's body. It appeared to Salazar that the body was not well preserved, although if he had been dead for a month and a half and not embalmed the decay should have been greater. It is also possible that the body carried on the stretcher was that of another person, dead or alive, since nobody was able to take a close look, as Cuban security officials surrounded the body, as Salazar confirms.

If there had been a fake transfer, it would have been carried out waiting for an opportunity to announce that the president had been sworn in for his new term in an event without any witnesses held at the Military Hospital, even if that were not true. This would have allowed the falsifying of Maduro's confirmation as vice president, who at the time served in that capacity via an act of legal fiction. In fact, the publication of the apparently doctored pictures of Chávez with his daughters on February 15 would have served the purpose of keeping up the appearance of a president fit enough to be sworn into office. Leaving aside Chávez's real situation, the Supreme Tribunal of Justice gathered the signatures of its members to testify about a swearing in ceremony that none of them attended, as I disclosed. Eventually there was no announcement.

Not even the highest military authority of the hospital was allowed into the ninth floor, which was guarded by Cubans. None of the hospital's employees ever witnessed the removal of garbage. The journalist Nelson Bocaranda drives this point home, and asserts that not even Chávez's family was allowed into the room. Few family members went there. When one of his daughters did make it to the hospital, there is no proof that she was able to access the place watched by the Cubans. "His daughters did not go up; neither did Maduro, despite his statements that he had been with him. They went up but did not reach the ninth floor; they waited for a while and came back down," he recalls.

Another strange circumstance is that Evo Morales, probably the South American leader whom Chávez held in highest esteem, arrived in the hospital on February 20 and was not allowed to visit the patient. Moreover, only one of his family members, his daughter María Gabriela, was present on March 1 when mass was celebrated in the hospital's chapel to pray for the head of state's recovery. These restrictions were surprising given how fetishist Venezuelans are with religious cult when it comes to praying for the health of the loved ones.

Despite these suspicious circumstances, Bocaranda trusts that his informants at this point were just as accurate as in the early stages of

Chávez's illness, although probably none of them personally witnessed that the Venezuelan leader, dead or alive, was in the Military Hospital. The Venezuelan journalist was assured, after the official announcement of Chávez's death on March 5, that he was taken off life-support mechanisms the same day at about 11 am. The calculation was that he would die after a couple of hours. Chávez would thus pass away approximately at the same time as Simón Bolívar, who expired on December 17, 1830, at 1:03 pm. But this process would have been interrupted, and Chavez would have been again placed on life support, to allow for Maduro's televised address, during which he accused the United States of inoculating Chávez with cancer. During the speech, Maduro spoke in a somber tone, in the same manner that he announced in the afternoon that the president had passed away. Taken of life-support again, Chávez would have died at 4.25 pm according to the government.

A source told doctor Marquina a different version at the end of the day, according to which Chávez died at 12:25 pm, but the official time of expiration was the moment when his daughters left the hospital room, after a period of time they were given so they could keep vigil over their father.

End of the Thriller

What if none of these scenarios was true? The body language of Nicolás Maduro and those with him during the televised announcement spoke volumes. None of the military officers or ministers who were standing next to the vice president, looking at the camera from a place of honor at the hospital's entrance, showed the emotion that would have been expected by the news that the charismatic leader had died there and then. Some of them turned towards Maduro, as if he were acting, when his voice began to tremble. Information Minister Ernesto Villegas glanced at his watch several times, as if the whole proceeding did not concern him. Chávez was either not there or he had died before arriving in Caracas. There is also the possibility that, for those assembled, who had not seen their leader for some time, Chavez was already in the distant past. Most probably they knew nothing and by this time did not trust any official version.

On the eve of the announced transfer of Chávez of February 18 to the Military Hospital, the medical team that had been treating him was completely dismantled, thereby breaking the communication link that had been a source of the intelligence reports I had been receiving for more than a year. During the last two months of Chávez's life the reports were less reliable, because the Cubans had tightened their grip. The information I obtained during the final two weeks was confusing. There was discussion about a possible return to Venezuela, but the transport would have been to "his secret medical installation on the island," an expression that had always referred to La Orchila. As I explained earlier, Chávez had previously undergone some medical treatment at the presidential residence on the island. Shortly thereafter, informants disclosed that the cancer in Chávez's left lung had spread quickly, believed that the patient had been flown back to Cuba on March 1, and that he died there on the early morning of March 5, a few hours before the official announcement.

At the time of writing it is impossible to know which is the true version of events: that Chávez died in Cuba between the 29th and the 31st of December, 2012; that he passed away on February 17, 2013, the day before he was officially flown to Venezuela; that he died in the Caracas Military Hospital on March 5, as the government announced; or that he expired on the same day but in Cuba. I regret to disappoint those who obviously expected to read the solution to this riddle. This chapter ends as the genre of novels which offer several possible endings, from which the reader can choose.

Given the facts that I have laid out, I personally find it hard to believe that Chávez passed away at the end of 2012. I am more inclined to believe that he was still alive, albeit very ill, until the middle of February 2013. But this is only speculation. In any case, it seems likely that he died in Cuba, and it is possible that his body was not flown to Caracas until the announcement of his expiration. I had access to information—which it was impossible to independently verify—that suggested that Chávez's body may have arrived in Cuba on the night of March 5 and been taken to the Hospitalito morgue, located within the Fuerte Tiuna compound, close to the Military Academy. His body would have remained there until the funeral procession reached the basement of the Academy, where it would be placed in the coffin so it could lie in state. These were not the only sources that pointed out that the casket paraded during seven hours in the Caracas heat amid throngs of people was indeed empty. The regime played with the feelings of thousands of Venezuelans, with a last deceit that crowned the hoax carried out in the preceding months.

Whatever option one chooses for the end of the story, there is an unquestionable fact that indicates who was in charge of this tragical comedy. Early on March 5, at about 7 am, a dispatch from Havana to the Miraflores Palace was intercepted. The message announced Chávez's death. Had he passed away in Cuba, was it the order to turn off the life support mechanisms in Caracas, or the green light to publicly disclose a death that had already occurred? The Castros were in charge, as they would be in the upcoming electoral campaign.

3

"IT IS TRUE, WE ADDED VOTES"

The Electoral Fraud

The chavistas' secret computers were very clear. At 6 pm, when on April 14, 2013, the polling places should close in Venezuela, the presidential elections had been won by the opposition candidate, Henrique Capriles Radonski. His was the victory that at the end of a manipulated process would officially be given to Nicolás Maduro. A parallel and secret computer system developed by the chavistas allowed them to know in real time during the day the amount of votes that each candidate was getting, thereby enabling them to calculate how many false votes they had to add to rig the election in Maduro's favor. This took place within the context of a completely automated electoral system, as is the norm in Venezuela, and with the complicity of the National Electoral Council (CNE), which was supposed to be an independent institution. Cuba also played a major role in rigging the elections.

At 10 am, Diosdado Cabello showed up at the Caracas city council building, in the municipality of Libertador. The Venezuelan regime's number two arrived with his security chief, Leamsy Salazar. Both went up to the floor where the mayor's office was located and headed towards a nearby conference room where computers secretly monitored the elections. Access to the conference room was extremely restricted. Cabello and Jorge Rodríguez, the mayor of Caracas and big *magician* of Chavismo's electoral fraud, had the clearance to enter the room. The mayor's sister, Delcy Rodríguez, later appointed Foreign Affairs minister, was present as well. Vice President Jorge Arreaza was also summoned when the need to speed up the deceit became apparent in the afternoon.

There were twenty-four electoral monitors arranged in a U shape around the room. Each one tracked the voting of one of Venezuela's twenty-three states. The central one tallied the overall result for the entire country. The need to maintain secrecy limited the number of IT personnel to one or two persons. Salazar had already witnessed several chavista secrets. He immediately realized that the computer screens were displaying the votes that Capriles and Maduro were garnering. This information was not available to anyone, even to the National Electoral Council, because the voting machines were only connected to the network after the polls closed and only then they broadcast the results. But in fact these devices could at any moment send or receive data wirelessly, because they have bidirectional capability, as the auditors have explained.

Polling places [here used as synonym for electoral centers, while polling stations or electoral tables will be used for each of the ballot boxes] had opened at 6 am. Within a few hours the Democratic Unity Roundtable (MUD) candidate was well ahead in the vote count. Around 11:30 am, Capriles, who was also the head of the Primero Justicia party and the governor of Miranda state, was beating Maduro by 400,000 votes.

Salazar had served Hugo Chávez until the announcement of the president's death one month earlier and had recently been appointed to head Cabello's security. He could gauge the increasing nervousness of Cabello, the president of the National Assembly, which was shared by everyone in the room. Salazar explains how they employed encrypted phones to call the CNE. The Libertador situation room coordinated the regional tallying posts spread secretly out around the country, which had direct contact with the polling places in each zone.

As time went by the likelihood of electoral defeat exasperated the chavista leadership. "Damn it! Are we going to allow that fag Capriles to win these shitty elections?" Cabello asked as he glanced around the room. Salazar gives an account of how the leaders of Venezuela's United Socialist Party (PSUV) then held an emergency meeting which Vice President Arreaza later joined. The measures to alter the result were making inroads into Capriles' lead. Chavismo deployed its well-honed practices of voter intimidation and forcible mobilization of its voters. But as late as 4 pm Capriles was still leading by 220,000 votes, according to Salazar. It was time to resort to extraordinary measures.

"This was the moment when that day the Internet stopped working. Arreaza publicly then announced that there was a glitch in the Internet which was being repaired. By the time the Internet was up again, the computer screens started to display bigger vote totals for Maduro." The chavista leaders' moods improved and they cynically began joking among themselves: "You were scared, right?" By the end of the night, the CNE proclaimed Maduro as the winner by a difference of 223,599 votes. According to the CNE, Maduro obtained 7,587,579 votes (50.6 percent), barely edging out Capriles' 7,363,980 (49.1 percent). What had happened?

Salazar alleges that the Internet was taken down on purpose in order to reduce the burden on the telecommunications network and hence be able to better manage the complex amount of data that poured into the parallel IT system developed by the PSUV. It was crucial to know the distribution of the vote in each state as election day was nearing its end.

Manufacturing fake votes on a massive scale required a vote distribution which did not blatantly deviate from the pattern at each polling place. All of the persons with fake identities had to cast their votes, and orders had to go out to the thousands of chavista agents deployed at the polling places across the country to create fake votes. The CNE had surreptitiously turned over to the PSUV the technical control of the voting machines and other key processes of the elections.

Chavismo needed time in order to carry out this final operation. Shortly before 6 pm, when polling stations were supposed to close, the CNE announced that they would remain open until 8 pm wherever it was necessary. The momentum swung in favor of Maduro during the additional two hours of voting. Moreover, the CNE's suspicious habit of not releasing results until there was an "irreversible trend" served as cover for the eleventh-hour manipulations. Chávez's victory proclaimed six months earlier also materialized towards the end of election day.

Bidirectional Devices

Salazar's account is backed up by the research conducted by several experts. Umberto Villalobos, who works for the Venezuelan company of electoral studies Esdata, was able to record the time at which each polling place sent its results to the CNE by examining the voting machines' printed registry. The data Villalobos compiled shows that polling places where closing time was delayed were predominantly carried by Maduro. It highlights the utter anomaly whereby the spike in votes for Maduro was especially large between 7:30 pm and 8:05 pm. Salazar, Cabello's chief of security, confirms that Capriles was still leading Maduro when 75 percent of polling places had sent in their results. The polling places that reported their results at the latest possible time overturned the pattern.

Were the votes from real people, were they from anonymous fingers that fraudulently worked the voting machines (let's call them *flat votes*), or had they been electronically engendered from a remote location (*virtual votes*)? Salazar was not sure. It was his first time in the Venezuelan United Socialist Party's secret room that monitored the election results. On previous election days he had remained by Chávez's side. The president delegated oversight of the elections to other officials. Salazar hence did not have enough information to reach a conclusion about the nature of the additional votes. But there was no doubt in his mind that he was witnessing the rigging of an election on a massive scale.

The real truth about what really happened on election night lies in the evidence garnered by the IT specialists Anthony Daquin and Christopher Bello. Daquin worked for the Venezuelan agency that produced identity papers during the early stages of the chavista manipulation of the identification system. Bello, for his part, was privy to the serious flaws that a wholesale audit of the Venezuelan voting system had uncovered in 2011 and 2012. Both conclude that the electoral census, officially called the Permanent Electoral Registry (REP), contained 1,878,000 voters more than the total number of Venezuelans aged 18 or over that appear in the official registry of identification. The National Electoral Council refuses to allow opposition's access to the REP. Chavismo therefore employed this batch of voters with several identification registries (or foreigners who were informally registered) as a cushion with which to adjust their margin of victory over the opposition. While overseeing the system's equipment, Bello ascertained that the voting machines had four BIOS (Basic Input Output System), an unnecessary complexity which ensured communication with external devices. This connectivity would have made possible the fraudulent recount as well as the issuance of *flat* votes.

The PSUV's leadership had deliberately taken down the Internet and caused blackouts in certain regions in order to fend off an attack against its parallel IT system. Mayor Jorge Rodríguez sounded the alarm bells in the PSUV's situation room when he realized that an anti-chavista hacking action was damaging the REP's database, specifically by targeting names that appeared more than once and other evidence of fictitious voters. The hacking operation had probably prevented approximately 900,000 fake identities from the ability of casting their ballot. After Internet service was restored, it is possible that part of these votes went finally to Maduro because during the blackout Chavismo managed to insert a back-up database into the system. But the closure of the polls was fast approaching. Between 6 pm and 8 pm, more than 600,000 votes were cast for Maduro, an amount that could not be accrued through the normal voting process. A significant number of this bevy of votes had to be *flat* votes.

The casting of such a large number of ballots in such a short period of time leads Umberto Villalobos to believe that Maduro's razor-thin victory was the product of digital voting, whose existence had always been feared: the possibility that a central server enabled the modification of the numbers in the final vote count. According to Villalobos, the deviations in the registered totals were the product of calculation methods that only a central server could execute. Since the voting machines were bidirectional, when they went online to transmit the results they could have received data that would alter them: the certificates of the final vote tallies were only printed after the results were transmitted.

Christopher Bello, on the other hand, discards the digital vote theory and instead asserts that the vote rigging was done manually. His research suggests that the fraud originated in the polling places themselves, an explanation that is consistent with the mass mobilization of the chavista apparatus which we will describe shortly.

Admission of Fraud

Some of the main chavista leaders privately admitted the electoral fraud to U.S. officials. The opposition denounced the abnormalities and some countries and international organizations called for a recount that would avoid a national confrontation. Initially, chavista officials publicly closed ranks behind Nicolás Maduro, the president-elect. But this was only an appearance. The hidden clash between Maduro and Cabello would soon resume. Several chavista officials reached out indirectly to contacts in the United States in order to clear their records. They wanted to ensure that they could be an alternative to Maduro that would receive international recognition. Or that, should they have to flee Venezuela, they would be safe from international arrest warrants issued by prosecutors who uncovered their illicit business practices.

This kind of meetings between chavista leaders' envoys and U.S. agents took place on Caribbean islands and some European capital. The meetings had to be conducted by the leaders' assistants given the inherent danger of undertaking a trip abroad with that purpose. Within a month of Maduro's alleged electoral triumph, couriers dispatched by Cabello and the new minister of Interior and Justice, General Miguel Rodríguez Torres, admitted what everyone had suspected.

–"Yes, it is true. We added 350,000 votes. Our people manned stages one, two, and three at the polling places.
–Capriles took from us 900,000 votes, and the figure could have gone to two million if we had not used assisted voting and other procedures."

The numbers could have been rounded up or down, and the term "adding" may refer only to the fake votes that had to be manufactured towards the end of voting day. In any case, this was an outright admission that they had stolen the presidency from Capriles. "It was not an easy admission for them to make," recounts one of the persons who attended the meetings. "Even if they were acting against Maduro by reaching out to U.S. contacts, they were loathe to delegitimize the entire electoral result as this entailed that any chavista replacement for Maduro as head of state was also illegitimate. In the end, they had to furnish answers to the questions persistently asked by the U.S. contacts in order to have a chance of striking some possible deal."

The confession admitted that Chavismo had lost track of 900,000 votes (due to the hacking attack) and calculated that two million votes was the security margin with which Chavismo confronted each election (the majority of them related with false identity). This admission should embarrass some international visitants, which on election day reported that everything had run smoothly and blessed the elections as free and fair.

It was not the first time that high-ranking chavista officials admitted in private that elections in Venezuela were rigged. Eladio Aponte was a judge in Venezuela's Supreme Tribunal of Justice (TSJ) until 2012, when he fled to the United States. He reveals that his colleague Francisco Antonio Carrasquero, vice president of the TSJ's Constitutional Court and president of the National Electoral Council (CNE) between 2003 and 2005, confirmed the vote rigging. Jorge Rodríguez was also president of the CNE between 2005 and 2006 and later directed Chávez's and Maduro's electoral campaigns. He told Aponte that the system was rigged. "Do not worry, everything is under control," Rodríguez once assured Aponte in a context that did not leave any doubt regarding Chavismo's complete domination of the electoral process. Some of these conversations took place within earshot of other Supreme Tribunal of Justice judges. The conversations also revealed that Cuba monitored the electronic electoral system through the underwater fiber optic cable that links the island to Venezuela.

This cable would draw attention from a foreign—but not U.S.—intelligence service. Shortly before the presidential elections of October 7, 2012, when a very ill Hugo Chávez sought another term, the intelligence service uncovered the spot on Venezuela's coast where the cable plunges into the sea. The agents also determined the exact location—very far from the coast—where divers needed to go underwater in order to deactivate it. But the operation was never undertaken. Since there was no clear evidence that the electoral trick had to do with the electronic creation of thousands of fake votes from a central server kept in Cuba, possibly the action wouldn't avoid the fraud; rather some countries or the opposition would be accuse of sabotaging the election. It was a very high price to pay. The connection center with Cuba was located on the ninth floor of the Banesco tower in Caracas. The operation's servers were installed nearby, on the second floor of the CANTV tower, and were run by Cuban and Venezuelan intelligence personnel.

The fact that Cuba's leadership knew about the election's results in real time is confirmed by the message of congratulations sent by Cuban President Raúl Castro to his Venezuelan colleague on October 7, 2012, several hours before the CNE proclaimed him as the winner of the presidential elections, as an intercepted communication revealed.

Judge Aponte witnessed the activities performed from the situation room that chavistas used to illegally monitor the voting process already in the 2006 presidential elections, as Leamsy Salazar would be a witness of the same behavior in the 2013 elections. According to Aponte, in 2006 the command-and-control center was set up in a house in El Placer development, in the Caracas metropolitan area. The house was close to the military installations of Fuerte Tiuna, the Ministry of Defense's headquarters, where the CNE had installed equipment to gather the official data from all of the polling places around Venezuela. Aponte had been summoned to the house in order to coordinate the *criminal security* on election day. The Criminal Court of Venezuela's Supreme Tribunal of Justice, whose president was Aponte, had already compiled lists of loyal chavista prosecutors who would be in charge of arresting opposition members who tried to tarnish the election with their denunciations, or to guarantee the release of chavista supporters locked up for intimidating voters. "There were policemen in motorbikes that required opposition voters to stand in line and produce their identity papers. This served to hinder the way of opposition voters to the polling stations and to intimidate them," Aponte recounts, admitting that prosecutors were instructed not to interfere with these activities.

"From the outside, the house resembled a bunker: it was completely closed and strongly locked. Nobody outside the house could see what was going on inside," Aponte goes on. "Every couple of hours the data on the votes garnered by each candidate was updated and decisions were made to mobilize supporters." Present at the house were, among others, Francisco Ameliach, who directed Chávez's 2006 presidential campaign; Diosdado Cabello, deputy leader of the Venezuelan United Socialist Party (PSUV) and president of the National Assembly, and Jorge Rodríguez, who until a few months earlier had been president of the National Electoral Council (CNE) and coordinated the incestuous relations between the PSUV and the electoral authority. Rodríguez recruited several CNE IT engineers with inside knowledge of the system when he left the institution. When he was elected mayor of Caracas in 2008, he installed a secret situation room at City Hall (the one visited five years later by Leamsy Salazar).

A Psychiatrist in Electoral Engineering

Jorge Rodríguez was a key figure in the perversion of Venezuela's electronic voting system. When he was president of the National Electoral Council, he arranged for the awarding of a contract to Smartmatic, a new company that had practically no track record. Smartmatic was put in charge of an integral IT solution for each step on election day: voting, recounting, vote totals, and adjudication.

Voting automation in the Venezuelan democracy was approved by a law adopted at the end of the presidency of Carlos Andrés Pérez. It was phased in by Indra, a Spanish company from the technological innovation sector with some track record in what was then a new field. In a gradual automation, Indra deployed several applications for the 2000 elections, called to legitimize the public institutions after the new Constitution was approved in December 1999, almost a year after Chávez reached power. Since the Bolivarian Constitution extended the presidential term to six years, Chávez would not have to seek re-election until 2006. This gave Chavismo plenty of time to prepare its takeover of the voting machines. But the 2004 recall referendum fostered by the opposition prompted chavista leaders to speed up their plans.

A psychiatrist by training, Jorge Rodríguez left the medical profession in order to take charge of the chavista vote production machinery. Rodríguez was the son of a Marxist leader who died in 1976 while in custody of the Venezuelan intelligence service. He had been a member of radical left-wing movements and thus was a committed revolutionary. He joined the CNE in 2003 as one of its councilors. His remit was to organize a bidding process to award a contract to a company that would be in charge of completely automating the elections.

The most logical option would have been to choose Indra's offer to expand and update its system since it had already installed seven thousand voting machines in Venezuela. Two other companies also took part in the bidding process. One was Diebold, whose U.S. parent company, ES&S, was a global leader in the sector. The third bid was led by Smartmatic, a small company headquartered in Florida, created in 2000 by several young Venezuelans. Smartmatic's technology had never been put to the test in an election. It was now planning to design and build touch-screen voting machines. Smartmatic was making its bid with Bista, a Cuban engineering company that would supply the software, and CANTV, the largest telephony provider in Venezuela, which would be assigned the task of transmitting the data. The joint venture had been labeled with the acronym SBC. In a very fast and opaque tender, SBC's bid was awarded the contract in February 2004.

The new system was quickly tested in the recall referendum of August 15, 2004, which Chávez won with 59.1 percent of the vote against 40.6 percent for those seeking his ouster. There was widespread surprise with the result, as analysts had thought Chavismo was against the ropes. The strong ties between Smartmatic and the Venezuelan government cast doubts from then on about the transparency of any election.

Before SBC was awarded the contract, the Venezuelan government had secretly purchased 28 percent of Bista's shares. Three years later Chávez renationalized CANTV. Given these actions, and the lack of transparency about Smartmatic's real ownership, its independence was called into question. By acquiring a U.S. company with more experience, Smartmatic had begun to provide services in some parts of the United States. But in 2007 it was forced to cease operations in that country as its brand had become tainted by its ties with Chavismo. It had been revealed, for example, that in April 2005 Smartmatic paid Jorge Rodríguez, then president of the CNE, to stay at a luxury hotel in Boca Raton, Florida, two months before the Venezuelan electoral authority renewed Smartmatic's contract in time for the legislative elections in December 2005. The opposition refused to contest the elections due to its absolute distrust of the voting system. This allowed Chávez's party and its allies to obtain a very ample absolute majority in the National Assembly and thereby appoint supporters to fill positions in many institutions.

Smartmatic always stood by its assertion that its system could not be tampered with. It was endorsed by international observers after its first trial in Venezuela. But it was never submitted to a comprehensive audit. The European Union, which drafted reports about the system in 2005 and 2006, hastened to add that its meetings regarding Smartmatic were "discussion fora among experts from political parties, members of civil society, and the election authorities, but they never amounted to an audit."

Voting automation underwent another strong trial run in the presidential elections of 2006. The voting system became even more sophisticated as a result of a setback that Chávez suffered a year later. In the referendum held on December 2, 2007, the government proposed constitutional amendments, among them removing term limits for the president, were rejected by 4.5 million votes and supported by 4.3 million votes. Chávez had received the votes of 7.3 million Venezuelans when he was re-elected president in 2006. "Where are the missing three million votes?" he angrily asked his advisors. Chávez dismissed the opposition's triumph in the referendum as a "shitty victory." The Bolivarian leader managed to upstage the opposition in another referendum, in February 2009, which finally approved the constitutional amendments. But the defeat in the first referendum was a wake-up call that induced the government into action. The Francisco de Miranda Front took charge of electoral mobilization. Cooperation between the different players was stepped up to ensure that Chavismo could efficiently rig elections.

The Francisco de Miranda Front and the Missions

Named after one of the heroes of Venezuelan independence, the Francisco de Miranda Front (FFM) was created in June 2003 in Havana by Hugo Chávez and Fidel Castro. Its purpose was to act in Venezuela in the same manner that the Committees for the Defense of the Revolution did in Cuba. In ten years, its membership grew to approximately twenty thousand Venezuelans, called Bolivarian Social Fighters. They were organized into seventeen hundred Integral Bolivarian Squadrons. Cuba had trained these officials so they would act as spokespersons—the eyes and ears—of the revolution among Venezuela's population.

According to its official statutes, this organization was created because the Venezuelan revolution needed "solid and exuberant" social actors among the population that contributed to the "consolidation of civil-military unity," and were ready to act decisively against foreign threats to national sovereignty. The Cubans acted behind the scenes and appointed the leadership of the Francisco de Miranda Front, including Elías Jaua, who would go on to serve as vice president and Foreign Affairs minister, and Erika Faría, who twice served as minister of the President's Office under Chávez.

The creation of the FFM occurred at about the same time as the government of Venezuela launched the Bolivarian Missions, some of which were founded with Cuban backing. One such example is the Barrio Adentro mission, which deployed thousands of Cuban doctors on Venezuelan soil. The social missions tended to specific needs of those with fewer resources. But their purpose went beyond providing assistance for the poorer. The government turned them into instruments of political and community control. In fact, the social missions were managed independently of the ministerial departments. It was PDVSA, the national oil company, and not the federal budget that funded the missions, thus turning them into charity work—as opposed to a right enjoyed by the population—whose recipients had to be grateful to the benefactor. The idea to create the FFM and to launch the missions was Fidel Castro's prescription when Chávez sought Fidel's counsel on how to tighten his grip on power after being briefly deposed from the presidency in April 2002.

In the run-up to the presidential elections of 2012, Chávez launched the Grand Missions in 2011. In stark contrast to the thirty missions undertaken previously—most of which had limited goals and their purpose was to provide certain services—the Grand Missions held out the prospect of salaries, pensions, or houses to those who fulfilled the requirements and enrolled. The Grand Missions committed to the construction and delivery within six years of two million housing units to families without adequate housing (Grand Mission Housing); monthly benefits for families with small or handicapped children whose income was below the minimum wage (Grand Mission Sons of Venezuela); training and placement of qualified workers (Grand Mission Knowledge and Work); pensions for older adults who were not enrolled with Social Security or did not otherwise qualify for a minimum pension (Grand Mission Major Love), and support for farmers with loans and the distribution of their products (Grand Mission AgroVenezuela). Around $26 billion were earmarked for the Grand Missions, whose funding was mostly provided by PDVSA.

The hope of earning the promised refrigerator or apartment, or to keep the public housing already obtained, was an efficient way to achieve and retain the population's vote. The beneficiaries feared that a change of government could take away their benefits. There was also widespread distrust about the confidentiality of voting in Venezuela. Why would Chávez otherwise demand of the officials who headed the programs that they cumulatively should reach ten million people? This milestone was attained in 2012 if civil servants were added to the list of those who received benefits. The number of civil servants in Venezuela grew from 1.3 million in 2002 to 2.4 million ten years later. This 83 percent increase in civil servants can be attributed to the nationalization of companies and expansion of the PDVSA work force. In 2012, almost 20 percent of the working-age population worked in the public sector, compared to 4 percent in Colombia or a little over 8 percent in Peru. In the case of those enrolled in the Grand Missions, the figure reached 7.9 million before the 2012 presidential elections. As civil servants were barred from enrolling in the Grand Missions, and a beneficiary could not sign up for more than one mission, both groups together reached 10,392,127 individuals.

Why was it so important to reach this threshold? Because half of the electorate therefore had a vested interest in maintaining their perks or benefits. The 10.3 million aforementioned individuals amounted to 54.9 percent of the census. This percentage was actually higher if we take into account that the electoral registry contained 1.8 million fake identities. Hence, in order to win at the polls, it was enough to get these loyal voters to the polling places. Chávez never aimed at convincing as large a number of Venezuelans as possible about his policies. His strategy was always to take care of the lower class and the poor, which accounted for a majority big enough to win elections. Moreover, he mobilized his supporters by using rhetoric about class struggle. Chávez employed a language of confrontation.

The Grand Missions were coordinated by the Ministry for Communes and Social Movements. This department was created in 2009 as a means to foster a network of communes that over time could replace the traditional administrative structure made up of states and municipalities. The ministry would be a launching pad for the expansion of the revolution following the Cuban model. The supporters enrolled in the FFM would permeate Venezuelan institutions. Erika Farías, leader of the Front, was the first to head the Ministry for Communes and Social Movements which later was placed in Elías Jaua's hands. The FFM was in charge of ensuring in the months leading up to the presidential elections that each and every one of the beneficiaries of the Grand Missions was going to vote *red*. To that end, the FFM employed the ministry's public infrastructure (IT network, installations, telephone directories, databases). Whoever believes that this operation was carried out with the usual Caribbean informality is naive—the same naiveté with which Chavismo was often judged. The delicate planning was worthy of the highest award to excellence in business leadership any capitalist business school regularly bestows.

The sophisticated and automated alternative electoral system and the vast array of missions and social programs had already been operational in the last presidential election that Chávez contested, on October 7, 2012. The government resorted to the same instruments in the presidential election held on April 14, 2013, when Maduro ran for president as the PSUV's candidate after Chávez's death. In order for Maduro to win, Chavismo had to commit a much bigger fraud, thereby making it easier for outsiders to see the regime's true colors. A great amount of internal and leaked FFM documents highlight the way in which the electoral mobilization was executed.

System Programmed from Cuba

Two days before the 2013 presidential election, instructions to cover up the deceit that would be carried out were transmitted from Cuba. "Order of operation number 004. Instructions for the information system: given the information leaked to the media about the use and management of the electoral IT system and in order to protect the data that will flow through the system, the following measures will be enacted."

This order was issued from the headquarters of the Francisco de Miranda Movement (FFM). It warned against what I had published that day in the newspaper *ABC*. The FFM's internal communications printed the exact first line of my article ("the chavista regime has a parallel electronic system to ascertain illegally and in real time how Venezuelans will vote next Sunday"), as well as the main paragraph: "thousands of chavista officials, with real-time access to data on the casting of ballots, what amounts to electoral fraud, will try to alter the turnout in the presidential elections on Sunday to favor their candidate and to the detriment of the opposition, with the apparent complicity of the National Electoral Council (CNE)."

The confidential transmission from the Cuban town of Pinar del Río admitted that the content of the article described "in a detailed and accurate manner" the alternative IT system that the FFM had set up and employed in the elections, and which had the internal code word Roque 2. The Front expressed its bewilderment about the "source used by the transmitter of the attack" and forced all of its members to modify their emails, issuing instructions to act secretly: opening of accounts with names completely unrelated to the organization and whose profiles, to throw off potential investigators, would be linked to sports, cultural, or academic activities.

The Front's order contained another recommendation: "considering the leak of information" to the media, "we must ensure that the Bolivarian Social Fighters deployed on the ground do not wear or sport any symbols related to the organization." The organization was therefore asking its members to disguise their presence at the polling places so they could carry out their tasks without alerting observers who could question the fairness of the process. This caution was completely warranted. Deployed across thousands of electoral centers, the activists' mission was to transmit cell messages during the entire day to feed Roque 2. With a certain frequency, they were called on to report to their superiors of the Front the number of *red votes* (Nicolás Maduro) and *blue votes* (Henrique Capriles) that were being cast.

There was no way to know this data without cheating. The documents leaked do not specify how the information was gathered. The Front's activists could have gleaned it from accomplices serving in key positions at the polling places: a second operation under way on election day involved chavista agents who were in charge of the technical voting process at the electoral centers, and whose political affiliation was not publicly known. PSUV supporters ran the official system to identify voters at the entrance to the buildings. They also monitored the voting machines, one of which was placed on each polling station.

All of these shenanigans could only be undertaken with the CNE's complicity. There were already vague suspicions at the time about these secret operations, but documents I examined later in order to write this book certify that the deployment did occur. Chavismo had drawn up lists assigning PSUV members to each district. The lists also detailed the complete name, identity card number, and cell phone of those who on election day would perform in the electoral centers as Voting Machines Operator and Information Station Operator, the latter by usually employing fingerprinting machines.

Whoever ran the official identification process knew the number of people who had entered the polling place. Besides, PSUV had a control point next to the entrance of polling places, the so-called *Red Points*, through which it forced its voters to go as additional information desk. By combining the number of people who entered the polling places and the information garnered by the Red Points, it was possible to deduce the amount of votes that each candidate had received. Another possibility is that the electronic identification information was enough for the chavista activists to determine how many of their voters had indeed cast a ballot. The secret information, which was anyway obtained fraudulently, provided input to the parallel electoral system Roque 2, whose main goal was to monitor and mobilize on election day. With the data in hand, the PSUV could pull out all the stops to mobilize its voters. As the closure of polling places neared, the objectives of the so-called 1x10 had to be fulfilled: each committed member had to accompany ten other persons to the electoral centers.

Christopher Bello, an engineer and owner of Hethical, a computer security company, confirmed during the audit he did on Smartmatic that the voting machines could have continuous wireless connectivity. Given these and other abnormalities in the elections, Bello rejected endorsing the system in order not to compromise his company's international certification. In 2012 he left Venezuela because he feared threats. Bello unveiled that the voting machines could be programmed in an improvised way so that during a certain period of time they would turn out a null vote whenever a vote for either candidate was cast. "I cannot take a vote in favor of Capriles and attribute it to Maduro, but I can program the device so that all of the mistakes disadvantage Capriles," he asserts. He is also certain that with a personal computer or even a cell phone connected remotely, in an adjacent room or simply on the street, the chavistas could know the tally of votes executed by the voting machines.

Bello's account hints at the existence of a third process. In addition to deploying the Francisco de Miranda Front to provide information for Roque 2 and those who were officially in charge of the technical management of the identification process and the voting machines, cloned polling stations managed apart from the CNE could have been set up. Bello explains that the unofficial ballot boxes could have been placed next to the official centers. Thus the alternative voting device could have been installed in a nearby house or in a mobile unit. This would happen in polling places controlled by chavistas, where monitoring by the opposition was rendered impossible. As both machines would be interconnected, the real vote registered in the official tally would also be transmitted to the duplicate, thereby allowing the latter to freely insert a great quantity of *flat* votes.

Last Days: Control and Blackmail

In the run-up to the elections of April 14, 2013, the Francisco de Miranda Front repeatedly reviewed in its multiple daily messages from its office in Cuba the lists of those entrusted with actions, the goals set, and their degree of fulfillment. In a dispatch sent eleven days before the election, for example, a letter from the national executive directorate addressed to the heads of the states, to the coordinators of the missions, and to the Ministry of the Communes reminded them of the goals. In order to attain the objective of ten million votes, the PSUV should rely on its 5.4 million members, to get started. The party should then focus on several "rings of research" to obtain more votes. The priority lay in the 3,307,543 persons that took part in the missions or received other benefits from the revolution and whose names did not show up on the 1x10 PSUV ledges.

It was not merely a case of excessive zeal which democratic governments also employ to extract electoral advantage from their policies. The FFM had registered each and every one of the names of the beneficiaries of aid, as well as their addresses, phone numbers, and even emails. The FFM was in a position to know who had cast a ballot and who had abstained in prior elections.

The Front had uncovered a "high degree of demobilization of the sectors directly assisted by the Revolution, grouped in the Grand Social Missions." It had recorded that 2,333,283 individuals, almost a third of the beneficiaries, had not voted for Chávez in the October

2012 presidential elections. The internal memorandum signed by María Isabella Godoy, executive national director of the FFM, set numerical objectives for each of the social missions and later added: "the way to contact these persons will be by telephone and a house-by-house visit to the housing developments. This plan requires the availability of all of the control and monitoring centers set up in the state and the deployment of a team made up of civil servants and Bolivarian Social Fighters, so that the daily total can be reached." With regard to the Grand Mission Housing, Godoy complained that, despite the 370,495 units already built and assigned, there were approximately 1.4 million "absentee beneficiaries"—meaning recipients of aid who had not voted. "In each apartment building of the new housing developments," the official ordered so as to reverse the situation, "Hugo Chávez Committees should be established in order to facilitate door-to-door visits and guarantee that the target population casts its ballot for the PSUV."

How is it possible not to see the similarity between the FFM strategy and the control exercised by the Committees for the Defense of the Revolution over each block of houses in Cuba? After all, it was Cuban officials who were pulling the strings. A transcript of a meeting of the FFM's national leadership from May 2012 detailed the presence of twenty-six Cuban advisors, who thus accounted for one third of those in attendance. In several months of preparations for the elections, there were 176 of these advisors deployed in the FFM's command posts over the country.

Nothing was left to chance. The FFM and the PSUV did reports for any action. One of them distributed the tasks to perform in order to take over control of the main power generating stations and sub-stations in Venezuela. The lists contained the names and phone numbers of those who, independently of the company's operational structure, would be in charge of the plants in case the chavista leadership decided that an action was politically required. The activists reported over a period of several days whether they had been granted access to the installations on election day or they had found obstacles in preparation of their tasks.

There are frequent blackouts in Venezuela, so ensuring the supply of electricity is crucial in order to guarantee a well-organized election that is free and fair. But the normal protocol would have called for the plants themselves to arrange for special units and technicians to be on stand-by. It was not normal that the supply of electricity remained in the hands of a political party that acted unilaterally with tacit approval from the government, and keeping the opposition in the dark. The control over the production of electricity could allow the government to pretend that a voluntary shutdown with a political motive was a technical malfunction.

The FFM kept a very watchful eye over both the Venezuelan and foreign media, as well as social networks. Fifty officials tracked and analyzed the information in shifts that began at 8 am and lasted until 11 am of the following day, with a three-hour overlap that enabled the drafting of reports about the morning press. This monitoring allowed the FFM to gauge the effects of the aforementioned information I had published. "The news item was known through its author's Twitter. Emili J. Blasco, who is the Washington correspondent for the Spanish newspaper ABC.es, at approximately 8 am tweeted, @ejblasco: This is how chavistas control the evolution of the real vote in the elections. Fraud." The report's transcript also included the article's URL, as I had inserted it into the tweet. The report went on to list the Twitter users that had retweeted or mentioned the news item. The bombshell created by my revelation increased the secrecy of FFM/Cuba, but the elections were nonetheless rigged.

Election Day, Roque 2 in Action

The chavista leadership arrived to April 14, 2013, knowing that things were not going well. Maduro's political discourse, with his references to the appearance of Chávez's spirit in the form of a bird, created the impression of a campaign built on smoke and mirrors. Despite Maduro's mishaps, his team was under no illusions about the real situation and had full knowledge of what was unfolding. Given the access to the full electoral database and the strict monitoring of the voters, the strategic plan which had been designed allowed the regime to keep track of the degree of mobilization on a day-to-day and parish-by-parish basis.

Three days before election day, only 54 percent of the *abstaining missionaries* singled out as a goal had been contacted. In addition, the surveys carried out by polling companies with links to Chavismo confirmed a steady decline in Maduro's support. Chávez officially defeated Capriles by ten points in 2012. Some pre-election surveys at the time had Chávez leading Capriles by twenty points, probably due to the distortion caused by voters' fear to reveal their true opinion. Now, two weeks before the 2013 presidential elections, Maduro's lead was diminished to eight points (Datin Corp), later to seven points (GIS XXI)...

Reporting for duty, from 2 am on April 14, 2013, four hours before the polls opened, the FFM's members had begun to take up their positions in the electoral centers. They focused on what they operationally labeled Priority Voting Centers (CVP): 3,433 centers, most of which had more than three polling stations (or electoral tables). The CVPs accounted for one fourth of the overall amount of electoral centers (13,638), but more than half of Venezuelans with a right to vote: 10.1 million voters, 53.4 percent in a census of 18.9 million. They were the places where the opposition received its biggest support. Tracking them thus facilitated quantifying with substantial accuracy how many votes Capriles was receiving.

The FFM militants—the Bolivarian Social Fighters—had been handed a flyer with instructions on the cell phone messages they needed to send and the automated numbers they had to call to provide input for Roque 2. This monitoring of an election by a political movement was undertaken with support from the Ministry of Communes and Social Movements, which acted as a cover for the FFM. The ministry had published the flyer with the instructions, whose logo was included in the printed copies. "If you require assistance about the System," a box indicated, "get in touch with the Office of Information Technology through the email: *elecciones2013@mpco munas.gob.ve*."

The instruction manual featured pictures of what the cell phone screens should show during each wave of messages. The messages were to be keyed in accordance with several codes: first the kind of information that was being handled at each stage of election day (IPV: beginning of voting process; PTM: presence of voting table witnesses; INC: incidence; FPV: end of the voting process), and then the first three letters of each state's name. The most important communication was deemed to be that regarding the evolution of the vote count. For example, the flyer read: VOTO AMA0001 VR30 VA15. This meant that, in the polling place of the state of Amazonas classified as number one, thirty persons (red vote) had already cast their ballots for Nicolás Maduro and fifteen (blue vote) had done so for Henrique Capriles.

Throughout election day on April 14, the sending of SMSs by the Bolivarian Social Fighters reporting the vote count in real time had to happen at three different times: the first after 10 am; the second about 2 pm, and the third at 5 pm. The FFM militants were in touch with their chavista colleagues employed as technicians in stations one, two, and three of the polling places throughout the entire process.

Venezuela's election process has several stages. When the voter arrives at the polling place, (1) shows the identity document and places the thumb on a fingerprint scanner, which recognizes the fingerprint if it has been stored previously, or which adds it to the fingerprint database. At this first stage, the voter is informed about the polling room to go to in order to vote. When the voter has reached the correct polling station, (2) the voter shows his identity document to the president of the station and places the thumb on a second fingerprint scanner; as soon as the identity is confirmed, the president unlocks the voting machine. The voter then proceeds to the machine and (3) touches the favored option on the screen. A paper ballot is printed, which the voter (4) deposits in a ballot box used to store the receipts. The voter then signs and stamps the fingerprint (5) on a registry notebook. Finally, (6) the voter dips the pinkie in a jar of indelible ink.

The verification of the voter's identity is performed in the first two stages, which are occasionally merged into one, as there is no information center in smaller polling places. In the latter case, the voter proceeds directly to the polling station, where the identity is confirmed anyway. The existence of a fingerprint scanner, often used twice throughout the process, has always raised suspicions among the Venezuelan population.

The fingerprint scanner is a machine connected to a personal computer that reads the fingerprints. The investigation carried out by Bello and Daquin estimated that the verification process was not on-line with the national database as the regime has officially asserted, as such verification would have delayed the process several days. According to Bello and Daquin's research, each polling station—with an average of five hundred voters—had an individual fingerprint file to collate. This would have made it possible to vote in several tables with the same fingerprint. One needed only to change the identity card number, and could therefore maintain the same name, picture, and fingerprint. The system would also have enabled them to determine a correlation between identity and vote as it monitored the vote in each table.

The fact that Cuba, through its framework agreement with Caracas, was in charge of managing and producing Venezuelans' identity cards and passports contributed to the doubt over the fairness of the electoral process. Intelligence sources were convinced that all of this information, as well as that of the census and previous election results, was being stored in a database in the Cuban province of Pinar del Río, precisely from where the Francisco de Miranda Movement's orders were flowing. In an interview broadcast by the television channel América Te Ve, the former Cuban agent Uberto Mario, who worked for Castro's intelligence service in Venezuela, indicated that the database was set up in the military base El Cacho, in the town of Los Palacios, in Pinar del Río province. He recounted that when in the 1990s the Soviet Union dismantled its SIGINT (Signals Intelligence) operation at the Lourdes base, near Havana, Fidel Castro developed El Cacho as a secret unit specializing in tracking cyberspace.

Uberto Mario attributed a substantial part of the electoral control work performed in Venezuela to a Cuban named Ernesto Raciel García Ceballos, nicknamed "agent Segundo," an engineer co-opted by the G2 for supervision and monitoring of information. García Ceballos had taught at the University of Information Sciences, which is located precisely in the former base at Lourdes, where the Soviet SIGINT was. Other sources claimed that the Cuban in charge of the specific responsibility for the identification system was someone named José Lavandero García.

Among the tasks carried out by the Cuban advisors was the withdrawal of the identity from Venezuelans who were chronic abstainers. "We froze the right to vote of those who always abstained. A group of more than two hundred persons examined the census and detected those who never voted. When it was ascertained that a certain person was always staying home on election day, his identity card was removed," explained Uberto Mario, who claims to have been in charge of this task in the 2006 presidential elections. He reckoned that several hundreds of thousands of votes were issued in favor of Chávez and Maduro by showing the duplicated identity cards.

Another source of votes for Chavismo was the number of Venezuelans who had passed away but remained on the census. The opposition was able to verify that, in several polling stations at which the participation registered 100 percent in the elections of October 7, 2012, people who had died cast ballots. All of these deceits and frauds inflated the electoral census. In 1998, the electoral census accounted for 50.5 percent of the total population; in 2013 the ratio had risen to 65 percent, an increase that could not be attributed to demographic factors.

The issuance of false identity cards resulted in surreal situations, such as voters with names such as "Free and Socialist Venezuela Marcano Vázquez," Superman, or Spiderman. These epithets were provisionally created at first to test the system. They were never removed from the system and in fact were sold to foreigners who illegally resided in Venezuela that wanted to obtain citizenship. There are therefore today in the country a few children and grandchildren of American superheroes.

An Electoral Council Judge and Jury

The government always boasted about international observer missions that supposedly legitimized its electoral system. This recognition occurred at the beginning of the generalization of the electronic vote. But as time went by, Chavismo rejected the presence of international observers during elections. In the 2012 and 2013 elections, there were only international "companions," as the government referred to them, who had almost no role nor itineraries in some of the electoral centers.

The renowned Carter Center in the United States, which at first was very acquiescent with the Venezuelan electoral framework, eventually criticized the climate favorable to Chavismo in which the elections were held. In March 2013, it inveighed against the electoral campaign of a few months earlier, censuring that Chávez was on the air nationally for forty hours and forty-seven minutes, in addition to the advertising time set aside for the political parties. All private as well as public radio and television channels were forced to broadcast Chávez's long speeches. Regarding the voting process in particular, the Carter Center pointed to probable arbitrary measures adopted by the electoral authority: "In the same manner as other Venezuelan institutions, the National Electoral Council is profoundly influenced by partisanship."

Everybody realized that the CNE was another instrument of Chavismo. How could someone expect independence from an institution whose president since 2006, Tibisay Lucena, occasionally represented her institution at events brandishing a bracelet that commemorated Chávez's 1992 military coup against democratic legality? The CNE was directly implicated in the preparation and execution of the chavista mobilizations of the last electoral processes. Members of the Council attended meetings before the elections with several chavista organizations in order to determine the distribution of polling places, the sharing of the voter registration rolls (always denied to the opposition), and the delivery of electoral registry machines by the National Electoral Council.

"The CNE will help to cross-check the data of the Social Missions and the Grand Missions in order to determine an operational plan for each territory," an FFM secret report concluded. The transcripts of several meetings, attended by representatives of the National Electoral Council along with officials from the United Socialist Party of Venezuela, the Francisco de Miranda Movement, and the Ministry for the Communes, revealed that the installation of new polling places more favorable to Chavismo was discussed, along with the sharing of the most updated data from the Permanent Electoral Registry, as well as the lottery for the selection of members of voting tables.

Several of these meetings took place in CNE offices, such as the one held in Guárico state, which was attended by the regional director. In New Esparta state, Joe Uzcategui, another CNE regional director, "opened the meeting by declaring that its goal was to set out the logistical details, unifying and strengthening proposed agreements between the MPPC, Fundacomunal, FFM, Inparques, PSUV, and the CNE." In the state of Amazonas, with the assistance of the regional coordinator, María Aragort, the same players designed the transfer of voters to new electoral centers.

The latter measures, following in the tradition of gerrymandering, were adopted especially to create and segregate polling stations dominated by Chavismo, so that even opposition voters would be overwhelmed by the PSUV's hegemony. Many of these polling stations subsumed most of the fake census and could operate without supervision, even after the official closure of the polling places. There was also an administrative transfer of voters to distant electoral regions: opposition supporters rebuked the fact that they were suddenly assigned a polling place far from their homes, even hundreds of miles away. This helped to delete traces of the creation of false identities and generated an environment less able to report possible electoral abnormalities.

The opposition gradually became aware of much of the data and developments this book describes regarding the electoral fraud. But the leadership of the Democratic Unity Roundtable (MUD) always publicly rejected that the elections were rigged. To do so would have decreased the incentive to vote and delegitimized elections that also hoisted opposition politicians to elected office. The opposition's strategy was to mobilize more voters than those which Chavismo added through deceit and fraud.

Burden of Irregularities

"I am not reaching agreements neither with lies nor with corruption. My agreement is with God and the Venezuelan people. I do not make pacts with illegitimacy. Today's big loser is you." The conviction with which Henrique Capriles spoke on the election night of April 14, 2013, addressing Maduro through the television cameras, took everyone by surprise. This was an altogether different Capriles from the one who six months earlier had quickly thrown in the towel, immediately conceding defeat to Chávez, although the numbers also did not add up, and his senior staff suspected that the election had been rigged, especially towards the end of election day. This time, however, Chavismo's efforts to turn the result around in favor of Maduro were much bigger and the reported irregularities piled up. "Our recount is different," Capriles reproached, alleging manipulation of votes.

The opposition alleged that more than 3,200 abnormalities had occurred. The array of abnormalities included different categories. Intimidation against voters and opposition witnesses had taken place. Capriles denounced that violence had occurred at 397 centers (persons threatened and assaulted near the polling places by motorized bands) and that in 286 centers the opposition representatives had been ordered to leave the place, in some cases at gunpoint. All of these illegal actions, according to the opposition, had affected electoral centers with a total census of more than one million voters. Although the law stated that polling places had to close by 6 pm except in cases where people were waiting in line to vote, there were electoral centers that closed ahead of time, especially in areas with strong opposition support. On the other hand, other polling places reopened to allow chavista supporters driven to the polls in buses to cast their ballot.

The abuse of the assisted vote was even highlighted in YouTube. People that clearly needed no assistance (the law required that the person be handicapped or old) were accompanied to the ballot box by chavista activists who oversaw the vote. The Electoral Observation Network, managed by a local NGO, claimed that it had detected this irregular practice in 5 percent of the polling places it oversaw.

The indecency which Chavismo resorted to knew no bounds: a mayor threatened through a local television channel to fire any civil servants who did not accept the assisted vote. This was a prelude to the witch hunt that would be unleashed in the ministries when chavista leaders realized that many public employees had not voted despite the pressure exerted on them. The warning by the Minister of Housing to fire disloyal civil servants, secretly recorded at an assembly of workers, went viral on the Internet.

Another abuse committed by Chavismo was the appearance at a polling place of a person who had forty identity cards, all issued in August 2012 and presumably already used in the previous presidential election. The person was stopped when he was handing out the identity cards to people getting off a bus whom witnesses described as having Cuban accents.

Given all of these developments, the opposition demanded a full recount of the vote. On the election night Maduro seemed to accept the opening of all the ballot boxes. They would "speak and say the truth," he said addressing his followers from the balcony of Miraflores Palace. But later he backtracked on his promise with the excuse that the National Electoral Council did not deem it necessary. The regulations of Venezuela's automated system call for the opening of 53 percent of ballot boxes that contain the paper receipts of the votes cast electronically. In practice, however, the number winds up being much lower: in the 2013 presidential elections it was 20 percent, and in the 2012 presidential ones only 5 percent. When this verification is carried out in electoral centers with several polling stations, only some of the boxes selected through a draw can be opened. There are some indications that point to the fact that this draw may also be rigged, so that chavistas could know beforehand which will be opened and which will not.

The official recount produced inconsistent results. In 1,776 electoral centers, Maduro's vote total surpassed that obtained by Chávez six months earlier, which seemed strange, because the CNE reported that the PSUV's share of the vote decreased by 4.46 points with a similar turnout of approximately 80 percent. The most extreme case was that of an electoral center located in Yaracuy state in which the PSUV and its allies increased their share of the vote by 943 percent. Another example mentioned by Capriles was that of a center in the state of Trujillo, where 717 votes were counted while the total amount of persons in the census was 536. A detailed analysis of the data in the ensuing days revealed interesting facts.

Size Matters: Capriles' Victory

Henrique Capriles should be the president of Venezuela. He won the election of April 14, 2013, with enough margin although difficult to quantify, given the variety of methods that Chavismo employed to commit fraud. There are the denunciations of the assisted vote, the intimidation exerted by violent groups, the coercion of public employees, and the pressure exerted on the beneficiaries of social programs. Moreover, there are the votes cast by persons with a false identity (multiple identity cards, dead people, foreigners), and the vote that here has been referred to as *flat* and was issued by activating illegally the voting machine.

According to a statistical research of the election results, the production of false votes was concentrated in the small electoral centers, which had been purposely increased over the years. Most of these small centers were created by grouping chavista voters, so that in a friendly atmosphere the voting the chavista agents in charge of the voting machines could activate them illegally as many times as necessary, although without exceeding the census: always a paper ballot were produced and inserted into the ballot box for a possible recount. The agent could then make up signatures and repeat his fingerprints in the voting notebooks, which would never be revised.

The electoral consultancy company Esdata revealed that in the centers with three or more polling stations, that made up 79.2 percent of voters, Capriles won by half a million votes. In the centers with two polling stations, he lost by 332.000, but adding the latter with the former, and including the vote by Venezuelans residing abroad, Capriles' lead in that 91.1 percent of the vote was 263,000. In polling centers with one station, which made up 8.8 percent of voters, Maduro won by 477,000 votes, and this allowed him to win the presidency. This constitutes a clear statistical anomaly. The chavista candidate won in electoral centers with one or two polling stations, which did not show a pattern of vote similar to that of the rest of the country.

One would think that smaller polling places would be more predominant in rural or remote areas in which, for socioeconomic reasons, the pro-Chavismo vote would naturally tend to be higher. But the proliferation of small centers happened as well in urban areas. It was apparently undertaken with the objective of operating with more impunity. Between 2006 and 2012, centers with only one polling station increased by 63.8 percent.

Moreover, small centers were the ones that had more people included in the census without having a fingerprint registered, which reduced the data that could be used to verify a voter's identity. The CNE published before the 2012 elections that 8 percent of Venezuelans in the electoral census (1.5 million people) did not have their fingerprint in the Registry for Fingerprints, an amount which had almost quintupled in nine years. In these 2012 elections, according to the official figures, 1.6 million people voted although their fingerprint did not match the one that had been previously stored. Therein lies with great probability the reservoir of fraudulent votes which Chavismo could resort to according to its needs.

A report by the organization VotoLimpio indicated that electoral centers with less than one thousand voters (all of the centers with one polling station and some with two) concentrated a number of voters without fingerprints that was two and one half times higher than the average. "This cannot be explained away by sheer coincidence," VotoLimpio emphasized. At the same time, the report censured that, although in 2009 the inclusion of a digital fingerprint was declared compulsory when the person was registered in the electoral census, between 2010 and 2012 a total of 456,290 people were registered without the enforcement of this criteria by the CNE. "Such a high amount of abnormal voters is bigger than the winning margin Maduro officially obtained," the institution concluded.

VotoLimpio concurred with Esdata in its suspicion of the anomaly of the results in the smaller electoral centers. In polling places with one thousand or more voters (15.6 million Venezuelans with the right to vote, 83 percent of the census), Capriles won by almost half a million votes. In the polling places with less than one thousand voters, (3.1 million Venezuelans with the right to vote, 16.9 percent of the census), Maduro officially obtained twice the number of votes than his rival and this small population segment allowed him to eke out a last-minute razor-thin victory. Was the opposition going to accept the fraud? Military and paramilitary units were on the street to sustain Maduro in the Miraflores Palace.

Military Officials, Paramilitaries, and Stuffed Food

The Republic Plan is activated in Venezuela in each electoral process or referendum to guarantee order during election day. A new feature was added to the plan in the presidential elections of October 7, 2012, the last that Hugo Chávez contested, and in the presidential ones of April 14, 2013, with Nicolás Maduro as candidate. For the first time, units of the Bolivarian Militia, made up of men of absolute loyalty to the chavista regime, took part in a military deployment intended to avoid unrest on election day. The Militia was created by Chávez in 2007 as a paramilitary corps made up of uniformed and armed civilians and directed by military commanders. The Militia had its own hierarchy and reported directly to the Strategic Operational Command of the National Armed Force (FAN).

The plan envisioned that the Militia would ensure public order in the 49 percent of the polling places, precisely in areas with more opposition support. The FAN would be in charge of 51 percent of the centers. The slightly higher degree of responsibility given to the regular armed forces aimed at allaying the suspicion with which many military officers regarded the Militia. In any case, the backbone of the military deployment was the National Guard, which within the FAN had proven to be the outfit most vulnerable to chavista interference.

The chavista regime's interest in getting the Militia to patrol the streets was that it could be better coordinated with actions groups organized as the Immediate Mobilization Network (REMI). This network enrolled in part members of armed street bands that were so useful to Chavismo in terms of social co-opting. According to documentary evidence that I published days before Chávez's last presidential election, the REMI had as a mission "the early alert and anticipation" in the face of possible opposition protests due to electoral irregularities. Trained for months, they were defined as a "street rapid reaction force, with the capability to block or open up key road transportation choke points, geographic areas, and municipalities," as well as to "defend the perimeters of state institutions." As was the case with the Francisco de Miranda Front with regard to the mobilization and monitoring of voters, the REMI also had a way to send cell messages for possible situations such as "reporting to agreed locations," "assemble near objective," and "guarantee assigned objectives."

Four months before the elections, commanders in the armed forces began to distribute AK-103 machine guns to the REMI, a Russian weapon which Venezuela is licensed to manufacture. The REMI were directed by Carlos Lanz, a radical who had always defended violence as a tactic. Lanz had maintained narrow ties with Iran, whose Basij forces, an instrument used by the ayatollahs to abort the

Green Spring in 2009, had inspired the Venezuelans' network. Lanz reported directly to the chief of the Militia, General Gustavo Enrique González López. After this general retired, Maduro urged him to return to active duty, naming him as head of the SEBIN, the Venezuelan intelligence services—the student protests of February 2014 had broken out and González had considerable experience in managing armed groups.

The Venezuelan armed forces had been submitted to pressure by the government in the run-up to the elections of 2012 and 2013. In 2010, the chief of the Strategic Operational Command, General Henry Rangel Silva, who would later serve as Defense minister, ruled out the possibility that the opposition could win the elections. "It would be selling out the country and people would not accept it; the FAN would not, and certainly neither would the people," he said in public remarks. "The National Armed Force do not has partial loyalties, but rather complete ones towards a people, a vision, and a commander-in-chief. We married this vision."

In order to keep the military happy, ensure their vote at the polls, and dilute the scruples of those who might reject the flagrant politicization of the armed forces, the government proceeded to raise their salaries by 40 percent. A month before the October 2012 presidential elections, the government launched the Grand Mission First Black (nickname given to the only black official in the ranks of Simón Bolívar) "to guarantee the socioeconomic protection of the soldier's family." The first measure implemented by the mission was the purchase abroad of twenty thousand vehicles, which would be sold at a subsidized price to those who signed up. With this purchase, the government made sure to get the vote of the military officers and soldiers who wished to own such a vehicle. To buy it otherwise was hard in a country with runaway inflation, no access to foreign currency, and big shortages.

This measure was a *bozal de arepa* (arepa is a typical maize dough here figuratively used as muzzle by filling the mouth), as people in Venezuela commonly say when a person is stuffed with food so as to get them to be silent. They had to keep quiet or look the other way when the Militia and the National Guard did the dirty work for the elections.

The Republic Plan included the operation, revealed by the opposition, to deploy on April 14, 2013, more than fifteen hundred motorcycles, buses, and military vehicles which would be made available to the chavista organizations to transport people to polling places. These would be the same motorcycles from which days later national guards and civilians would shot at Capriles supporters when they demonstrated against the official results. The post-electoral street protests claimed the lives of nine persons in several regions of Venezuela.

The Venezuelan armed forces had played a key role in allowing the electoral fraud. A change of attitude on their part resulted on December 6, 2015, in the proclamation of Chavismo's first defeat in a national election since 1999. The manufacturing of fraudulent votes was not sufficient to counter the overwhelming support for the opposition. On this occasion, nine deaths would not have sufficed. Stealing the parliamentary elections was not something that could be easily disguised. The National Armed Force's leadership chose to ensure public order and recommended the acceptance of the electoral results, which after all did not change the fact that Maduro remained president.

Deluge of Votes against Fraud

The chavista political leadership had every intention of stealing the parliamentary elections of December 6, 2015, using the same procedure already described earlier. The sharp decline in the popularity of Nicolás Maduro and his government heralded a vote of punishment whose size would be impossible to counter with the usual cheating. Chavismo was thus undecided about convening and confirming the date of the elections. In the weeks leading up to election day, violent events took place, such as the firing of shots that almost struck Lilian Tintori, the wife of imprisoned opposition leader Leopoldo López. Was the regime looking for an excuse to postpone the vote? In the run-up to local elections held two years earlier, Maduro had warned some of his ministers that they would not take place if the regime was not assured of victory, as one of the ministers acknowledges.

Four days before the December 2015 parliamentary elections, Maduro called an emergency meeting at Fuerte Tiuna, the main military compound in Caracas. Surveys continued to predict a bad result for the government. According to the transcript of the meeting, which was later leaked, those in attendance were the members of the military leadership, the heads of intelligence and counterintelligence, some members of the government, and the PSUV's electoral campaign chief. A Cuban general whose identity was not revealed also took part in the meeting. The minister of Defense, General Vladimir Padrino, highlighted that a tally conducted among the armed forces had the opposition leading by 35 points, the same margin that polls among the population at large were forecasting. The minister then remarked that, given the state of mind among the military, it would be "dangerous" to "tamper" with the electoral results.

The possibility that Chavismo would resort to violence in the face of electoral defeat catalyzed the international community. On the day before the elections, President Barack Obama and Pope Francis called Raúl Castro so that he would restrain Maduro, according to sources who were in close contact with the Department of State. The White House had been working a back channel in the preceding weeks in order to be able to reach the Venezuelan Defense minister, and thus relayed that on election day it would be on permanent stand-by to help prevent violence in Venezuela. The White House mediator had transmitted a special telephone number, written on a small piece of paper, to one of the individuals who was serving as an emissary.

There is every indication that on election day chavista agents took the usual steps to commit fraud in the accustomed manner. The National Electoral Council helped them out by officially postponing the closure of polling places by one hour, although some locations remained open even longer. But Chavismo was not able to rig the elections on this occasion. Mostly, because the swing in favor of the opposition was so massive that it rendered insufficient the up to two million fraudulent votes (a combination of voters with fake identities and fake votes) that Chavismo employed. The Democratic Unity Roundtable (MUD) candidates received 7.7 million votes, while the PSUV ones garnered 5.6 million (an amount that was even presumably inflated by the fraud). In addition, the chavista electoral *engineers* were partly in the dark about how many votes they were collecting during the day. Ironically, many traditionally staunch PSUV voters whom the regime was so efficient at turning out wound up breaking ranks with the ruling party and supporting the opposition.

The chavista officials' efforts were also hampered by the fact that opposition activists placed signal inhibitors at sixteen hundred polling centers, as the head of the operation asserts. These devices would have suppress the signals that chavista officials had sent in previous occasions from the electoral centers in order to feed their parallel IT system or perhaps to produce fraudulent votes. Also it should be noted that the chavista fraud apparatus was much more efficient for presidential elections or referendums than for regional or local ballots as the latter featured many more candidates and the vote was dispersed among many electoral districts.

At about 6 pm, the members of the military high command were aware of the exit polls, which all indicated that the opposition would win by a landslide. But the chavista decision-making command—at the campaign headquarters and at the presidential palace—continued to privately insist that the PSUV was ahead by one seat. A struggle was clearly under way. Just before the 2013 presidential elections, the head of the intelligence services, Miguel Rodríguez Torres, who was thereafter promoted by Maduro to Interior minister, warned the Defense minister at the time that a governmental electoral defeat was unacceptable, as one of those present during the conversation confirms. But this time the opposition trounced the PSUV, which made it very hard to cover up the real results. Moreover, the opposition had easily defeated the PSUV in the special precincts where members of the military and their families voted. Hence Defense Minister Padrino, fearing a split in the ranks of the military, advocated for respecting the MUD victory. He was the first government official to appear in public the evening of election day, "forced by rumors" making the rounds about attempts to steal the election. Padrino's stance prevented some in the regime from ordering loyal violent groups to take to the streets to abort an orderly closure of the polls and therefore the absence of an official result.

"You are a rat," Diosdado Cabello, the deputy leader of Chavismo, later lashed out at the minister. "Rats are the first to jump ship," he upbraided him, according to sources in General Padrino's entourage. The heated exchange took place a few days before the new National Assembly was convened, on January 5, 2016, and which Cabello would not be able to chair any more due to the opposition's victory. Padrino, a staunch chavista, was again avoiding that street violence might derail the institutional chain of events.

But it was soon plain to see that General Padrino was more worried about public order, because of the divisions within the military that the use of force could spark, than about constitutional order. He did not object when Maduro used the Supreme Tribunal of Justice to render null and void the work of the National Assembly. In order to buy silence through complicity, Chavismo implemented a new scheme to reward the military—another *bozal de arepa*. This time it was not a Bolivarian mission financed by the oil company PDVSA, but rather a direct stake in the oil business itself. The regime created a new company named Military Company of Mining, Oil, and Gas Industries (CAMIMPEG). The revolution could not survive without oil revenue.

4

THE REVOLUTION'S PURSE STRINGS

The Oil Wells Dry Up

P *rriiiii...* "Out you go!" Live on television, just as a referee would send a player off the field with a blow of a whistle, Hugo Chávez fired some of the members of the board of the public holding company Petróleos de Venezuela Sociedad Anónima (PDVSA). The announcement was made on the program *Aló, presidente* on April 7, 2002. Chávez had already been host of the popular TV show one hundred times. He spent most of Sunday live on TV in *Aló, presidente*: the program began at 11 am and sometimes would run until 5 pm, depending on how talkative Chavez was on that particular day. During the talk show, usually seated at a table, the president reviewed current events and gave his take on an array of matters, often rambling and continuously improvising. During program number 101, broadcast from the Miraflores Palace, it suddenly occurred to Chavez to ask for a whistle: "Doesn't anyone have a whistle? Get me a whistle, because I am going to whistle them *off-side.*" But the announcement to fire seven PDVSA managers was not improvised, as he had previously drawn up a list. After reading each name and position, Chávez sent them packing by declaring "out you go, you are fired mister," while the audience chanted "out, out!"

A week later, Chávez himself was fired from the presidency. In his confrontation with the opposition parties and the business association Federation of Chambers (Fedecámaras), and amid massive strikes called by the labor union Confederation of Workers of Venezuela (CTV), Chávez was overthrown, but restored to power by loyal officers three days later. After the shock of being removed from power, albeit for so short a period of time, Chávez was more determined than ever to pursue his take over of PDVSA. High and medium-ranking officials at the state-owned oil company refused to cave in and organized the so-called *Oil Strike*, which lasted between December 2002 and February 2003. Chávez crushed the strike by firing half of the company's staff. Analysts have described the aforementioned confrontation as a blessing in disguise for the Bolivarian leader. It gave him the perfect justification to execute the most far-reaching move of his presidency. PDVSA became the sponsor of the revolution.

Without control over the company, the revolution did not stand a chance of succeeding. Without tapping its resources, Chavismo would not have been able to buy off groups of voters and thus tighten and lengthen its grip on power. Nor would it have been able to purchase foreign support for the revolution or at least silence from some of its critics. The government was able to turn PDVSA into a cash cow by thwarting supervision or independent parliamentary audits of the oil company. In fact, without PDVSA's funding Chavismo would probably not have undertaken so many disastrous economic experiments, nor would corruption or money laundering have flourished to such an extent as to contribute decisively to Venezuela becoming a major drug-trafficking player. In the end, many *apparatchiks* were able to line their pockets and PDVSA's coffers were emptied.

Chávez was lucky in two regards: he was president during a period of continued increases in the price of oil, and he passed away precisely at a time when, as oil prices tumbled in global markets and Venezuela's production sagged due to underinvestment, serious financial difficulties were in store for the government. The grave economic crisis that unfolded under Nicolás Maduro was not of his making, although he dug his country into a bigger hole, but rather the result of having pillaged for so long a company that furnished 45 percent of the state's resources and generated one third of Venezuela's GDP.

Venezuela has the world's largest proven oil reserves, with approximately 300 billion barrels. Of the overall amount, 27 percent is conventional crude (light as well as medium and heavy) and the rest, almost three-fourths, is crude extra heavy, which is more difficult to extract. Only 5 percent of Venezuela's reserves have been tapped. The country was traditionally able to manage its vast oil wealth and achieve a higher degree of economic development than its regional neighbors. Although Venezuela underwent grave political and institutional problems at the end of the 1980s and during the 1990s, the oil sector remained the country's economic cornerstone. When Chávez died, however, PDVSA was in a financial mess: its cash deficit reached 40 percent of its budget, and its production had decreased by 26 percent. Actually the entire economy faced a dire situation.

In 2013, Venezuela's budget deficit reached 15 percent and inflation soared to 56.3 percent, already the highest in the world. Matters would only get worse. In 2015, Venezuela's budget deficit exceeded 25 percent of GDP. The International Monetary Fund forecast an inflation rate of 720 percent for 2016, which could triple the following year and reach 2,200 percent.

The shortage of food products was highlighted by daily news accounts of empty shelves in grocery stores and long lines to buy specific products. Venezuelans' inability to purchase basic items such as toilet paper or diapers made news around the world. The shortages spread to many everyday necessities such as powdered milk, sugar, olive oil, and flour, which were unavailable in 80 percent of grocery stores. The private sector shrunk due to the expansion of the public sector and the difficulty to get hard currency with which to import goods. The supply of markets therefore worsened. Not even the government, with a combined internal and external debt that surpassed $300 billion, was in a position to solve the problem by resorting to the purchase of imports.

How could such a scenario develop in a country that in the preceding fifteen years of a boom in oil prices had produced $1.1 trillion in crude oil? Chavismo's story is that of its abuse of PDVSA. By the end of the Chávez era, Venezuela had become a net importer of gasoline. This symbolism speaks volumes about Chavismo's terrible mismanagement of PDVSA.

What at First Was a Black and Viscous Hole

Venezuela realized it was sitting on vast reserves of oil in the 19th century. The nascent global oil industry charted the country's reserves, which were known to its inhabitants for many centuries. In 1539, colonial officials sent emperor Charles V a barrel of oil to allay his gout attacks. Little did the Spanish crown suspect at the time that this commodity would become as important as the gold it searched for throughout its empire. In fact, Spanish conquerors had lost interest in the Venezuelan provinces because of their absence of gold. In the same manner as the precious metals in Spain's overseas possessions—large shipments of silver—spawned a wealth which Spain squandered, Venezuela also was misusing its black gold.

Venezuela's oil industry developed in the 1920s, when foreign companies with the adequate technology were able to begin to exploit their concessions. Multinational corporations remained the leading actors in the oil sector for fifty years. Significant levies and taxes on capital gains were adopted in 1943 so the state would also profit from its own wealth. The oil boom that the country benefited from towards the end of World War II spurred the spectacular economic development of the 1950s under the dictatorship of Marcos Pérez Giménez. A lot of the infrastructure that led Caracas to be labeled the Miami of the South was built during this period. The nationalization of the sector during Carlos Andrés Pérez's first presidential term in 1976 significantly modified the business model. Venezuela was following in the footsteps of several Arab countries, which had also taken over their oil sectors in the preceding two decades, a period that witnessed decolonization on a global scale and the creation in

1960 of the Organization of the Petroleum Exporting Countries (OPEC), of which Venezuela was one of five founding members. This association's goal was to wrest control of the oil markets away from multinational corporations, which kept prices at a low level. Despite the low prices, multinationals recorded big profits due to the global scale of their operations. For the individual countries, however, production and revenue levels were small. It was precisely a Venezuelan, Juan Pablo Pérez Alfonzo, minister of Energy and Mines in the government of Rómulo Betancourt, who was the brains behind the creation of OPEC, alongside his Saudi colleague, Abdullah al-Tariki.

With nationalization, Venezuela's oil exploitations continued to operate as different business units, but now under a model of vertical integration and public ownership. Petróleos de Venezuela was then created as holding company for the sector. This transformation was described as a calm transition, in contrast to the shocks that Hugo Chávez would cause in the oil sector. After the purchase of the multinationals' assets, the personnel that already worked in the wells and offices was hired, and the Venezuelan managers were promoted to high-ranking positions which were previously the exclusive domain of the foreign corporations' nationals. This ensured the maintenance of a high level of technical expertise and management best practices.

Having created a brand, at the beginning of the 1980s the Venezuelan oil sector sought foreign operations to expand its markets in a process of internationalization. It purchased refineries in Switzerland, Denmark, and Germany, as well as storage tanks in several Caribbean islands. This internationalization strategy was carried out to counter the fall in oil prices. It was designed by Humberto Calderón Berti, who was appointed president of PDVSA in 1983 under the presidency of Luis Herrera Campins. The plan also resulted in the purchase of the U.S. company Citgo, a refiner and distributor of gasoline in the United States. Citgo became PDVSA's main subsidiary outside of Venezuela.

During the 1990s the overall trend was of downward pressure on prices. In order to counter a drop in revenue due to the lower prices,

PDVSA's companies made an effort to scaled up their production levels. In 1998, for example, with the barrel of oil dropping to a low of $10.5, a record 3.3 million barrels a day were extracted. In order to further ramp up production by a fresh capital injection, the government under President Rafael Caldera had opened up the oil sector to foreign competition in 1997. This *oil opening up*, as it was known, entailed letting the multinationals operate in Venezuela again after a twenty-one year hiatus. But the foreign companies were awarded contracts to operate residual fields which PDVSA was not exploiting because they needed higher investment levels and had lower returns.

Within this plan, the development of the Orinoco River region was stepped up. The Orinoco Belt's reserves of extra heavy crude could only be exploited with more advanced technology. The oil extracted from the Orinoco Belt had previously been commercialized as orimulsion, a bitumen-based fuel that can be used in power plants designed to run on coal. The opening up of the oil sector also allowed multinationals like Exxon and BP, thanks to their new technology, to extract the oil and sell it as synthetic crude.

During this phase, all operations with foreign companies were carried out as joint ventures, whereby the foreign partners extracted the oil, PDVSA sold it, and the profits were shared fifty-fifty. PDVSA had just become a large holding which incorporated the state companies that owned Venezuela's oil fields. Chávez reached power at that time of low prices and maximum production. These variables would be soon completely changed.

Taking on PDVSA and Running OPEC

Hugo Chávez won the presidential elections in December 1998 and started his mandate in February 1999. He took power with an agenda that included taking over political control of PDVSA in order to employ it to bankroll the revolution. "To this end, he first had to rid the company of its internal culture of meritocracy, inherent in a competitive enterprise, and which enabled upward mobility towards more senior management positions for those with the appropriate knowledge and track record." Antonio de la Cruz, oil analyst and executive director of Inter-American Trends, had been employed at PDVSA for sixteen years when he and all other managers were fired by Chávez after the oil strike. An engineer by training from the state of Zulia and manager of maintenance planning at PDVSA, De la Cruz had worked his way up the corporate ladder over many years, as was the case with many of his colleagues who also lacked political godfathers. "The people that made it to the top of PDVSA had garnered experience in many areas. To politicize the company, Chávez had to end this culture," he recounts.

De la Cruz explains that the criteria for internal promotion based on the employees' ability and experience—the norm at private companies—also applied to this state company, which had to compete with multinational corporations whose owners or largest shareholders were not states and thus did not operate according to bureaucratic whims or submission to constant political pressure. After many years of intense professional activity, PDVSA placed very high in international rankings, occupying the first or second place in some instances. It was a prestigious and admired company which defied the usual clichés about Caribbean laxity. Although it was a public company, PDVSA was organically separated from the rest of the government, and its accounts were audited by Parliament.

Chávez's disagreements with PDVSA's management began with his initial appointments for president of the company. He first named Roberto Mandini, who had moved up the ranks in the previous administration. He held the top job for only a few months. Then Chávez appointed Héctor Ciavaldini, who had worked in the company time ago. But he was perceived as someone who would apply a political agenda given his well-known left-wing credentials. His appointment spawned internal strife and turned many employees against Chávez. They viewed Ciavaldini's appointment as a violation of PDVSA's corporate governance culture.

Chávez exhausted many presidents of PDVSA during his confrontation with the oil company. Ciavaldini was succeeded by a military officer, General Guaicaipuro Lameda, who was better received because he understood the company's hierarchical structure. But he was forced to resign after heeding the advice of the company's technicians instead of Chávez's orders. The Bolivarian leader then named Gastón Parra Luzardo. A left-wing economist from the University of Zulia with no background in the oil sector, he was rejected by the employees, who organized protests and backed strikes called in other sectors of the economy at the beginning of April 2002. These massive protests helped to trigger the crisis that unseated Chávez from the presidency from the 12th to the 14th of April. After Parra's resignation, Alí Rodríguez Araque was appointed new president. He was a former communist guerrilla who had just been promoted to the posts of Energy minister and secretary general of OPEC. Under Araque's stewardship, PDVSA's activity ground to a halt beginning in December 2002. The walkout at the state-owned company was part of the general strike which formally lasted until February 2003. The walkout was the biggest lockout in Latin American history. But Chávez would not be overthrown on this occasion, and he took advantage of the clash to take over control of PDVSA.

The oil strike was a direct struggle between Chávez and PDVSA's core managers and employees disgruntled with the government. The public holding stopped producing and refining crude oil, alleging that it was forced to cease operations due to the general strike across the economy, which affected sectors such as transportation. The company blamed its shutdown on an external factor because its staff was constitutionally defined as a strategic labor force and could therefore be accused of sabotaging the country as it was not supplying gas stations. After two weeks, Chávez managed to get the company moving again by hiring other crews that took the tankers out of the ports. PDVSA's professional elite was thus denied its justification for remaining idle.

The firings at the oil company had begun during the April 2002 showdown, when the president announced the layoffs and early retirements live on *Aló, presidente*. Now the armed forces took over control of the installations and, deployed at the gates, prevented the management (about 120 persons) from returning to work. The regime prevailed in its struggle and wound up firing twenty-two thousand employees (half of the staff), with an average experience at the company of fifteen years. They were replaced by employees who were already engaged in the company's work through subcontracting practices, but also by others with absolutely no experience in oil operations. A new purge of PDVSA's staff took place in 2004, when those that signed the petition to hold a recall referendum against Chávez were forced into early retirement, harassed, or fired. This same fate befell all those in any labor sector or social group who signed the petition, which would later be known as the *Tascón List*.

With PDVSA's submission, in 2004 Rafael Ramírez took over as president of the company. He had impeccable revolutionary credentials as the cousin of the well-known terrorist Ilich Ramírez, alias Carlos *The Jackal*. The public holding would henceforth be kept on a short leash. Rafael Ramírez had already been appointed minister of Energy and Mines two years earlier. Since then he held always both positions, even though Venezuela had traditionally avoided this overlap to maintain a system of checks and balances and enable the company's independent supervision. In September 2014, Nicolás Maduro split the two positions, but not in an effort at transparent management but rather in his quest to brush aside potential contenders. Maduro appointed Ramírez as Foreign Affairs minister and later dispatched him to New York to serve as Venezuela's ambassador to the United Nations. After strengthening his grip on power, Maduro again merged the two positions in August 2015. Eulogio del Pino, who was already head of PDVSA, was appointed Oil minister too.

When Ramírez was named president of PDVSA, Chávez had already managed to win over OPEC's members to his oil policy, which was not based on prioritizing production volume but rather on prices. Displaying skill in international diplomacy, the Bolivarian leader had already forged a consensus among enough countries and convened the second OPEC summit in Caracas in 2000. Holding the summit in and of itself was already a success, as it was the organization's first in twenty-five years. OPEC's official numbers were misleading: given the low market price, OPEC members publicly announced and committed to production levels which they regularly flaunted by surpassing their targets in order to increase their revenue. At the Caracas summit, the participating countries pledged to really stick to their respective individual production quotas. In so doing, the real supply of oil dropped, demand increased, and the price of a barrel of oil rose. The strategy paid off.

Oil Harvest with Electoral Benefit

Chavismo's consolidation of power cannot be explained without considering the surge in oil prices which happened after Hugo Chávez was inaugurated as president. Having to pay more to fill up their cars' gas tanks would obviously not be popular among consumers in the rest of the world. But the new president fostered a policy that should have benefited his country. The price of a barrel of oil had remained relatively stable during the preceding ten years, fluctuating between $13 and $18 per barrel—the price of the so-called *Venezuelan basket*, an average of the different crudes that Venezuela produces. In the decade that followed Chávez's rise to the presidency, the oil price surged: from a low of $10.5 a barrel in 1998 to $25.9 in 2000, $46.1 in 2005, $83.7 in 2008, $101.7 in 2011, and $103.4 in 2012.

The surplus revenue was not channeled to finance substantial improvements in Venezuela's infrastructure. There was little investment in roads and airports, and the persistent blackouts highlighted the electricity network's deficiency and its need for a significant upgrade. The petrodollars were also not allocated to structural improvements among society's most disadvantaged sectors. It is true that substantial funds were earmarked for the population groups with lower income, known as C, D, and E (lower middle class, poor, and very poor), which accounted for more than 70 percent of Venezuela's population, but the progress achieved was not bigger than that registered in other countries.

According to the government's own figures, during Chávez's fourteen years in power $500 billion were invested in social policies.

This amounts to almost half of the oil revenue, since between 1999 and 2012 Venezuela produced crude worth $1.1 trillion. Social spending was clearly of an extraordinary magnitude. But the reduction in poverty was smaller than in neighboring countries. As the United Nations Economic Commission for Latin America and the Caribbean (ECLAC) points out, between 1999 and 2011, Venezuela cut its poverty rate by 38.5 percent, a lower amount than in Peru (41.4 percent), Brazil (44.3 percent), and Chile (49.3 percent). In fact, the entire region achieved substantial reductions in poverty, as the decreases in Colombia (33 percent) or especially Uruguay (63 percent between 2007 and 2011) also attest. The World Bank's statistics rank Venezuela in ninth place in Latin America in terms of poverty reduction in the last decade.

The funding for social policies was not more effective because the goal of improving the situation of the poorer in a sustained and permanent manner took a back seat to another objective. What Chávez dubbed as *oil harvest* formally sought to spread the wealth to the most far-flung places of the country through social aid or provision of services. But, in the final analysis, the *oil harvest*'s real intent was to collect votes. Chavismo's precept that the beneficiaries of the revolution should reach ten million adults in order to win over the political loyalty of a little more than half the electoral census underlines the clientelist mechanism with which the PDVSA's resources were employed. This was probably the subconscious thought of the Education minister when in February 2014, in the midst of the street protests against Maduro's government, he declared: "We are not going to lift people out of poverty to turn them into a middle class, so that they will strive to be *scrawny*." By *scrawny*, Héctor Hernández was referring to opposition voters, as Chavismo designated them. One can infer that the minister preferred that Venezuelans be poor rather than troublesome.

Chávez did not start lavishing money on social policy until he was forced to do so because of the 2004 recall referendum; he even dismantled some programs developed by previous governments during his first years in office. ECLAC's statistics and graphs reveal an extraordinary fact: the poverty rate did not budge during Chávez's first five years in office, and only dropped sharply after the Bolivarian missions were deployed at the end of 2003. After Chávez survived the 2004 recall referendum and was re-elected in the 2006 presidential elections, the poverty rate stagnated again despite the fact that spending on social policy remained high. The economic legacy inherited by Maduro resulted in a rise in poverty, proving that the progress had not been sustainable. In 2013, Venezuela was the only country in the region where the number of poor people increased. A study carried out by several Venezuelan universities concluded that in 2014 the poverty rate (48.4 percent of homes) surpassed that at the time of Chávez's rise to power (45 percent). In 2015, as the economy collapsed, the poverty rate skyrocketed to 73 percent.

The state-owned company became a distributor of funding, and was directly in charge of financing the Bolivarian missions. Between 2006 and 2011, PDVSA appropriated $56.1 billion for the missions; only in 2012, the year in which Chávez contested his last election, the amount was $26.4 billion. The company also contributed significant amounts to the National Development Fund (FONDEN) aimed at making the necessary payments for the execution of public-works projects, goods, and services. PDVSA's transfers did not diminish even during the credit crunch brought about by the international economic and financial crisis that began in 2008.

The government nationalized a range of companies not related to the oil sector and incorporated them into PDVSA's holding structure. Alleging that they operated in arguably strategic sectors, the government carried out nationalizations that were bankrolled by PDVSA. Petróleos de Venezuela therefore grew in size as it was forced to take over companies from a wide range of sectors and with differing goals. The most important one was PDVAL, which produced, distributed, and sold basic foodstuffs at prices set by the government. PDVSA also managed construction companies in the context of the Housing Mission.

PDVSA became Chavismo's purse strings. As Antonio de la Cruz summarizes, "PDVSA became the Venezuelan state's financial arm, was a key player in the development of its social projects, the buyer of social assets, and the instrument of its foreign policy." This latter goal was the international dimension of the *oil harvest's* strategy, which Chávez reaped in the form of direct advisory services from Cuba and support for Venezuela's stance in key votes at the Organization of American States (OAS) and other regional organizations. The approximately 100,000 barrels of oil a day given away to the Castro regime and the almost 200,000 sold at subsidized prices to the countries integrated in Petrocaribe substantially curtailed PDVSA's revenue. The state-owned oil company was therefore also footing the bill for Chávez's international public relations and defraying the cost of the regional podium he lectured from.

From a financial standpoint, PDVSA was the tool that enabled the state to maintain its liquidity. The revenue from 96 per cent of the exports and 95 percent of the hard currency that flowed into Venezuela did so through the oil business and the capital markets spawned by PDVSA. The government resorted to Petróleos de Venezuela's issuance of bonds whenever it faced a budget shortfall. Instead of promoting Treasury bonds, the government relied on the higher-yielding *petrobonds*, which unlocked $35 billion of capital between 2003 and 2011. As a commodity whose future price could be traded, oil enabled Venezuela to receive loans from China and Russia. From 2006, when the so-called China Fund was created, until 2016 Beijing lent Venezuela $54 billion. Russia provided a loan of $2 billion in 2014 as an advance on oil that Venezuela would deliver.

Fleeced Wells

Devoted to financing the revolution, in Venezuela and abroad, Hugo Chávez strangled the goose that laid the golden eggs. One of the main tenets of the oil industry is that constant investments are necessary in order to at least sustain a company's production potential. Wells' natural decline, which varies according to the kind of drilling and exploitation employed, must be offset by a demanding task of well maintenance. The chavista PDVSA neglected this obligation and production began to dwindle. The drop in production was also caused by the firing of thousands of highly-skilled employees in 2003 and their replacement by less experienced workers. This loss of experienced human capital was particularly harmful in an industry with mature wells as essentially was the Venezuelan. As PDVSA had been well-run for many years, the negative effects of these actions were not immediately felt. But production went to a progressive decline. As long as the price of a barrel of oil was climbing in world markets, a drop in production did not excessively concern Venezuela's leadership. But the situation took a turn for the worse when, with Maduro as president, prices started to tumble. Indeed, the price of the *Venezuelan basket* was $103.4 per barrel in 2012; $98 in 2013; $88.4 in 2014, and $44.6 in 2015. At the beginning of 2016 it plunged to $24.3 per barrel.

According to OPEC's annual reports, which the organization outsources to an independent auditor, Venezuela's peak production level was in 1998, when the country churned out 3.3 million barrels a day after a steady climb in the preceding years. Production nose-dived after 1998, with a spectacular crash in 2003 due to the *oil strike*. After the return to work at PDVSA, production increased slightly before dropping again. It was at 2.3 million barrels in 2013, the last year of the Chavez era (the figure in 2016 probably was 2.1 million). In stark contrast to past presidencies under which production registered continuous growth, Chávez's time in office ended with a cut in production of one million barrels a day. Venezuela, which had been among the world's leading producers, sank to number thirteen in 2012. In Latin America it was surpassed by Brazil, with 2.6 millions barrels a day—the Brazilians doubled production in ten years.

Eager to raise cash to finance the attainment of Socialism in the 21st Century, as Chavismo labeled its ideology, PDVSA was transformed into "a company that predominantly exported crude, and which employed oil as a financial resource for a political project and therefore did not act as a mercantile company," Antonio de la Cruz concludes. The evolution of PDVSA's labor force underscores its bureaucratization and politicization. In ten years its workforce was tripled despite the fact that production shrank. Chávez sought to increase the number of staff dependent on a public salary. All employees were admonished in public by the company's president to vote for the PSUV. At the beginning of 2002, PDVSA's workforce numbered forty thousand; by 2012 its staff had reached 110,000. Productivity dipped from one hundred barrels per employee to twenty-five. The stumble in productivity was constant: between 2001 and 2008 operational costs per barrel doubled and total costs trebled.

The slide in production was also the result of a process of renationalization. Foreign companies, which had been kicked out of Venezuela after the 1976 nationalization, returned with the opening of 1997 to operate marginal oil fields. Joint-venture agreements were signed whereby the multinationals extracted the oil and later split the benefits fifty-fifty with PDVSA, which was in charge of distribution and sales.

Venezuela was interested in this kind of arrangement because the required investments—usually high due to the fact that the oil fields were more costly to operate or provided lower returns—were shouldered by the foreign companies. But when oil prices rose, multinationals' benefits reached a level higher than that envisioned by the government. Chávez then proclaimed that Venezuela had struck a bad deal and decided to unilaterally change the rules. He demanded that multinationals turn over their operations to joint companies where PDVSA would be the majority shareholder. This amounted to a new nationalization. Some multinationals had undertaken long-term investments, especially in the Orinoco Belt, and rejected the compensation provided by the government for the nationalization of their assets. The main plaintiffs were U.S. multinationals ExxonMobil and ConocoPhillips. International arbitration ultimately ruled in their favor and against Venezuela, which was forced to pay more than $1 billion in compensation.

Chávez's neglect of the oil sector is surprising given that he regarded it as an engine to power his Bolivarian revolution. Previous presidents obviously also based their policies on the revenues accrued from oil sales, but none of them allowed the oil fields to languish to such an extent. Economists Javier Corrales and Michael Penfold highlight this fact in their book *Dragon in the Tropics* (2011), and underscore the contradiction of a PDVSA turned into the financier of social programs while its productivity was allowed to sag, thereby jeopardizing the government's own social policy goals. According to Corrales and Penfold, the politicization of the oil company "resulted in a worrying decline in PDVSA's operational capability, which actually undermined the socialist goals of helping the poor." Having compromised production for a barter of services, as was the case with Cuba, or of goods, as was done with part of the oil bill in Petrocaribe, weakened the financial position of the Venezuelan state-owned company.

Due to the aforementioned trends, over time the public holding lost the managerial, technical, and technological abilities needed to expand oil production, as Corrales and Penfold conclude. "Billions of dollars in investments and know-how are needed to turn tar into heavy crude that can be refined, and this is the only kind of crude production that Venezuela can easily scale up. PDVSA has thus become increasingly reliant on foreign investment to rebuild its oil industry." Playing with their book's title, Corrales and Penfold assert that oil "might have been the fuel for the dragon's fire, but in the end the dragon itself was burned by its own fire." One could add that it was not only the dragon that got burned, but that the country's terrain was also seared: Venezuela's source of wealth had been battered and mortgaged.

Present Chinese Money for Future Oil

Chavismo's enormous spending, the clientelist strategy, the discretionary funding the president used to further his immediate political needs, and widespread corruption across the system with time required more money than even PDVSA could furnish. Hugo Chávez then chose to mortgage the oil that should benefit future generations of Venezuelans in order to stay in power. His two traditional international allies would not provide cash: Iran suffered special difficulties accessing financial flows due to the imposition of sanctions, and Russia had other priorities. Chávez thus knocked on China's door, thereby including it in its alternative geopolitical calculations.

The Chinese loans were negotiated at the same time Venezuela launched the Petrocaribe operation. The fact that a big portion of PDVSA's oil no longer was sold in global markets, and the slow drip-feed with which Venezuela's allies returned Chávez's largesse deprived the Venezuelan state of revenue and hard currency it needed to obtain from other sources. Chavismo was withdrawing funding from the goal of promoting the revolution in Venezuela in order to pursue it abroad. But it needed to tap additional financing. After the shipments of tankers to its allies in the Caribbean started in 2006 (the comprehensive agreement with Cuba had begun earlier), the president concluded with China in 2007 a line of credit that enabled Venezuela to access $54 billion over eight years. The amount was split up into different installments, and was provided in return for future oil and refined products. Chávez thus made it to the last elections he would contest with financial breathing room, but Venezuela was forced to deliver barrels to the Chinese until at least 2021. It was the first time the country had paid with future production.

The negotiations to open up the credit line were conducted by Rafael Isea, who at the time served as deputy minister of Finance and president of the Venezuelan Economic and Social Development Bank (BANDES). Isea recounts from Washington, where he fled to after falling out of grace following Maduro's inauguration, the tough negotiations that he held to get the first loan installment of $4 billion from the Chinese. "Rafael, look," Chávez pleaded, "I need you to reach an agreement with the Chinese, because everyone here is full of talk but nobody can seal the deal." Isea remembers the difficult give-and-take with the Chinese, who showed up with a new negotiating team each time, and with whom matters that had been settled had to be renegotiated. China wanted that part of the loans to be earmarked for projects that its own companies would execute.

Isea pushed for a resolution in his visit to Beijing. In his final dinner with his counterparts of the Chinese Development Bank

(CDB), he announced that on the following day he would fly to Spain on his way back to Caracas and that he would not be able to take a concluded agreement to Chávez. At 3 am, with a knock on his hotel room door, he was presented with the signed agreement. The first disbursement would take place on February 18.

"The Chinese believe in the number eight," Isea explains. He learned that the Chinese business world is attracted by this number, deemed to be a bearer of good fortune, and that many Chinese businessmen open their businesses on a day of the month that ends with eight. Chávez also got lucky, in a manner of speaking. "The $4 billion were delivered to the president in cash. Nobody knows where they wound up." The money did not make it into the state's accounting, to the bewilderment of its deputy minister of Finance.

For the following loans the Chinese imposed the condition that their companies be in charge of executing different projects in Venezuela. But many of the joint ventures were not undertaken. Of the 243 projects that were considered up until Chávez's death, only three were carried out, and ten failed. There was no real intent to bring all of these projects to fruition because, as Isea attests, many were just a cover to launder Iranian money. In order to circumvent the international sanctions, Tehran sought to recover the funds it had placed in China with the transfers that Beijing made to Venezuela. The deals were also fraught with corruption: Ramírez, president of PDVSA, claimed for himself 20 percent of the value of the contracts that Venezuela would conclude with Chinese companies, such as those awarded for projects to build units of public housing. The Chinese retorted with a demand for a 10 percent share of kickbacks for each side.

Everything related to this credit line was called the Chinese Fund. As with many things under Chavismo, the name belied its true nature. Although a fund had been established, it did not contain investments but rather loans which Venezuela would have to return. Formally it was a loan to the Venezuelan government from the Venezuelan Economic and Social Development Bank (BANDES), with a small contribution by the National Development Fund (FONDEN).

But in reality it was the Chinese Development Bank (CDB) which was injecting the loans into BANDES. As an offset of the deal, PDVSA delivered the agreed amount of crude to the China National Petroleum Corporation (CNPC), which sold it in international markets or assigned it for domestic consumption. If the actual oil price was higher than that set when the loan was valued—what usually happened in the first years because the initial estimates were too low—the remainder was deposited by the CNPC, after taking the interest, into an account held by BANDES in China.

The management of this remainder was a strange mechanism that generated a fascinating result: an account beyond the reach of the Venezuelan people and beyond the jurisdiction of the Venezuelan Central Bank. As some experts pointed out, by the middle of March 2012 the account could have amassed approximately $24 billion. These funds were available to BANDES and to whomever Chávez authorized. But the money was not returning to PDVSA's coffers, despite the fact that it originated in the oil it produced. Maduro ended this practice when, upon taking office, he was forced to scrape together all available resources to ensure the daily functioning of his government. Beginning in 2013, the barrels delivered to China were valued at market price, generating no remainder, thereby decreasing the burden of delivery from 670,000 barrels a day to 470,000 and to 350,000 from 2015.

Paying and Keeping the Goods

The negotiation of the Chinese loans became even more arduous. After the civil war that resulted in the end of Muammar Gaddafi's dictatorship and life in 2011, China demanded that the agreements take the form of decrees that the Venezuelan National Assembly should approve. This added legitimacy to the agreements, and insured that, in the case of a political change, the new government would be bound by the decrees. China had investments of nearly $40 billion in Libya, and many were reneged on by the new leadership in Tripoli.

Initially, Caracas exclusively decided the specific use of the money in the China Fund aimed at financing projects that fostered economic development in Venezuela. But over time Beijing linked half of its loan to contracts awarded to Chinese companies. For example, the government of Venezuela bought between 2010 and 2012 three million air conditioning units, television sets, and household appliances from Qingdao Haier for the government program My Well-Equipped Home; the China Railway Engineering Corporation took the lead in building a 312 mile rail line in the state of Guárico, and CITIC Group was entrusted with the construction of 33,000 housing units. Moreover, the big engineering company CAMC signed contracts with the Venezuelan government worth $1.6 billion in 2010, which accounted for more than half of its global operations.

As the economist Emilio Nouel put it, "with the China Fund we pay and they keep the goods." China charged twice for the loan it was offering: with PDVSA's crude and with the benefit that Chinese companies derived from the awarding of contracts to carry out projects or selling their products.

This amounts to what the expert Antonio de la Cruz refers to as *neocolonialism 2.0.* "The country that receives the credit line commits future generations to the production and transfer of raw materials, and fosters a technological dependence on the Chinese companies, thus jeopardizing the development of national industry. This is a model that generates economic wealth for China and destroys it for the recipient of the credit line." In this model, which China has used in other Latin American countries and in Africa, the national companies lose market share as the country commissions Chinese companies to execute projects or purchases its goods. De la Cruz recalls that in the 20th century the theory of dependence developed by Cardoso and Faletto censured the United States' neocolonialism. The United States obtained natural resources from developing countries at market prices, turned them into manufactured products, and sold them to poor countries through its multinationals. "Through the credit lines given to countries, China is rewriting new forms of domination and neocolonialism of the 21st century, obtaining in exchange natural resources which it transforms into products that are included in the projects that big Chinese companies execute in these countries."

The money that arrived in Venezuela from China vanished almost immediately due to corruption, interest payments, and thousands of political urgencies Chávez needed to deal with. PDVSA was caught in a vicious cycle which was only sustainable—if it wanted to avoid bankruptcy—if it received more funding. After begging the governments of China and Russia, and with no other ally to turn to, the next step was to resort for loans to the foreign oil companies that had entered into joint ventures. Having honed the technique of current financing in exchange for future oil, it was a matter of applying this formula to other partners.

Resorting to multinational oil companies was the last idea floated before the *comandante*'s death. The regime labeled them *remedy plans*. It conveyed to public opinion that the investment from the foreign companies would serve to remedy the decline in oil production. The government often offered excessively optimistic forecasts for the increase in the production of oil that these investments would engender. In its strategic plan drafted in 2010, PDVSA's management envisioned attaining a production level of five million barrels a day by 2015, and 6.5 million in 2020. In all, between the end of 2012 and the middle of 2014, PDVSA was able to secure more than $11 billion through credits and investments by foreign oil companies operating in Venezuela. In reality, no significant increase in production was registered by 2015, when PDVSA didn't even arrive to half of the goal.

Cash Deficit and Sale of Assets

PDVSA's situation was further aggravated by the fact that gasoline was completely subsidized in the domestic market. Viewed as a national good that belongs to everyone, Venezuelans have traditionally paid very little to fill up at gas stations, regardless of the ideology of the government in power. In fact, Venezuelans enjoy the lowest gasoline prices in the world. As the price of exported gasoline more than trebled between 1999 and 2014, the price of the one set aside for domestic consumption not only remained the same, but actually dropped in real terms given the depreciation of the bolivar against the dollar. Hence, in 2014 the price of a liter of ninety-five octane gas was only $0.015, so that filling up a tank of forty liters cost just $0.60. Gas for cars was cheaper than water. The amount paid for a bottle of mineral water could buy seventy-two liters of gasoline. The price of fifty liters of diesel was the same as that of a soda. With such prices, managing a gas station was a very bad business proposition given the absence of profit margins.

The massive subsidies were taking a toll on PDVSA, as the more than 300,000 barrels of gasoline consumed by Venezuelans daily (out of a total of 700,000 barrels of oil a day allotted for the domestic market) were subsidized to the tune of $12.5 billion a year. The subsidies paid for all of the fuels supplied to the domestic market during the Chávez era amounted to 7 percent of annual GDP; in 2013 the subsidy reached $28 billion, an amount that exceeded the budget's appropriation for education and health care and accounted for 60 percent of what PDVSA earned that year from its exports.

Starved of public revenue, Maduro decreed in February 2016 the first increase in gas prices in twenty-seven years. "We are going to charge for gas because we were paying to waste it," he said. Maduro had put off the decision, fearing a wave of public unrest. The biggest popular unrest in memory, the *Caracazo* of 1989, had broken out precisely because the government of Carlos Andrés Pérez had decreed a rise in gasoline prices.

The government brought up as well the need to cut consumption. Venezuela is surpassed only by the Gulf countries in terms of per capita consumption of gasoline. Consumption increased from 2.8 barrels per person in 1999 to 3.7 in 2012, which amounted to 1.6 daily liters per person. In 2012, Venezuelans consumed twice as much gasoline as Brazilians and five times the amount used by Colombians, as a report by the Institute of Business Administration (IESA) indicated.

To make matters worse for the national accounts, part of the gasoline pumped from Venezuela's gas stations was imported. In 2013 it amounted to 6 percent of daily consumption, a volume that increased after a fire in August 2012 at the big refinery of Amuay claimed the lives of forty-two people. PDVSA purchased gasoline from the United States only to give it away to Venezuelans: at a market price of $110, it lost $107 per barrel.

This was yet another dimension of the fraud that Chavismo was committing against PDVSA. The regime was gutting a company that previous generations had turned into a global leader and whose benefits would be curtailed for future generations. Production dropped by 23 percent between 1998 and 2013. Of PDVSA's daily production of 2.3 million barrels, only 30.2 percent—the share sold to the United States, which had been diminishing—provided regular earnings at market prices. The rest of the production was set aside for purposes that only burdened PDVSA: subsidized national consumption (29.3 percent of production); cancellation of loans already received from China (23 percent); energy cooperation ventures with countries from Petrocaribe and ALBA (9 percent), which had payment periods of twenty years and could cancel them with agricultural products; and the agreement with Cuba (4.1 percent), which envisioned that all of the oil delivered could be paid for through the provision of services.

Such management of the public holding resulted in a growing constriction in PDVSA's income statement. In 2016, the external financial debt reached $46 billion; commercial debt was $35 billion. Moreover, the company owed the Venezuelan Central Bank more than $100 billion. It meant that the liabilities were bigger than the assets. "Given this state of affairs," De la Cruz concludes, "the sale of company assets appears to be one of the few options available to PDVSA in order to face its severe financial situation and meet the onerous internal and external obligations that the government of Venezuela has committed to." Chavismo had regarded nationalizations as a hallmark of its economic and social policy. It now had no other choice than to embark on a program of privatization of state assets.

In this regard, PDVSA announced in 2014 that it intended to sell Citgo, its subsidiary in the United States. It is one of its main assets as it owns refineries in Louisiana, Texas, and Illinois, as well as a network of six thousand gas stations across the United States. Given the plunge in oil prices, there were no bidders. "Citgo should not be worth less than $10 billion," Hugo Chávez had averred. This was the price the government had in mind. But it needed to factor in $2 billion in liabilities and the large commissions that corruption would extract—for the personal enrichment of some and the laundering of money from the business of others.

5

PROFITING FROM SOCIALISM
Economic and Judicial Corruption

I f Diego Salazar Carreño had not been so drunk on that night at the end of 2012 in Paris, his cousin Rafael Ramírez Carreño might still be comfortably living off of the fortune which he acquired by ripping off the people of Venezuela in his capacity as president of Petróleos de Venezuela (PDVSA). In the universe of chavista economic corruption, Ramírez was by far the most shining star. It is estimated that the personal wealth he accumulated exceeded $10 billion. But in March 2015 U.S. officials came knocking on Ramírez's door. While Ramírez pretended to lead a normal life as Venezuela's ambassador to the United Nations, in the very city he lived in—New York—prosecutors based in southern Manhattan were poring over new evidence. There was more proof about the role that PDVSA had played as a cover to launder money from drug trafficking by the chavista regime, the Revolutionary Armed Forces of Colombia (FARC), and Hezbollah, the Lebanon-based Shia group. Prosecutors were investigating as well how PDVSA had been used to evade the sanctions imposed on Iran because of its nuclear program.

Diego Salazar may have been very generous when it came to tipping. But on that night at the end of 2012 at the Hôtel de Crillon in

159

Paris, in his stupor, he got carried away. Placed at the upper echelons of PDVSA by his cousin, Salazar managed the insurance and reinsurance business of the state oil company. This is a particularly lucrative part of the oil business. His bank account was thus very full, and on that night in Paris Salazar signed a check for $100,000 as a tip for an employee of the Hôtel de Crillon. Taken aback, the employee told the hotel manager, who alerted the police. The check was from an account located in Andorra, the small country in the Pyrenees that attracted a lot of clients with murky money. When French officials relayed the information to their colleagues in Andorra, the latter froze the account with $200 million that Salazar held at the bank Banca Privada de Andorra (BPA).

The former manager of PDVSA was able to stop the investigation by paying a $80,000 bribe (in effect, another tip for him), which was spent on the services of prostitutes for the agents in charge of the investigation in Andorra, as the press later revealed. The famous former Spanish magistrate Baltasar Garzón was involved in BPA's decision to unfreeze Salazar's account. When the news broke, Garzón alleged that he had only dealt with the bank, and not with Salazar, and that his law firm had merely drafted a report for BPA's legal department.

Diego Salazar believed he was untouchable because of his direct family ties to Rafael Ramírez. Their bond also owed a lot to special family circumstances. Part of the family had supported revolutionary guerrilla movements. One of Salazar's second cousins, Ilich Ramírez Sánchez, attained notoriety as the international terrorist Carlos *The Jackal*, who since 1994 has been serving a life sentence in a French jail. When Rafael Ramírez's father was arrested in the 1960s by the Venezuelan authorities due to his involvement in guerrilla activities, Diego Salazar's father took care of Rafael, who at the time was only a boy. Before he passed away, years later, the uncle instructed Ramírez to look after his son Diego, who was twenty years younger. In his role as a godfather to Salazar, Ramírez appointed him to key positions and promoted him up the ranks of PDVSA. In turn, Diego became Ramírez's main middleman.

U.S. officials had been investigating Salazar's dealings in order to track down and expose Ramírez's illegal business practices. But it had been to no avail. The U.S. Treasury Department did not pass up the opportunity to follow the trail left by the tip at the Hôtel de Crillon in Paris and looked into the Andorra accounts. In the middle of March 2015, the Treasury Department's anti-laundering unit Fin-CEN (Financial Crimes Enforcement Network) published a report revealing that executives at BPA had enabled financial activities that served to launder money by groups and individuals that committed crimes, corruption, smuggling, and fraud. In addition to denouncing Russian and Chinese mafias, FinCEN's report also accused Venezuela. It quantified the money transfers allegedly stemming from money laundering by Venezuelan officials at $4.2 billion, $2 billion of which was related to PDVSA. Current or former chavista government officials would have laundered these billons of dollars through a network of hundreds of fictitious companies registered in Panama.

The investigations of BPA and its subsidiary in Spain Banco Madrid (the latter investigated by the Spanish Commission for the Prevention of Money Laundering and Monetary Infractions) uncovered a list of almost thirty Venezuelan clients whose accounts apparently had illegal or tainted assets. Diego Salazar was on the list, as well as Nervis Villalobos, Javier Alvarado Ochoa, and Francisco Rafael Jiménez Villarroel. All of them served in senior positions at PDVSA or in the Ministry of Energy under Ramírez's stewardship of both. The blow delivered by U.S. and Spanish officials concerned not only the oil czar Ramírez, but also Diosdado Cabello, president of the National Assembly and narcotics czar. The list contained the names of two of Cabello's close associates: former Interior Deputy Minister Alcides Rondón and Carlos Aguilera, a former military officer who had ran the intelligence services and whose business dealings were in part intended to funnel money to Chávez's daughters.

Although Ramírez was worried about these developments, he felt relatively safe. His position as Venezuela's ambassador to the United Nations afforded him diplomatic immunity. It offered him as well high-level contacts that could allow him to explore a deal with U.S.

officials. But as U.S. authorities pursued their investigations into corruption and laundering of drug trafficking funds, it was not clear how long it would take for them to catch up with Ramírez. In October 2015, *The Wall Street Journal* published an investigative report by José de Córdoba and Juan Forero. Under the title "U.S. Investigates Venezuelan Oil Giant" it said that "former PDVSA officials [are] suspected of looting of dollars through kickbacks and other schemes."

The $4.2 billion held by clients of Banca Privada de Andorra paled in comparison to the conservative estimate of $6 billion that the some involved people privately admitted they had transferred to bank accounts in Liechtenstein and Luxembourg. And these amounts were only a fraction of the $16 billion that Ramírez's network and his front men had allegedly at least acquired illicitly while they ran PDVSA. Oil sales had generated approximately $1 trillion in revenue during Ramírez's time at the helm of PDVSA and the Ministry of Energy. The $16 billion figure was based on the illegal commissions and bribes of at least 3 percent charged on multiple operations.

Authorities had finally found the thread with which to unravel the main hank. A lot of attention had been spent for a long time pursuing partial clues. One of them was the Illarramendi case.

Nuclear Alarm

It all started in the basement of a house located in Bethesda, a suburb of Washington, on a weekend in 2008. While the children played upstairs, a private investigator worked overtime on a task entrusted to him. He was reviewing documents about José Zambrano, a Venezuelan whose career had started as a salesman of men's clothing and, in a strange turn of events, had wound up owning one of Venezuela's banks. The BaNorte was a small bank founded in 2004. Zambrano was managing it in a risky manner. The Venezuelan Financial Supervisory body carried out inspections when Zambrano was poised to purchase the Federal Bank, which was ultimately liquidated. The inspections led to the takeover by authorities of BaNorte. The Financial Supervisory body alleged that BaNorte faced solvency problems, had lent money to itself, and was dependent on public funding. The bank was taken over in December of 2009 and it was nationalized the following year. Zambrano's business operations were no different than those of other so-called *new bankers* in Venezuela. But in his case he fell out of favor with chavista authorities. He would not be the only one.

On that weekend in Bethesda, the computer mouse opened several files and discovered unexpected information. In the United States are legend great discoveries in basements or garages. Many now want to claim the same epic start as Steve Jobs (Apple) and Jeff Bezos (Amazon). In this case it is true: from that basement in Bethesda, an investigation was launched that grew and eventually uncovered a corruption case that would unearth how PDVSA's executives took personal profit from the company's funds, and how other chavistas managed to increase their ill-gotten fortunes.

Among Zambrano's banking transactions was a loan of $30.7 million from a hedge fund. This was an unusual loan as it seemed to have no conditions. The person operating out of the Bethesda basement called the Manhattan District Attorney's Office, which pursued the lead. It exposed that the hedge fund had invested heavily through the company Michael Kenwood Energy in an Oregon-based firm that planned and developed nuclear power plants. These investments were financed with money from PDVSA. At a time of very close cooperation between Venezuela and Iran and international concern about Iran's access to nuclear technology, this prosecutor's discovery set off alarm bells. The Securities and Exchange Commission (SEC), one of the bodies that regulates and supervises U.S. financial markets, began to untangle the web of corruption of what would come to be known as the Illarramendi case.

In January 2011, the SEC filed a civil suit against Francisco Illarramendi and his companies and funds, integrated into the Michael Kenwood Group. This was followed up by a criminal charge. Francisco Illarramendi, whom family and investors call Pancho, is a well-built Venezuelan who achieved early financial success. When the case broke, he was forty-one and by then had accumulated fifteen years of experience on Wall Street. During a decade (1994-2004) he served as director of emerging markets at Credit Suisse. From this position, which involved frequent travel between the United States and Caracas, Illarramendi advised the Chávez government. He presented it with an operation that appeared to be a magician's trick: the *permuta,* in effect a currency swap.

In a heavily controlled currency exchange market such as the Venezuelan one, the government set a fixed exchange rate between the dollar and the bolivar. Venezuelan individuals and companies thus had trouble purchasing hard currency. Illarramendi explained to the government how it could maintain the dollar-bolivar exchange rate while giving individuals, importers, and companies a safety valve. The *permuta* system created stock exchanges that allowed Venezuelans to buy shares of companies that listed both in Caracas and New York. They could buy the shares in bolivars in the Caracas stock exchange and sell them in dollars on Wall Street. Both operations could be performed almost simultaneously. This amounted to a currency swap at a more favorable rate than that set by the government of Venezuela. The currency swaps were carried out especially with shares of CANTV, a public telephony company that was privatized in 1991, purchased by U.S. funds, and which was listed in both countries (it was renationalized in 2007). These operations became commonplace and resulted in the dollar swap. It allowed companies to access hard currency and eased the pressure on the official exchange rate, thereby containing the dollar's rise against the bolivar in the black market.

Well-versed in the intricacies of currency markets, Illarramendi quit his official position at Credit Suisse in 2004 in order to directly manage the speculative operations undertaken by Petróleos de Venezuela from its office in New York. Illarramendi thus became a senior advisor to PDV USA, Inc., the international financial consulting arm of the state-owned Venezuelan oil company. Internal clashes prompted him to set up his own company in 2005, but PDVSA soon became one of his clients. His reputation spread as a financial magician capable of delivering juicy returns by speculating with the dollar-bolivar exchange rate. Illarramendi managed funding from Venezuelan companies closely tied to the chavista elite. He operated out of Connecticut, with bank accounts in Panama, the Cayman Islands, and Switzerland.

Illarramendi's funds executed many financial operations that went beyond the realm of currency markets. But the swift exchange of currency remained at the core of his business model. In the purchase and sale of assets, the amount in bolivars was converted into dollars at the official exchange rate, which overvalued the Venezuelan currency. These dollars were then converted into bolivars in a parallel market that reflected the real value of both currencies, thereby increasing the original sum. These operations could be repeated indefinitely. This practice was not restricted in the United States, where there are no currency controls. In Venezuela it was legal until May 2010, when Chávez banned it to staunch what had become an instrument of capital flight. Despite being a state-owned company, PDVSA's currency speculation remained unabated under Illarramendi. It only ceased in 2011, when U.S. authorities froze the assets of the Connecticut financial company.

Interest Rates of 82 Percent

The Securities and Exchange Commission (SEC) did not object to Francisco Illarramendi's currency operations. It did censure that between December 2009 and November 2010 he used $53.7 million from one of the funds to make purchases on behalf of companies he owned or controlled. The SEC referred to these operations as "asset appropriation" and "fraud" because they withdrew money from a fund whose clauses did not authorize personal investments such as those carried out by Illarramendi. Of the money diverted from the fund, $23 million were set aside for the purchase of a majority of shares in NuScale, a company that developed prototypes of small nuclear power plants. At the time of the filing of the lawsuit, the hedge fund where the money originated (Short Term Liquidity I Ltd) was worth $540 million, 90 percent of which was owned by the pension fund of PDVSA's employees.

The trial made headlines for the wrong reasons. Firstly, it was wrongly described as a Ponzi scheme. In this type of fraud, the first investors' interest payments are paid with the new investors' funding. In Illarramendi's case, the operations did yield profits. Secondly, the losses were not astronomical. Clients initially claimed $2.1 billion in compensation. But the receiver lowered the amount to $300 million, because the majority of clients had exaggerated their claims. One of the main investors was one of Venezuela's leading businessmen, Oswaldo Cisneros, who had been Illarramendi's partner at one of the funds, Highview Point Offshore. Cisneros reduced his initial claim of $1.3 billion, made under oath, to only $20 million. Some investors sought to take advantage of the situation in order to massage their own accounts. Illarramendi's defense alleged that no losses were registered as investors had initially benefited handsomely. In fact, PDVSA ultimately asserted that Illarramendi's operations had not caused any detriment to its pension fund. The judge discarded the argument regarding past real profits and sentenced the financier to thirteen years in jail for fraud.

Illarramendi was really not more than an operator who can be censured for having looked the other way when flooded with money obtained illicitly. The real news was the profit margins earned by leading officials in chavista Venezuela. In some cases, the investments yielded annualized interest payments of up to 82 percent. "Venezuelan government officials made billions of dollars through Pancho's operations. They can therefore not allege they incurred any losses. They made a lot of money," retorts Ramón Illarramendi, the father of the financier who ran the hedge funds. He adds that when he was introduced to Jorge Giordani, the Venezuelan minister of Planning and the person who exerted the most enduring influence on the government's economic policy, Giordani told him: "So, you are Pancho's father. You do not know how much we owe your son!"

A veteran supporter of COPEI, the Christian democratic party that took turns running Venezuela with the left-of-center Democratic

Action for forty years, Ramón Illarramendi served as minister, ambassador, and strategic consultant under President Rafael Caldera. Aged 76 when the lawsuits against Pancho were filed, Illarramendi Sr. devoted himself to securing the release of his son. He represented him in court during the civil trial because the freezing of the accounts made it impossible to hire a good attorney. After all, it had been Illarramendi Sr.'s idea to purchase NuScale, the operation that had prompted the launch of the investigation. NuScale was a company based in Oregon which developed its own model of Small Modular Reactors (SMR), a new generation of smaller nuclear plants.

The idea of investing in NuScale had gained traction because of its potential and the perseverance with which Ramón Illarramendi pleaded his case. This was his *modus operandi*. For instance, Illarramendi Sr. claims that in the 1960s he sparked Robert F. Kennedy's interest in affiliating the Democratic Party with the Christian Democratic International, where Venezuelans always held a big sway. RFK's assassination in 1968 foiled any plan in this direction.

The farsightedness of investing in a company involved with the development of small nuclear power plants was soon confirmed. In December 2013, the U.S. Department of Energy announced that it would appropriate up to $226 million to foster NuScale. After shutting off the Venezuelan capital injection, the U.S. administration hastened to fund NuScale's plans to design and commercialize miniature reactors in order to prevent future foreign investors.

A Climate of Extortion and Intimidation

Given the high corruption in Venezuela, wasn't Francisco Illarramendi aware of the fact that the money was raised illegally? Or that public companies' investments yielded profits that wound up in personal bank accounts? "Pancho realized that the money's origin was shady. He thought he should not worry about the money's origin because, given the principle of unity of account that public companies operate under, the funding originated mostly with Venezuela's Treasury. But then he was told to deposit a payment in one account, another one in another account... He actually had suspicions, but there was a climate of intimidation and extortion," Illarramendi Sr. recounts in an attempt to justify his son's actions. "The coercion and threats were couched in friendly warnings. He would be told, 'listen, be careful'. But this apparent advice was really a clear warning. Pancho worried about cases of unresolved deaths and concluded that he was not safe, even in the United States."

On one occasion, according to his account, the threat came from one of the straw bosses for some of the regime's most powerful men, and who handled most of the illicit money: Diosdado Cabello and Alejandro Andrade. The middleman, Danilo Díaz Granados, demanded from Francisco Illarramendi during one of his trips to Caracas that he pay the promised amount stemming from the sale of Credite Lyonnais bonds whose price had decreased and were yielding lower profits than expected. Díaz Granados represented the interests of more persons, among them Rear Admiral Carmen Meléndez de Maniglia, who would go on to serve as minister of the President's Office during the transition from Chávez to Maduro and later as Defense minister. In this climate of intimidation, Illarramendi paid the amount that was demanded, thereby incurring a deficit of $5 million in his accounts.

The SEC alluded to these losses as alleged proof of the existence of a Ponzi scheme. "But this is not true," objects Illarramendi Sr., "because there were dozens of daily operations that accrued profits. The issue at hand is that many people are afraid to testify." Many were hiding the substantial profits they had obtained. The Venezuelan National Assembly, controlled by the chavista party, rushed to quell suspicions with a swift and perfunctory investigation that concluded that all of the civil servants named in the case were innocent. All innocent? The receiver appointed in the Connecticut case, John Carney, documented that a leading financial executive at PDVSA, Juan Montes, had been paid $30 million in bribes. Montes served at the time as manager of investments at the company. The report also indicated that "other civil servants" at the oil company had benefited as well.

Illarramendi Jr. provides an estimate of the profits that PDVSA registered in its links with its hedge fund companies through the practice of consecutive currency exchanges—from dollars to bolivars and vice versa on multiple occasions and taking advantage of the difference between the official and market exchange rates. Illarramnedi projects that the gains reached a minimum of $900 million and could have easily exceeded $1.3 billion, depending on the exchange rate. Many of these gains were amassed with public money and wound up lining the private pockets of chavista officials, the financier suggests from jail. "PDVSA makes such a big profit on the arbitrage between the official exchange rate and the market rates that the level of corruption skyrocketed."

"It is clear from the receiver's reports that civil servants from PDVSA, directly or indirectly, committed several acts of corruption and, in some manner, of administrative coercion, pocketing hundreds of millions of dollars," he concludes. It is therefore surprising that when U.S. authorities were investigating murky transactions related to executives of PDVSA, as was the case with some of the huge sums deposited in accounts at Banca Privada de Andorra, the Connecticut court with jurisdiction over the matter ruled in favor of the company, ordering that it be paid the amounts it claimed. And this fact did not take into account that the funds invested in the hedge funds had generated much higher returns than the amounts invested when the takeover of the companies managed by Illarramendi took place.

In addition to the *permuta* designed by Illarramendi during his tenure as consultant to the government of Venezuela in the early stages of Chávez's presidency, the Ministry of Finance also employed another important financial product known as *nota estructurada*. It involved the packaging of Venezuela's public bonds issued by its Treasury with those of other countries such as Argentina, Ecuador, Bolivia, and even Belarus. In order to commercialize these products, financial operators with close ties to the government's high-ranking civil servants were hand-picked in a process without an auction and devoid of any transparency. The bonds were sold to

Venezuelan banks in bolivars and with a spread. The banks in turn sold them in dollars below their nominal price. After obtaining the dollars, the banks traded them in the free currency market and made immediate profits.

As Carlos Tablante and Marcos Tarre describe in their book *Estado delincuente*, 60 percent of the profits were doled out to the Ministry of Finance and the remaining 40 percent for the banks endorsed by the government. According to the authors' conservative estimate, in the first two years of use of the packaged bonds the Venezuelan people and taxpayers were fleeced to the tune of about $20 billion. The government had argued for the need to facilitate access to hard currency and for reining in the parallel dollar market to justify the launching of the packaged bonds, but the scheme backfired and resulted in higher levels of capital flight. Chávez terminated the packaged bonds in 2010.

Since the international press was delving into the Illarramendi case, many people who profited from the financial engineering started to keep a lower profile in order to avoid appearing in the newspapers. One such person was Víctor Vargas, president of the Banco Occidental de Descuento (BOD), an important institution in Venezuela. According to Illarramendi Sr., Vargas had invested about $200 million, but chose to write off his investment rather than claim the return of his assets. He thus avoided being summoned and questioned by the receiver. Vargas' successful career, which did not have chavista origins, was predicated on his calculated decisions regarding whom to engage with. This is the only way to explain how he rose to the top during Chavismo and was not a victim of the purge of bankers that took place in 2009.

Vargas' Horses, as in *The Godfather*

A U.S. State Department report from July 2008, leaked by Wikileaks, highlighted Vargas' good standing with Chavismo. The dispatch also underscored that Vargas had accrued substantial profits through investments in the packaged bonds: "Vargas, whom sources claimed had benefited from the negotiations, is a banker whose star has been on the rise during Chávez's presidency". He remained in the good graces of the government under Maduro as well. One of the transactions he handled for the new government was to finance with 500 million bolivars the purchase of the communications group Cadena Capriles in October 2013. As the minister of Communications would privately confess, according to the Venezuelan press, the operation's mastermind was Tareck el Aissami, the powerful former Interior minister. Chavismo thus gained control over one of the opposition's media conglomerates, which included the most widely read newspaper, *Ultimas Noticias*, and the financial newspaper *El Mundo*.

Vargas was a smooth operator. Moreover, as love knows no borders, he was able to forge family links with members of the Spanish and French nobility. In 2004, his daughter Margarita married the Spaniard Luis Alfonso de Borbón, son of the duke of Cádiz, Alfonso de Borbón, and of María del Carmen Martínez Bordiú, granddaughter of the late Spanish dictator General Francisco Franco. Margarita's husband Luis Alfonso, who worked for his father-in-law's bank, is deemed by French royalists as the legitimate successor—as he is the duke of Anjou—to the French throne. This marriage brought glamour to the Vargas family and was often featured in the tabloids. But the marriage of Vargas' other daughter, María Victoria, with the businessman Francisco D'Agostino did not generate positive publicity. In fact, it linked the Vargas name to news about chavista corruption. D'Agostino had links to Derwick, a company that had been awarded an unusually high number of contracts in the Venezuelan public sector.

Vargas, in any case, acted with caution. What happened to him on April 19, 2009, was reminiscent of one of the most famous scenes of the movie *The Godfather*, in which one of Vito Corleone's enemies awakens in his bed to find the head of a prized horse among his blood-soaked sheets. At the Polo Open of the United States, held at the Palm Beach International Polo Club in Wellington, Florida, the stands were packed with members of the social elite. They looked on in horror when the horses of the Lechuza Caracas stable, owned by Vargas, emerged from their trailers before the start of the competition only to collapse. Twenty-one horses in all. Two collapsed immediately, and the others, dizzy and dazed, also wound up laying on the grass. Veterinarians tried to resuscitate them with ventilators and water, and some assistants put up a canvas to spare the crowd the horses' agony. Seven horses died on the spot at the club, and the other fourteen passed away despite the best efforts of an emergency veterinarian service. All of the horses' blood samples presented abnormally high levels of selenium, a common mineral that helps muscles recover from fatigue.

The death certificate determined that the overdose of selenium had been caused by an imbalance in the medical product's formula which Vargas's team had ordered from a pharmaceutical laboratory in Florida called Franck's Compounding Lab. Franck's admitted that the formula was incorrect, but the person that manufactured the product claimed to have followed the indications in the prescription the lab received. Vargas estimated the financial loss at $4 million, or almost $200,000 per horse.

Andrade, the Treasurer Who Hoarded

The investigation did not turn up a smoking gun that could be directly linked to the poisoning of the horses. But with the scene from *The Godfather* on everyone's mind, the instinctive inference was that a *consigliere*, as in Francis Ford Coppola's movie, had intended to send a warning. And the *consigliere* could be no other than Alejandro Andrade, also newly rich and owner of a big horse stable. A participant in the failed coup of 1992, Lieutenant Andrade was a bodyguard and assistant to Chávez in the 1998 presidential elections. The following year, after retiring from the military, he became a member of the Constituent Assembly. In 2002 he was appointed president of the Common Social Fund, and in 2007 was promoted to head of the National Treasury and deputy minister of Financial Management. In 2008, while continuing to serve in both two positions, he was also named president of the Venezuelan Bank for Economic and Social Development (BANDES), a position he held until 2010. Born in a humble neighborhood of Caracas, he rose to power with no wealth. By the time he left the government, he had amassed a fortune estimated at several billion dollars. Andrade was entrusted with the right high-level positions that enabled him to make a killing. Chávez's hand guided his career.

It was probably Chávez's way of compensating Andrade for an accident that occurred as they played *chapita* at the Miraflores Palace. *Chapita* is a poor boy's baseball played with a bottle cap and a broomstick. The president batted the bottle cap into Andrade's eye. Since the accident, Andrade wore a glass eye and was always appointed by Chávez to positions that offered the possibility of personal enrichment. Being the president's protégé provided him with impunity. But over time several accusations were leveled at him for alleged irregularities in the Treasury, leading to his resignation. Andrade left his position without Chávez ordering a probe, and he was replaced by a trusted aide, Claudia Díaz, who had been Chávez's nurse. Nicolás Maduro would later name a nephew of his wife, Cilia Flores, to the post of national treasurer. It was loyalty that dictated the appointment to this—and other—positions.

Chávez's death left Andrade without his political and personal sponsor. His troubles began in earnest in May 2013, when the Securities and Exchange Commission (SEC) of the United States uncovered a fraudulent scheme developed by the Venezuelan BANDES during Andrade's presidency. The SEC detected that between 2009 and part of 2010 BANDES had undertaken illegal operations with Direct Access Partners, a brokerage in New York. The brokerage bought bonds which it later sold at a higher price to BANDES' treasury department. BANDES in turn offered the brokerage house part of its bonds at below-market prices. The investigation conducted by U.S. authorities revealed that these operations had generated earnings of $66 million. The profits were transferred to a company registered in Panama, which held five bank accounts in Switzerland. The accounts for two semesters that contained BANDES' transactions were signed by Andrade, while a third bore the signature of his successor as president of BANDES. The charges against Andrade were leveled at the same time as U.S. officials arrested María de los Ángeles González, a former manager at BANDES, during her visit to Miami.

The Federal Bureau of Investigations' probe of Andrade left him without a visa to enter the United States. He could therefore not visit his crown jewel: Hollow Creek Farm, his horse farm in South Carolina. These are first-rate facilities that take care of racehorses and train riders, many of whom are originally from Latin America. They are trained so they can compete in international equestrian events. Andrade's son Emanuel became an outstanding rider with several trophies. His father had vowed to sacrifice everything for his son's career.

Andrade was a frequent visitor of the Caracas equestrian clubs. The elites of the Venezuelan capital have always been fans of horse-racing. Andrade's money enabled him to sponsor some of the clubs. But if he wanted to attend his son's races around the world without the threat of being arrested, Andrade had no choice other than to negotiate a plea agreement with U.S. officials. He was facing the FBI investigation stemming from the SEC's charges regarding the BANDES bonds. Moreover, the U.S. Drug Enforcement Administration and the U.S. Treasury were looking into his laundering activities. In 2013 the former military officer struck an agreement to cooperate with U.S. authorities and in return received permission to reside in the United States.

Billionaires in Barely Ten Years

It is impossible to ascertain how much was stolen by those who regarded themselves as the owners of Venezuela. "If the Venezuelan state reported its accounts to independent auditors, an estimate could be made," according to Alek Boyd, a Venezuelan journalist based in London whose blog has brought to light many details about his country's rampant corruption. "The problem is that Venezuela does not report its accounts, but rather makes them up to try to keep up appearances. PDVSA's exact production level is unknown, as is the case with the revenue collected by the SENIAT, Venezuela's internal revenue service. The exact amount in the funds available to the array of bodies created by Chavismo (FONDEN and others) is also unknown. This applies to all of the public funds in Venezuela."

A good estimate is the difference between the amounts cleared by the Commission for the Management of Currency (CADIVI) and the currency used to pay for imports. CADIVI was created in 2003 with the aim of authorizing the exchange into foreign currency for the payment of invoices from foreign purchases. But until 2012, CADIVI cleared $75 billion more than the official figure for imports into Venezuela. This quantity amounts to capital flight from Venezuela. The real total is probably higher as some of the imports reported were fake. It cannot be ruled out that businessmen who backed the opposition contributed to the capital flight, but such operations would only amount to a fraction of the corruption facilitated by the government.

Alek Boyd points to many other corrupt practices: misappropriation of assets, overpayment in public tenders, issuance of debt, unauthorized lavishing of free goods or services to other countries, unnecessary purchases, irresponsible spending, payments for nationalizations, and financing for political allies. "These practices are not unique to Chavismo. What distinguishes Chavismo from all other previous Venezuelan governments is the sheer amount of funding involved. According to an estimate of total revenue, since 1999 the chavista government has had more revenue than all of the governments of the 20th century put together. Chavista corruption has hence multiplied to the nth power." Boyd estimates the total sum related to corrupt transactions during Chávez's presidency at $150 billion. But other sources project that it could have reached $400 billion, an amount equivalent to Venezuela's GDP.

Several international institutions have repeatedly underscored the pervasive corruption that afflicts Venezuela. The country places near the bottom when it comes to measuring corruption levels. In its corruption perception index, Transparency International ranked Venezuela in 2013 as the most corrupt country in Latin America; in 2015 it was the ninth most corrupt in the world, just behind states such as Somalia, North Korea, Libya, or Guinea-Bissau.

When Chávez's death weakened internal discipline, chavista leaders began to publicly voice their concern about graft. Freddy Bernal, a historical PSUV congressman, publicly admitted that "red [chavista] corruption is even worse than the white, green, or yellow ones," referring to the colors of the political parties of the pre-Chávez era. Other leaders warned that the country was being drained due to the outflows of hard currency carried out by phantom chavista companies. All this was the *robbolution*.

What degree of responsibility does Chávez bear with regard to the spread of corruption? Did he look the other way, did he encourage it, did he take part in it, or was it a combination of all three? Boyd's response is categorical: "By structuring a one-man populist regime, where all of the relevant decisions had to be made by him, because all of the state's institutions were subordinated to him, his responsibility cannot be questioned nor avoided. There can be no doubt that he resorted to graft to advance his political objectives, within Venezuela as well as beyond its borders. So the answer is that he is responsible for all three."

There can be no doubt about Chávez's involvement in the use of discretionary resources and the design of corrupt practices, as the previous pages have described. It is harder to link Chávez himself to operations that resulted in his personal enrichment because the use of front men and the transactions' shady nature complicate any probe. Clues that emerged from investigations undertaken for this book point to a possible transfer to Chávez's daughters of bribes worth several hundred million dollars related to construction and infrastructure projects. A key figure in this operation could have been Carlos Aguilera, a businessman related to the public works sector who was involved in projects such as the Caracas metro.

The wealth that was swiftly acquired by the rest of the Chávez family is also suspicious. His brother Adán, governor of the state of Barinas, is one example. His brother Argenis is another. He served as deputy minister of Electric Energy and president of the National Electrical Corporation. The opposition accused him, among other fraudulent practices, of buying outdated equipment at inflated prices. The list of family members who might have benefited from corruption also includes Asdrúbal Chávez, one of the president's cousins, as well as several nephews, whose activities are suspicious. Asdrúbal Chávez was promoted in 2007 to the position of vice president of PDVSA, where he was in charge of the commercialization of crude; Maduro appointed him minister of Oil and Mining (2014-2015).

Casto Ocando is another Venezuelan journalist who has documented chavista graft as a Miami-based investigative journalist for *El Nuevo Herald* and the Univision television network. He portrays corruption as pervasive among those who served in key positions within the chavista regime, from the military to civil servants and businessmen. "There are extraordinary fortunes among military officers, who due to their management of troops, resources, and vehicles and their control of Venezuela's roads or its borders have illegally profited from drug trafficking. They have also profited from smuggling of gasoline and stolen resources such as aluminum, and from other illicit activities. There is as well the category of civil servants, who also accrued exorbitant wealth, such as Lieutenant Alejandro Andrade, who is an iconic case: a man who rose from his position as a low-level official in the Caracas city council and became one of the richest men in Venezuela thanks to his appointment as national treasurer. And then there are the businessmen and bankers, such as Víctor Vargas, who also racked up great wealth by obviously using their contacts with the system, especially with regard to the *management* of hard currency. There are also straw bosses, operators…"

Neither Socialism nor Death: *Petrobonds*

The full list of those who committed fraud in the name of the Bolivarian revolution is very long. The purpose in this chapter is not to name them all. Some have already been mentioned in previous pages and others will be unveiled later on. But if we had to single out one person who stands out in terms exceeding all others in the sheer magnitude of the fortune he acquired, it would be Rafael Ramírez. This is why we have to write about him again. Appointed minister of Oil and Mining in 2002, after 2004 he also served as president of Petróleos de Venezuela. In 2014 he swapped both positions for that of Foreign Affairs minister. He was later named Venezuela's ambassador to the United Nations. While he proclaimed the motto "PDVSA, Socialism, or Death," he and his straw men employed their version of the revolutionary tax to line their pockets. During his ten years at the helm of PDVSA, he managed not only the company's extraordinary oil revenue, but also the company's operations in other sectors: production and distribution of foodstuffs and public housing development, which is inherently prone to the payment of bribes and commissions.

There were also illicit gains to be reaped from the private use of PDVSA's public funds, as the Illarramendi case highlighted, or even agreements to manipulate the price of the state-owned company's bonds. In November 2009, days after the issuance of bonds worth just over $3 billion, Ramírez announced a new issuance. According to an insider, his remarks were intended to send the price of the first package of bonds tumbling. It was an arranged operation carried out with some of Ramírez's investment friends, who took advantage of the situation to buy a high amount of bonds. When the markets realized that the double issuance did not signal problems at PDVSA, the bonds' price rose and the investors sold them at a handsome profit. The investors had agreed to share half of the gains with Ramírez and his accomplices at PDVSA. The corporate secretary was the one who signed off on the transactions and distributed the profits from these illicit operations.

The chavista elite's abundant purchases of PDVSA's bonds explained why the company met its payment obligations in a timely manner, distributing billions of dollars to its investors while Maduro's government, on the brink of bankruptcy, delayed payments to suppliers of food, medical products, and other basic goods. This was not done in deference to Wall Street: the payments were not bound for the accounts of international corporations, but rather to swell the fortunes of socialist Venezuela's millionaires.

Ramírez's actions were endorsed by Hugo Chávez, and subsequently by Nicolás Maduro. They caused huge losses of capital at PDVSA and risked its bankruptcy. The U.S. Treasury Department was uncovering evidence that the state-owned oil company had laundered through its financial accounts funds that originated in drug trafficking. In doing so, it was providing a service to the chavista chieftains, to the FARC, and to Hezbollah. U.S. authorities had evidence as well that PDVSA had helped Iran circumvent the sanctions that the international community had imposed. All this could qualified PDVSA itself for sanctions by the United States. As the guarantor of the operations that are conducted worldwide with its currency, the United States has the power to ban certain actors from using dollars to conduct their business. If it were not allowed to commercialize in dollars, PDVSA would be reduced to barter agreements and financial isolation.

The U.S. Drug Enforcement Administration (DEA) dangled the threat of such sanctions in its contacts with Ramírez to force him to cooperate. Was the DEA going too far in trying to turn him into an informer? Where should the line be drawn between the need to gather information and the fitting punishment of criminals? Should he face trial in the United States, Ramírez's sentence could certainly include jail time, but his cooperation with the investigation would be rewarded with a reduced sentence. However, if he faced the prospect of a tough punishment, Ramírez might decide to hold out inside of Venezuela, although Chavismo's new rulers could also eventually decide to settle scores with him.

The road to Washington was well-traveled and had its enablers. Some of the Venezuelan officials who turned to the United States and sought to live there legally hired an attorney named Adam Kaufmann. Until 2012, Kaufmann worked in the Manhattan District Attorney's Office, where he investigated many of Chavismo's murky accounts. The website of the law firm Lewis Baach, where he became a partner, indicates that Kaufmann specializes in representing white-collar criminals and helping clients to "navigate crises and mitigate their exposure to regulatory and criminal risks."

Venezuela's own budget was managed with great leeway. Planning Minister Jorge Giordani kept the different ministries on a short leash with regard to the drafting of their ordinary budget, which was submitted to the National Assembly. But the budget was later stretched to include additional appropriations. "Sixty or 70 percent of the additional funding for the ministries was personally embezzled by the ministers and governors," asserts another Venezuelan who struck an agreement with U.S. authorities. "When Chávez visited a place, he was told, 'President, here we lack this or that,' and Chávez then promised to provide it. The governor would then approach the minister and tell him, 'the president ordered that a university be built here' or whatever it was, and the minister turned over the funding. And if the project had a price tag, they made sure to increase it."

In addition to these dealings, overt nepotism was rife. A few months after taking office as president, Nicolás Maduro created the Presidential Corps of Inspectors. He appointed his son, Nicolás Ernesto Maduro Guerra, to head the Corps. Known as Nicolasito, Maduro's twenty-three years old son had no experience or studies related to the position. He also lacked experience in the film industry, but was later named coordinator of the newly founded National School of Cinematography. The president's wife, Cilia Flores, already doled out positions when she was president of the National Assembly: the opposition counted up to forty-two appointments of brothers, nephews, cousins, daughter-in-law, a former husband, and other relatives or associates.

Bolibourgeois and *Boliboys*

Caribbean wit made up the term *bolibourgeois* to refer to those who, in the Bolivarian republic, stacked up great fortunes during what was supposedly an anti-capitalist revolution. While Hugo Chávez and Nicolás Maduro lambasted the United States, the *bolibourgeois* and their families filled flights to Miami to go shopping. "To Bal Harbour, please." The cabs flocked to the famous mall at Miami Beach, known for its brand stores and high prices. "Those people like to buy lots of things. It is not for me to explain the purpose of the purchases. But I know they are chavistas, you know. There are people who are well-known," remarked the owner of one of the stores to the journalist Casto Ocando and his Univision camera. "We are buying a line of gold iPads, which is a limited edition... there are many Venezuelans who come, see the product, and purchase it." The iPhone with inlaid diamonds was priced at $75,000, and the solid gold iPad at $45,000.

As Ocando recounts in his book *Chavistas en el Imperio* (2014), the Venezuelan armed forces had a purchasing office in Miami, in the Doral neighborhood, close to the giant discount mall Walmart, "where many coronels and generals ordered to buy everyday goods." During the first seven years of Chavismo, a C-130 from the Venezuelan Air Force took off every week from Miami "loaded with all kind of supplies, such as TV sets, HD equipment, toiletries, motorboats, and even vehicles, alongside the usual supplies of munitions and military equipment." Ocando himself flew on the plane, and on that occasion the main load was a full fitness center for a general. The closure of the office "caused outrage among high-ranking chavista military officers."

Not all who have acquired wealth were referred to as *bolibourgeois*. Such status was reserved for those who could especially flaunt their wealth: show off a Gucci belt or a thick golden bracelet; own one or several private jets parked on runways; gather race horses on the polo fields, or mansions in Florida... And the members of the Venezuelan government had gone to great pains to not display their biggest trophies. Regardless of the label, Chavismo's list of bourgeois and those with bourgeois inclinations was long. It also included left-wing ideologues such as José Vicente Rangel. The online media *La Patilla* unveiled that he wore an eighteen carat gold Rolex worth almost $30,000. Or like Mario Silva, who during years served as the regime's propagandist with his TV program *La Hojilla*. Silva fell out of favor after Chávez's death due to a recorded conversation during

181

which he criticized other factions of the party. This was quickly followed by the release of pictures of him undertaking private trips on PDVSA airplanes. "Airplanes which are not justifiable, they bought airplanes and more airplanes... with the state's money, which belongs to the people," Chávez had censured when he rose to power in 1999. Fourteen years later, when his death ended his time in office, Silva stood out as a symbol of populist hypocrisy.

The corruption has extended to the new generations. The offspring of chavista officials or those who accrued fortunes with Chavismo's endorsement practice what they always witnessed their peers do. They are the *boliboys*. The most talked about case is that of the executives of Derwick Associates, Alejandro Betancourt and his cousin Pedro Trebbau, whom Francisco D'Agostino is linked to. They are well-connected youth who are no strangers to tabloids. Betancourt is the son of a former wife of the Spanish bullfighter Palomo Linares. D'Agostino is the brother-in-law of the *royal* Luis Alfonso de Borbón. They resorted to their contacts to engage in business dealings in the Venezuela of arranged contracts.

Derwick, a company incorporated in the United States, was awarded without any public tender twelve contracts worth $3 billion for electrical projects approved by the government of Venezuela in only fourteen months, between 2009 and 2010. This was an extraordinary amount. According to the lawsuit filed against them in New York by the former U.S. diplomat Otto Reich, after the contracts were awarded and the money transferred to bank accounts in Manhattan the accused then pocketed millions and subcontracted the execution of the energy projects to companies based in the United States.

The charges asserted that D'Agostino admitted to a friend that they "of course" paid bribes, because in Venezuela "you always have to pay." For four contracts with PDVSA they had bribed its president, Rafael Ramírez, and for three others signed with the National Electric Corporation they had paid off the minister of Basic and Mineral Industries, Rodrigo Sanz. The judge dismissed the case of Derwick on procedural grounds.

In addition to PDVSA leadership, mid-level officials at the Venezuelan state oil company also benefited from the bribes policy. In a separate case, in December 2015 the Venezuelan oil tycoon Roberto Rincón was arrested in Texas. He and his partner allegedly paid bribes to five PDVSA officials to get their companies selected for energy contracts. About $1 billion was traced to this conspiracy.

From Newcomer to Banker

Hugo Chávez rewarded the political favor that several businessmen did him during the difficult period of the 2002-2003 strikes. Wilmer Ruperti used his fleet of tankers to export the PDVSA production that piled up due to the oil strike. Ruperti later increased his contracts and became a naval merchant with a net worth that he himself quantified at $1.4 billion. The businessman always nurtured his relationship with the president. In 2012, he presented him with the gift of two guns that had belonged to Simón Bolívar and his romantic partner Manuela, estimated at a value of $1.5 million. Another businessman awarded for his initial generosity with the president was Ricardo Fernández Barrueco. The owner of parking lots in the Venezuelan capital, Fernández Barrueco made his fleet of vehicles available to President Chávez to transport food when the distribution networks froze in 2002. Between 2008 and 2009, Fernández Barrueco gained control of four banks: Confederado, BanPro, Bolívar Banco, and Canarias.

These were years when businessmen with no experience in the financial sector became bankers. The banking business was especially attractive as a means of racking up profits quickly. If one had the right connections, there were plenty of public contracts to bid for. After raising capital, the aspiring bankers registered companies that soon had a portfolio of clients and contracts. The bankers without many scruples borrowed from their clients' savings or lent themselves money. These were times when it appeared that the price of a barrel of oil would never stop increasing and excessive financial risks were being incurred everywhere. Moreover, banks were obtaining revenue from the operations with the packaged bonds, which was the means to have access to dollars in a controlled foreign-currency market.

The bursting of the global financial bubble resulted in a Venezuelan banking crisis in 2009. Because many packaged bonds had been negotiated when the parallel dollar was higher, banks now had no other choice but to sell them at lower prices, resulting in losses in their accounts. The government used the crisis to settle scores. It reported that bankers were using their clients' savings to buy companies, place debt, or buy bonds. In all, between the end of 2009 and the middle of 2010 twelve banks were taken over, seventeen bankers were arrested, and another twenty-five fled.

The first banks to be taken over in this crisis were those of Ricardo Fernández Barrueco, who at the end of 2009 was jailed and charged with embezzling his clients' assets; he was not released until 2011. The next to fall out of grace was Arné Chacón, an executive of the banking institutions Baninvest, Central, and Real, who was charged with misappropriation of savings and fraudulent use of public funds. "I cannot understand how Arné Chacón, who is from the Navy, and is a newcomer like us, now presides a bank," Chávez said on television. Chacón's case had special political fallout because Jesse Chacón, a fellow comrade-in-arms to Chávez in the 1992 coup, resigned from his position in the government after his brother's arrest. After Arné was released from jail in 2012, Jesse joined Nicolás Maduro's government.

One of the accused who evaded justice was the owner of BaNorte, José Zambrano, whose shady accounts led to the discovery of the Illarramendi case. Zambrano's initial godfather was Pedro Carreño, who chaired the National Assembly's Investigative Commission into Smuggling of Dollars, was a member of the group Parliamentarians of Latin America against Corruption, and made it all the way up to minister of Interior. As opposed to what one might infer given the positions he held, Carreño got Zambrano involved in illicit dealings. One of these activities was the sale of fertilizers to the FARC for their use in cocaine growing fields. Zambrano acted as a middleman between PEQUIVEN, the national petrochemical company, and the Colombian narco-guerrillas.

Zambrano also founded a company in Honduras that sold inputs to PDVSA in exchange for the fuel that it delivered to the Central American country. This deal was part of the barter system agreed upon so that countries in Latin America could receive supplies of oil from Venezuela. The transaction was carried out at the price that Zambrano agreed on with Eudomario Carruyo, PDVSA's financial director, so that both men could reap a profit. To avoid raising any suspicions, Zambrano divorced his wife, although they were not formally married. He could thus pretend not to have any links with the Honduran company, which was registered under his wife's name. This information was reported to U.S. authorities by the private investigator who worked out of the Bethesda basement mentioned before.

When he fell out of favor with the regime, Zambrano fled to Miami, where he flaunted his wealth by driving among the beaches in a Rolls Royce. Another Venezuelan banker who sought safe haven in Miami was Eligio Cedeño, whose relationship with Chávez got off on the wrong foot. Cedeño was charged at the end of 2003 of having allowed one of his banks (Banco de Canarias) to carry out a fraudulent operation to obtain dollars. The computer equipment company Microstar, owned by the young businessman Gustavo Arráiz, had requested $27 million from the Commission of Currency Management, but it appeared that the equipment slated for export did not exist and fake invoices were issued. Actually the real problem lay elsewhere. Cedeño had been able to swim with the tide in the early stages of Chavismo, but his banks were sought after by others who had closer ties to the PSUV.

Cedeño's unwillingness to sell his assets was not well received. Gustavo Arráiz had had an affair with Rosa Virginia, Chávez's oldest daughter, and had recorded a videotape of their intimate liaison. Arráiz would have shown it to Cedeño, and the banker would have been denounced by one of the bank's security heads to the president's inner circle. Chávez concluded that Cedeño was trying to blackmail him using his daughter. His fury could not be contained and the banker was jailed without a trial for several years. The president's anger was also vented at the judge who eventually allowed Cedeño to get away.

Judicial Corruption

The outrageous case of Judge María Lourdes Afiuni is a testament to the elimination of the judiciary's independence under Chavismo. "She is a bandit," Hugo Chávez exclaimed from the Miraflores Palace in a nationally televised prime time broadcast on October 11, 2009, a day after Eligio Cedeño fled and Afiuni was arrested. The president even ask for a tough sentence directly to the president of the Supreme Tribunal of Justice, Luisa Ortega, who was present in the room: "I demand toughness... This judge should receive the most severe punishment, thirty years in jail. She should be in jail. The full weight of the law should fall on her and any other judge who thinks about doing something similar."

Afiuni had simply applied Venezuelan law, which banned that someone be in preventive custody—without a trial—for more than two years. Cedeño had spent almost three years in preventive custody. Each time his case came up for a court hearing, the prosecutors simply did not show up, and Cedeño was sent back to jail. There was thus no prospect that his trial would begin. When the banker appeared before Afiuni, the magistrate in charge of Court 31 in Caracas, the judge granted him parole. Cedeño left the courthouse, took a motorbike taxi, and vanished amid the Caracas traffic. He emerged months later in Miami.

The judge was immediately accused of corruption, being an accomplice to Cedeño's escape, abuse of power, and criminal conspiracy. In his appeal for a harsh punishment against Judge Afiuni, Chávez invoked the holy name of the Liberator. "Simón Bolívar decreed that anyone who takes a cent from the national Treasury should be summarily shot, meaning executed. This also applies to judges." The prosecutor's office alleged that Cedeño had bribed Afiuni, without examining, for example, the illegality of extending the banker's detention in jail without a trial to almost three years.

The United Nations' Human Rights Council Working Group on Arbitrary Detention deemed the proceedings against Afiuni as "particularly severe," and labeled them arbitrary detention and an act of reprisal. Under a harsh detention regime, Afiuni developed some ailments and had to undergo surgery on several occasions. In February 2011, she was placed under house arrest, but she continued to need hospital care. Her trial in absentia began in November 2012. In June 2013, she was released on parole.

For the non-governmental organization Human Rights Watch (HRW), the Afiuni case marked a turning point—from bad to worse—in the state of the judiciary in Venezuela. Since Chávez "manipulated" the composition of the Supreme Tribunal of Justice "stacking it with loyal appointees" in 2004, the result was a "partisan judicial system committed to legitimizing abusive practices," according to José Miguel Vivanco, president of HRW for the Americas. Under such circumstances, judges were reluctant to issue rulings that could upset the government. If they were initially afraid to lose their jobs, after Afiuni was jailed in 2009 they also feared being put on trial for applying the law. This had been referred to as the "Afiuni effect": judges were intimidated and blackmailed with threats of criminal charges. Jesús Ollarves, professor at the Central University of Venezuela (UCV), explains that "the judge who tries to follow the law receives a phone call from the Supreme Tribunal of Justice or the disciplinary regime's entities." In Venezuela, Ollarves concludes, "there is a judicialisation of politics and a politicization of justice."

At the center of the judicial meddling was Eladio Aponte, who presided over the Criminal Court of the Supreme Tribunal of Justice. His testimony after fleeing Venezuela in 2012 was devastating. In remarks to the news media in Costa Rica, before seeking refuge in the United States as a protected witness, he described a system that systematically rode roughshod over individual rights.

Aponte recounted to the Miami-based SoiTV television channel that every week on Friday morning, a meeting was held at the Vice

President's Office. Its purpose was to determine the orders that judicial bodies should follow in their proceedings. He attended these meetings, as did the vice president of the government, the head of the Supreme Tribunal of Justice, the attorney general, the president of the National Assembly, the solicitor general, and the general accountant. One of the police chiefs would occasionally join the meetings. What was discussed at these gatherings? "The pending cases and what will be done. In other words, the orders were issued according to the political climate."

Calls from Miraflores to Arrange Trials

Hugo Chávez closely followed the main judicial cases. "In Venezuela nothings happens without the president's consent," Eladio Aponte asserted. Occasionally the president intervened personally in the case. As the magistrate in charge of the Criminal Court of the Supreme Tribunal of Justice, Aponte received phone calls from Chávez so he would bring about the convictions of innocent defendants. This happened with the so-called Paracachitos case. It involved a group of young Colombian peasants recruited and trained as paramilitaries who were arrested in 2004 in Caracas when they were allegedly plotting to assassinate the Venezuelan president and stage a coup. There were suspicions that the group had been created by chavista officials in order to frame the opposition and purge the armed forces. But Chávez was asking Aponte "to proceed with the investigations, exposing that the operation was directed against the government, that this should be proven." They were sentenced to long jail terms. Chávez later pardoned them.

Another instance of personal meddling by Chávez, according to Aponte, was in the case of the eleven persons convicted for the Puente Llaguno events. Puente Llaguno is a transit overpass in the center of Caracas, close to the Miraflores Palace. The bridge was the scene of clashes between demonstrators on April 11, 2002, which led to the brief overthrow of Chávez. The disturbances claimed the lives of nineteen persons, both supporters of the regime and of the opposition. Several members of the extinct Metropolitan Police were charged with the shooting. In April 2009, a court convicted three police commissioners (Iván Simonovis, Lázaro Forero, and Henry Vivas) and eight officers. It handed down sentences of up to thirty years in jail. Before the ruling became final, the defendants filed a cassation appeal before the Supreme Tribunal of Justice. That brought the case under Aponte's writ. The prosecution's case had many flaws. For the head of the Supreme Tribunal's Criminal Court, it was obvious that political pressure had been exerted from the top during the entire process. Now he would be the one to feel the pressure. "The president directly ordered me to bring the case to a final resolution, without more delay," reads the statement signed and notarized by Aponte in Costa Rica. "Convict them once and for all," Chávez urged Aponte. The magistrate relayed the president's orders to his colleagues, and they all "rushed to sign." The opposition lambasted the political persecution, and international organizations undertook several campaigns aimed at securing their release, especially that of Simonovis, whom the government treated with special harshness. In September 2014, after nine years spent behind bars, Simonovis was put under house arrest due to his deteriorating health.

The magistrate Aponte received more frequent instructions from Attorney General Luisa Ortega, and especially from the president of the Supreme Tribunal of Justice, Luisa Estela Morales. They instructed him about "when someone was going to be indicted, when a person would be arrested, when their homes should be broken into." With such information, Aponte was expected to "organize" the necessary proceedings and find the "most appropriate" judge. Arranged cases? "There were many."

On a particular occasion, Aponte was urged to certify a double injustice. "They looked for a convict, put a hood over his head, and used him as a witness" to charge someone. The convict was freed as a reward for his false testimony. The innocent man who was so flagrantly accused, José Sánchez Montiel, known as Mazuco, was convicted of homicide and sentenced to nineteen years in jail. He was charged and convicted of the murder in 2007 of an officer of the Military Intelligence Directorate. The murder took place in the state of Zulia, whose governor, Manuel Rosales, was the opposition presidential candidate whom Chávez defeated in the 2006 elections. Mazuco was Zulia's police chief and the charges brought against him were interpreted as an attempt to politically intimidate Rosales. Elected to the National Assembly in 2010 and convicted shortly thereafter, Mazuco was finally able to serve as a member of parliament in 2013 despite the fact that he had not served out his sentence. Aponte's confession from exile did not prompt the judicial authorities to review the sentence that they had handed down against Mazuco.

The farce also was commonplace in the military justice system. Aponte himself was a military prosecutor before he served in the Supreme Tribunal of Justice. He was pressed by the government to convict Francisco Usón. He was a retired general who had held a senior position in Chávez's government and was appointed Finance minister at the beginning of 2002. He resigned after a few weeks in disagreement with the government's repression of the street protests that took place in the context of that year's tumultuous events. Usón rejoined the military, but was forced to retire after voicing criticism against the government. As a civilian, Usón in April 2004 appeared on television. He hinted at the possibility that a fire which had burned eight soldiers alive in a punishment jail cell at the military base of Fuerte Mara in March could have been set intentionally with a flamethrower. Aponte was pressured to "manipulate" the case, because Usón "had to be indicted." He was charged with slandering the armed forces. In October 2004, a military tribunal—a clear violation, as he had returned to civilian life—sentenced him to five and a half years in jail. He was paroled in December 2007 under the condition that he not publicly discuss his case nor take part in political events or meetings.

Chavismo transformed the judiciary, removing judges who did not yield to its aims and replacing them with retired employees of the military justice system. This amounted to a partial militarization of the courts. Some judges were replaced as well with persons without the necessary qualifications who were quickly promoted. Some persons went from selling counterfeit CDs or cold meat to serving in important judicial positions; a judge with a criminal record of having looted a bank was promoted. These practices stoked even more corruption.

In addition to the Friday meetings at the Vice President's Office of all of the high-ranking judicial officials, on Mondays a gathering of each circuit was held. All of the cases that affected leading opposition or regime figures were discussed, with the aim of distributing the assignments among the judges. These meetings were the brainchild of José Vicente Rangel, a veteran left-wing ideologue who exerted a lot of influence on Chavismo and the political agenda through his weekly television program of interviews and analysis.

During his tenure as vice president (the longest of anyone who held the post under Chávez, from 2002 to 2007) Rangel made sure that the courts would go after political enemies as well as *class* enemies. This development contributed to the appearance of a group of lawyers willing to manipulate records and to exert pressure on some judges. The so-called Band of the Dwarfs took on a life of its own when it turned economic gain into its main goal. They had good connections with the prosecutor's office, although it sometimes cracked down on them as perceived rivals. The Dwarfs openly engaged in extortion, covering up criminal records or using false witnesses depending on the defendant's willingness to accept payment of big sums.

Someone who prospered within the group was Raúl Gorrín, who in 2013 became the owner of Globovisión, the last remaining generalist private television channel that had eluded the regime's grasp. Globovisión's purchase was carried out with Alejandro Andrade's funding, which multiplied after he served as national treasurer of Venezuela. "Andrade is not just my friend, he is my soul mate," Gorrín told the journalist Nitu Pérez Osuna, one of Globovisión's stars, shortly before she was fired. Pérez Osuna had probed the Band of Dwarfs and her program "I promise" made Chavismo uncomfortable.

The purchase was backed by Diosdado Cabello. But when the president of the National Assembly realized that he was not able to seize control of the television channel, he used the businessman Rafael Sarría as a front man to buy the newspaper *El Universal* in July 2014. The purchase was carried out through a complicated web of companies. *El Universal* had managed to survive beyond the government's control as a beacon of independent information and opinion. In less than a year, three non-governmental communications groups (Cadena Capriles, Globovisión, and *El Universal*) buckled under the government's pressure after funds of murky origin were employed to buy them.

Eladio Aponte's testimony about the total submission of the Venezuelan judiciary to the chavista regime explained other proceedings, such as the harassment by courts of opposition leaders like Leopoldo López, Antonio Ledezma, and María Corina Machado, who was stripped of her parliamentary immunity and banned from traveling abroad. Another prosecutor, Franklin Nieves, admitted in October 2015—from Miami, after fleeing as well from Venezuela—that, following orders from the attorney general, he had fabricated evidence in order to bring charges against Leopoldo López. The trumped-up charges resulted in a conviction and jail sentence of more than thirteen years for the opposition leader. Nieves' confession reaffirmed the corruption of the judicial system described by Aponte. But Aponte's revelations also pointed in another direction...

6

THE BOLIVARIAN DRUG CHANNEL
Narco-Trafficking Directed from Above

On a weekly basis, the head of the Directorate of Military Intelligence (DIM) reported to Hugo Chávez on the operations under way. General Hugo Carvajal included in his report a review of the involvement of high-ranking military officers in drug trafficking activities. Carvajal, nicknamed *The Chicken*, briefed Chávez about a business that the president didn't direct in its entirety but certainly oversaw. The involvement of Venezuelan state structures in the purchase of drugs from the Colombian guerrillas and their distribution from Venezuela was a product of Chávez's geopolitical worldview. To manage a narco-state with strategic aims degraded the Venezuelan armed forces and were the source of the ill-gotten wealth accumulated by many of the regime's officials. Chávez endorsed the business, giving his narco-generals free rein and intervening only when the spoils had to be divided between drug lords. Chávez also directly called the judiciary so they would turn a blind eye in some cases and convict scapegoats in others.

The magistrate Eladio Aponte was an extraordinary witness as president of the Criminal Court of Venezuela's Supreme Tribunal of Justice (TSJ). When Aponte fell out of favor and went from being the accuser to being the accused, from *organizing* the prosecution to being the object of an *organized* cause against him, he unveiled several secrets after he fled from the country in 2012. In his accusations, he aimed at the top by asserting that Chávez was not only aware of the drug trafficking carried out in Venezuela, but actually one of its prime abettors.

It should come as no surprise. When examining a map of South America, Colombia was the missing link in the great pan-Bolivarian chavista project. Without Colombia, there could be no talk of fraternal political links and an alliance between all of the peoples liberated by Simón Bolívar in the 19th century, despite the enthusiastic addition of Ecuador and Bolivia. Ollanta Humala's Peru seemed to align itself with the Bolivarian revolution at first, but would soon distance itself from it. But in the Colombia of presidents Alvaro Uribe and later Juan Manuel Santos there was never any thought of toying with Bolivarianismo. Chávez's interest was to weaken the government of Bogota by supporting the terrorist groups that had been fighting it for decades, basically the self-styled Revolutionary Armed Forces of Colombia (FARC) and the National Liberation Army (ELN).

"The way to strengthen the narco-terrorists was to increase the sale of drugs. Since their traditional distribution channels were being undermined by Plan Colombia, Chávez opened the gates of Venezuela to them," according to a Venezuelan who closely collaborated with the U.S. Drug Enforcement Administration (DEA). "Chávez ordered his military not to obstruct the narco-terrorists' operations in Venezuela, and ultimately the Venezuelan military itself became embroiled in them." Up to 90 percent of the drugs produced in Colombia were distributed from Venezuela.

The regime provided an ideological cover for the consciences not already spoiled by corruption: in the *asymmetrical war* that Venezuela had to wage against the United States, any tool was legitimate as long as it harmed the enemy. This *weapon,* as opposed to expensive ones, came with the added advantage of generating revenue for the Bolivarian revolution and, especially, for its standard-bearing agents. Within this scheme, Chavismo required a judicial system that would also act in an *asymmetric* way, and some judges that would rule accordingly. Eladio Aponte was one of these judges.

"One was made to feel important because the president called you, because you were invited to the Miraflores Palace," he recalled with embarrassment. After months of living in Washington, the former magistrate viewed the situation in a different light. In several interviews I held with him regarding his work in Venezuela, Aponte surprised himself praising the separation of powers in the United States. He did not disown his communist upbringing, but he realized that Chavismo had been a flight forward which had destroyed the rule of law. He admitted his guilt in the process, but he did not disclose certain matters and alleged a range of excuses to justify his behavior. He was keen to redeem himself by gaining the respect of Venezuelans. The most straightforward way to achieve this goal was to tell the truth, and calling out Chávez, he assured, was a mandatory part of this truth.

Hence, Aponte recalled how he was often summoned to Miraflores in the early hours of the morning. The time of day had nothing to do with an attempt to cover anything up. It was simply the consequence of the president's work schedule. Although Chávez did not wake up late, he tended to accumulate tasks towards the end of the day. If he was unpredictable by day, the more so he became at night—reading books, calling in to some live television programs, and holding unplanned meetings with Chavismo's main players. The result was insomnia among the high-ranking government officials. Nobody could rest easy without fearing a phone call from the presidential palace asking about data or requiring answers to presidential questions. "He would call at 2 am, and although it could be a pain, someone like me felt honored to be summoned. Diosdado Cabello, Jesse Chacón, and Rangel Silva all attended the presidential palace regularly. They were all friends of mine at the time, and these meetings made you feel you belonged to something."

Those whom Chávez called for sometimes had to wait their turn whiling away in the corridors before seeing the president. On other occasions, some appointments overlapped. That is how Aponte was

195

able to be present sometimes when General Carvajal, the head of the Directorate of Military Intelligence, briefed Chávez on the drug trafficking operations undertaken by officers in the armed forces. Judge Aponte had experience in the military, as he had served as the chief military magistrate before his promotion to the Supreme Tribunal of Justice. These meetings kept him abreast of developments, so he could know how to deal with operations whose cover had been blown. But Chávez's instructions did not always arrive at such moments. Chávez also contacted him at any time of the day without waiting for the quiet early morning hours, as happened in one urgent case involving several well-connected officers.

An Army Marred by Drug Trafficking

The voice message was recorded on the cell phone. "*Maracucho*, this is López, tell Ricardo not to panic, that things will work out, that he needs to tough it out, that all doors are still open, that he should not despair, ok?" But the *maracucho*, a colloquialism that refers to those from the city of Maracaibo (Zulia state), was not able to listen to the message, which had come from a member of the Army. Despite the reassurance the message sought to provide, the doors had closed: the *maracucho* had been arrested, and he was not the only one. It was November 19, 2005. At about noon, two members of the National Guard stopped a vehicle with military license plates. The white Chevrolet Kodiak was brought to a halt at a checkpoint located in the town of Torres (Lara) after it had covered half of its planned route. As the judge concluded, the loaded vehicle had departed the municipality of La Fría (Táchira), on the border with Colombia, and was en route to Puerto Cabello (Carabobo). It was enough to know this itinerary to suspect about the nature of the trip. Many of the drugs that were shipped out of Venezuela were first delivered by the FARC at the border and then transported to the country's main port, where the drug barons had their own warehouses. But the members of the National Guard were not acting on unaided suspicion of wrongdoing, but rather on a likely tip-off from a rival group.

During the inspection, two thousand bales of cocaine with a weight of 2.2 tons were found. They were hidden under almost 300,000 packages of a type of brick (Colombian *caico*). The driver of the vehicle, Edgar Alfonso Rincón, a civilian who had been working in the Army for more than ten years, and Second Lieutenant Ricardo Antonio Lacre were arrested. A cell phone impounded from the driver contained several recordings with messages that conveyed an increasing sense of concern. "Edy, do me a favor. When you hear the message, this is the friend of the gentleman who put you in charge of this little job." "Look, *maracucho*, get in touch with the major, and do so now, as I have been calling you all afternoon and you are not answering. Call the major urgently, and let Lacre know." The telephone numbers and the review of the communications led to the arrest of two additional military officers: one was Major Héctor José López; the other, Lieutenant Colonel Pedro José Maggino, the gentleman who "commissioned the little job."

Lieutenant Colonel Maggino, Major López, and the Second Lieutenant Lacre had spent the previous night in the small hotel Stancia's Suite in the town of La Fría, as the guesthouse's registry indicated and some of its employees testified. At that meeting, they had supervised logistics for the shipment of the drugs, which would be supplied by a couple of Colombians. The drugs arrived through the nearby border crossing of Orope and were loaded onto a Chevrolet van. A military license plate taken from an Army vehicle had been attached to the Chevrolet, which was guarded overnight by troops at the Orope military base. Early in the morning, the shipment was transported to Puerto Cabello in order to be loaded onto a ship bound for Europe. Until a few months before these developments, Lieutenant Colonel Maggino had served for two years as head of the hunting battalion in charge of patrolling that section of the border with Colombia. In all likelihood, similar operations had been executed in the past because Maggino, now serving in another posting, was assisted in that operation by previous deputies, such as Rincón, who had been his chauffeur, and Second Lieutenant Ismael Andrés Barrios, who was also arrested and was in charge of the Orope base.

The state tribunal which initially dealt with the case was especially outraged that the shipment was stacked up in a military installation. "The place of storage was none other than the border protection base of Orope, where officers and soldiers deployed there kept watch over the vehicle loaded with an illicit substance," the judge underscored. Second Lieutenant Barrios admitted to having ordered his rank and file not to activate the reaction or defense plan upon the arrival of Major López despite the fact that neither the major nor the vehicle were authorized to enter the base. Due to the solid evidences presented by the public persecutor the operation's kingpin, Lieutenant Colonel Maggino, was jailed pending trial and indicted as an "accomplice to illegal and aggravated transportation of narcotic and psychotropic substances." It appeared that a sentence would be handed down against Maggino until Eladio Aponte, the Supreme Tribunal of Justice magistrate, stepped into the judicial fray.

Following orders from above, Aponte called off the prosecution. He decreed that the case be withdrawn from the state tribunal's jurisdiction, ruled that some of Maggino's rights had been violated, overturned his preventive detention, and returned his case to a lower court for it to be investigated from scratch. The charges against Maggino were dismissed in May 2007 although the investigation revealed that his assets far exceeded his salary. The authorities accepted his statement to the effect that on the night of the delivery of the drug shipment he was not at the border area. Maggino was promoted to colonel even before his official acquittal.

Maggino had a number of powerful supporters, as Aponte's testimony would later attest. The judge asserted that he exonerated Maggino under orders from the Miraflores Palace and other high authorities. He received phone calls from "the president of the republic on down." "Defense Minister Baduel called me. Rangel Silva called me [the head of DISIP, the intelligence services]. Hugo Carvajal [head of DIM, military intelligence] called me. An admiral called me... Aguirre, I believe [Luis Enrique Cabrera Aguirre, of the President's Joint Chiefs of Staff]. In other words, many heavyweights vouched for this man."

–"What did they tell you exactly?
–Well, that Maggino was a good guy, that the president was very interested in the outcome of the case.
–But did these people know that he had stashed drugs in the military's barracks?
–Yes, how could they not know? Maggino was apparently an aide to Chávez's mother. This was a strong bond."

These were questions put to Aponte by the journalist Verioska Velasco, who was able to interview him for SoiTV in Costa Rica on his layover as he fled from Venezuela. During the interview, Aponte publicly accused two high-ranking Venezuelan military officers of involvement in drug trafficking: General Clíver Alcalá, then head of the Armored Division, and General Néstor Reverol, who actually directed the National Anti-Narcotics Agency (ONA) and later served as Interior minister. "I handled and continue to have a lot of information," Aponte stated. During three months, Aponte had been smuggling classified files out of Venezuela, as he suspected that events were turning against him.

Aponte saved some of his darkest secrets for his negotiations to turn himself into the U.S. Drug Enforcement Administration, such as the regular briefings in which he reported to Chávez how the state-run drug trafficking was proceeding. Aponte also accused Diosdado Cabello, deemed as the regime's number two strongman, of being the biggest drug lord. Aponte was the first defector who directly and forcefully implicated Cabello, whom he charged of organizing the money-laundering network comprised of a web of companies and banks controlled by the regime. In his account of his escape from Venezuela, Aponte did not forget that the most serious threat against him came precisely from Cabello.

Aponte, the Great Getaway

"Remember what Fidel did to Ochoa." Eladio Aponte immediately recognized the voice of the person who was conveying the warning.

It was that of a high-ranking chavista official with whom he had become friends with. As the head of the Criminal Court of the Supreme Tribunal of Justice and former chief military magistrate, Aponte was part of the circle of chosen ones whom Chávez summoned in the early morning to the Miraflores Palace. Many of them looked the other way when they realized the judge was falling out of favor; others even joined the chorus of accusations leveled against him. In this lawless kingdom of corrupt power-players, which Aponte served with his rulings while he was in the government's good graces, nobody could feel safe. Just as Arnaldo Ochoa had not been safe in Cuba, despite being the most decorated general on the island.

Aponte had immediately identified the caller and just as swiftly understood the warning: his life was in danger. Venezuelans had widely followed the events surrounding the purge of General Ochoa. Fidel Castro had him executed in 1989 although the military officer had been a key figure in the revolution against Batista, and was named "Hero of the Revolution." In the 1960s he had directed the incursions of guerrillas into Venezuelan territory, and he had personally led daring ambushes against the Venezuelan armed forces. In 1989, Ochoa was accused of conducting drug trafficking operations in cooperation with the Medellin cartel. The televised trial lasted for a month. Ochoa confessed to the charges, that also accused thirteen other officers of involvement, and requested that he receive the death penalty. Ochoa's execution in the same year as the fall of the Berlin Wall was a statement by Fidel showing that he still wielded all power in Cuba. It amounted as well to a bang of Castro's fist on the table akin to the one the Chinese authorities delivered to protesters in Tiananmen square at about the same time.

Though the caller would help him no further, the message was enough to move Aponte to work swiftly to protect his life. It was the morning of March 16, 2012. It was Friday and a session of the National Assembly had been scheduled for Tuesday, March 20. It had been officially convened by the Moral Power (a fifth power established by Chávez) to formally hear from Aponte regarding the charges leveled against him by a leading drug trafficker. It was obvious that, in the course of the session, Aponte would be stripped of his immunity, removed from his position as a judge, and turned over to the judiciary. And Aponte knew first-hand how Venezuelan tribunals followed the regime's orders. Lest there be any doubt about the regime's plan for how events should turn out, on the day prior to the National Assembly's session, its president, Diosdado Cabello, met with several opposition parliamentarians. "I am going to make Aponte available so you can do with him as you please," he told them, according to the judge. By that time, the man who had been the head of the Criminal Court of the Supreme Tribunal of Justice had already fled Venezuela.

After he had heard the warning over the telephone in his office, Aponte had taken a cab to his house to retrieve his passport. He contacted several friends, with whom he charted his escape route. At about 11 am, he left Caracas in a car with two of them; one did the driving while the other looked out for potential trouble. It took them about three hours to reach Tucacas, a coastal town in Falcón state where Aponte hired a fisherman to take him to Curaçao, a Dutch island located only forty miles from the Venezuelan coast. The boat ride lasted three hours on a small motorized boat. During the journey, Aponte worried that a Venezuelan coast guard vessel might appear from behind the waves breaking around the craft. At about 5 pm, the boat reached Curaçao and the passenger stepped ashore. He was arriving as a tourist, not as a fugitive. Despite the accusations that had been made against him in Venezuela, no formal charges had yet been brought in the courts. Hence, Aponte's plan called for him to stay abroad for a certain period of time—maybe two or three months would be enough—until matters settled down and he could return to Caracas.

Aponte hopped from one country in the Caribbean to the next; each time the maximum time period for a tourist stay was about to elapse, he crossed the border into another country. From Curaçao he flew to the Dominican Republic, and then on to Panama. There he ascertained that the Venezuelan authorities had finally managed to locate him, allegedly with the help of Cuban espionage. He thus decided to move again, this time to Costa Rica. Aponte believed that he could apply for political asylum in the Central American country. But his plans were ruined when the local press, quoting Venezuelan government sources, implicated him in drug trafficking crimes. "That is when I contacted the *gringos*. It was my only way out," Aponte recounts. In accordance with the news of his appearance in Costa Rica, which provided the first public information about his whereabouts since he had fled Venezuela, the government in Caracas rushed to file an application for extradition and for an activation of an Interpol red alert.

Aponte's escape then became a race against time. Since it was weekend, the bureaucracy in Washington was not working over and the State Department was not inclined to urgently process a visa for the fugitive. For this reason the Drug Enforcement Administration enlisted the help of veteran Republican Congressman Frank Wolf, whose northern Virginia electoral district encompasses Langley, the Central Intelligence Agency's headquarters. Wolf had previous experience assisting federal agencies in urging U.S. presidential administrations to move on similar decisions.

Meanwhile, that same weekend—April 14 and 15, 2012— the Sixth Summit of the Americas was taking place in Cartagena, Colombia. There was concern that Venezuela's Foreign Affairs minister, Nicolás Maduro (Hugo Chávez did not attend due to his illness), could persuade President Barack Obama not to grant asylum to Aponte. Hence, Costa Rican President Laura Chinchilla began to tell summit participants that the judge was already in the DEA's custody. This gave time to Congressman Wolf to work his contacts in the administration and obtain the asylum visa for Aponte. Wolf himself also managed that the Pentagon send an Air Force plane to the Costa Rican capital because the DEA aircrafts that cover the Caribbean, whose operational base is in Puerto Rico, were all deployed on other missions.

But Aponte's thrilling escape to the United States was not yet over. The plane landed at the San José airport about 7 pm on April 16. The Costa Rican police had held Aponte in their custody for the previous forty-eight hours. It was past midnight by the time they transferred the judge to the DEA agents and the flight to the United States was ready to take off. At that time, with no other scheduled flights, part of the airport's operation center had shut down. There was therefore no way to pay for the U.S. Air Force plane's refueling. Costa Rica's Interior minister had to show up at the airport, with the airport's director at his side, in order to receive the payment. On April 17, Aponte finally arrived in Washington, having managed to stay a step ahead of Venezuelan authorities: on April 18 the Venezuelan attorney general issued a warrant for his arrest. By the time the international red alert was activated, Aponte was already being grilled by the DEA in debriefing sessions on U.S. territory.

The National Guard Protects the Narco-State

U.S. authorities had been gathering information about the web that Chavismo had been spinning in the drug trafficking business for some time. The network was deeply embedded in the state apparatus, as it was underscored by the implication of high-ranking military officers and governors, the use of armed forces infrastructures, the complicity of the Supreme Tribunal of Justice, and the laundering of funds through bonds and invoices issued by Petróleos de Venezuela (PDVSA).

By that time, U.S. government agencies had already drafted a list, which was never published, of thirty Venezuelan officials considered of interest due their relation with drug trafficking. The most significant ones were the following (the positions they then held are in brackets): Diosdado Cabello (president of the National Assembly), Adán Chávez (the president's brother and governor of Barinas state), Rafael Ramírez (president of PDVSA), Tareck el Aissami (Interior minister), Henry Rangel Silva (Defense minister), Hugo Carvajal (head of military intelligence), Manuel Barroso (president of the Commission for the Administration of Currency Exchange or CADIVI), and Wilmer Flores (director general of the Body of Scientific, Penal, and Criminal Investigations). Other top-ranking military officers, such as Inspector General Haissam Dalal-Burgos and General Luis Felipe Costa Carlez, were also on the list.

A more complete picture would result from the testimonies of officials who later left Venezuela, such as Judge Aponte, Treasurer Alejandro Andrade, and Captain Leamsy Salazar, or cooperated with U.S. authorities while remaining in the country. Their collective account spoke of unquestionable involvement in the drug trade by the head of state, first Hugo Chávez and later Nicolás Maduro, leading to the conclusion that Venezuela was a narco-state.

To describe Venezuela as a narco-state does not imply that the governmental drug cartel held an ironclad monopoly over an activity that inherently spawned a growing number of criminal groups, nor that all Venezuelan institutions were involved in crime. But there is no question that government officials' participation in drug trafficking networks was part and parcel of their entrusted duty. They simultaneously held their official positions and engaged in this illicit activity with high-level protection.

The top priority of those involved in the Venezuelan drug trade was to establish their country as a transit point for the cocaine shipments, mainly produced in Colombia and supplied by the FARC. They also wanted to ensure that the shipments could be taken to the final markets by Mexican cartels. The harvesting of cocaine also began to take place in Venezuela itself, and some of the manufacturing of the drugs could be finished in its laboratories. Moreover, cocaine from Peru or Bolivia also reached Venezuela. In any case, the collusion of the state's institutions in this criminal undertaking was first and foremost focused on enabling the transportation of the shipments.

"They are using Venezuela as a big highway; to assure safe passage of the drugs, they need to secure the access to and control of roads, ports, and airports. It is the law enforcement authorities in Venezuela who are in charge of road safety and customs control," Carlos Tablante explains. Before the Chávez era, in President Caldera's second term, Tablante directed the National Commission Against the Illicit Use of Drugs. Hence it was the armed forces, and especially the National Guard, who were deployed on all of the country's roads as well as its borders, that were the most active institution in the drug trafficking business.

Drug trafficking ran parallel to smuggling of gasoline, extortion, kidnappings, bribes, and corruption. These manifold crimes were carried out by thousands of gangs—Tablante reckons there were eighteen thousand. The military commanders, governors, and other officials worked in tandem with criminal groups. Although this amalgam was largely anarchic, there was an organizing mind that ensured the maintenance of the channels used by certain *official* operators.

When Chávez committed the state's institutions to support the drug business, he decided to expel from Venezuela the region's preeminent agency engaged in combatting drug trafficking. In 2005, he revoked the resident permits of DEA agents stationed in Caracas who liaised with their Venezuelan counterparts. The agents were expelled after the DEA accused six officers of the National Guard of involvement in narco-trafficking and banned them from entering the United States. One of the six was General Frank Morgado, head of the National Guard's anti-narcotics unit. The British National Crime Agency (SOCA) had already denounced the "large magnitude of corruption in drug trafficking among the National Guard of Venezuela."

Without the DEA's monitoring, the orders instructing how to smuggle FARC shipments or how to set aside some of the business for Hezbollah could be executed more easily. The National Anti-Drug Office (ONA) could give the impression of activity, arresting traffickers who operated outside of the *friendly* networks, or interfering in internecine *vendettas* within law enforcement, meanwhile it paved the way for shipments that were given safe passage.

By opening the door to narcotics trafficking and fostering the routing of drugs through Venezuelan territory, Chávez inflicted great harm on his country. We can again attest how, in the pursuit of its own political and economic interests, the chavista high command buffeted the most distressed in Venezuela, as Tablante denounces. In his book *Estado delincuente*, co-written with Marcos Tarre, he high-lights that "he who rose to power in the name of the poor and social-ism, and who sought a parliamentary hegemony to support the poor, was actually the one who especially hurt them." The high and upper middle classes could afford to hire private security agents and install safety systems in their homes. They could also shoulder the econom-ic and social costs of drug dependency. It was the inhabitants of the poor neighborhoods who were most scarred by the personal and community scourge brought about by drugs.

From Makled to the Cartel of the Suns

At the outset of Chavismo, Walid Makled García stood out among drug traffickers. A Lebanese-Venezuelan businessman nicknamed *The Turk* (or *The Arab*), he enjoyed the protection of the authorities in his areas of operation. As Chávez progressively militarized institu-tions, appointing officials from the armed forces to key positions, military officers close to the president took over control of several states—as governors—via the ballot box. The governors and those in charge of the military garrisons gradually became a part of Makled's network. Between 2000 and 2006, Makled directed a network that retrieved the FARC's drugs from the Colombian plains through the border of the Venezuelan states of Apure and Táchira. These state's governors, captains Luis Aguilarte and Ronald Blanco, respectively, secured the operations. The shipments were then sent to the city of Valencia and were loaded at nearby harbor of Puerto Cabello. This happened in the state of Carabobo, whose governor, the retired Gen-eral Luis Felipe Acosta Carlez, also harbored the network. Makled was also sheltered by the president of the port, Admiral Carlos Ania-si, as the drug trafficker himself would reveal after his arrest in Co-lombia.

These relationships involved a never-ending exchange of favors. During the 2002 general strike, Makled made his fleet of transport vehicles available to the chavista government. As a reward, he was granted the concession of selling urea, a fertilizer employed to grow coca as a cash crop. This fact was well known to the state-owned company that supplied it, Petroquímica de Venezuela or PEQUIVEN. "In gratitude" for a donation of $2 million for the chavista electoral campaign, as the businessman described, he was awarded control of Puerto Cabello, Venezuela's biggest harbor. Counting wages and bribes, Makled shelled out $1 million a month to high-ranking officials. "My payments were how many in high government positions made a living," he claimed to the Colombian TV station RCN after his arrest. Makled claimed to have amassed a fortune of $1.2 billion.

As time went by, Makled's network, known as the Beirut cartel due to its drug lord's Lebanese origin, encountered the competition of military officers due to the armed forces' direct involvement. These officers were no longer satisfied with a share of the proceeds; they wanted to distribute the drugs themselves. The opportunity for the Venezuelan armed forces to step up their drug trafficking operations presented itself when the Colombian narco-guerrillas FARC and ELN achieved complete freedom of movement in Norte de Santander, a Colombian region neighboring Venezuela. The town of Puerto Santander has its own border crossing, which is connected to the Venezuelan township of Orope (Táchira sate), where an Army garrison is located.

Protected by the head of the military region, General Wilmer Moreno, the drug trafficking business began in this area with the use of the base as a staging point. The military's direct involvement led to the appearance of the cartel of the Suns, which was named after the insignias on the uniforms of Venezuelan generals. Makled regarded these developments as an interference and presumably was the one who tipped off the National Guard about the 2.2 ton stash of cocaine which Lieutenant Colonel Maggino had retrieved in Orope in November 2005, as described earlier.

He who lives by the sword, dies by the sword, especially in this criminal underworld of clans and mafias. When in 2007 General Clíver Alcalá was transferred to the state of Carabobo he sought to wrest control of Puerto Cabello from Makled. Puerto Cabello was a strategic location for the loading of narcotics. The showdown between the military and Makled ended with *The Turk* on the losing end. In November 2008, officials from the Directorate of Military Intelligence (DIM) *discovered* in Makled's ranch eighteen boxes with the Red Cross emblem that contained almost nine hundred pounds of cocaine. His brothers were arrested, but Walid managed to flee. In August 2010, he was arrested in Colombia and extradited. Makled averred that the stash uncovered in his estate had been planted by DIM agents in order to frame him and accused officials left and right.

The United States had closely monitored the Makled case. Among the evidence against him was the April 2006 Mexican detainment of a DC-9 jet without passengers loaded with 5.5 tons of cocaine. The plane departed Maiquetía, Caracas international airport Simón Bolívar, bound for the Mexican city of Guadalajara, but was forced to perform an emergency landing in the Yucatán Peninsula of Mexico due to a hydraulic malfunction. One of the pilots was able to flee after the emergency landing at Ciudad del Carmen, but the other one was apprehended. The cargo was made up of 128 identical black suitcases filled with cocaine.

The investigative press found out that the DC-9 was owned by a phantom Florida company, Titan Group, which in turn was the property of L-3 Communications. The latter provided transportation services to the DEA and had signed other contracts with the U.S. government. These facts prompted some blogs to accuse L-3 of corruption and murky dealings with someone of Makled's reputation and to brand the DEA's officers as inept, as it appeared that they had been played right under their noses. This, in fact, was far from the hidden truth.

Sources familiar with the operation insisted that the DC-9 was provided by the CIA to lay a trap for Makled. In fact, L-3 had supplied several airplanes to the CIA for its controversial rendition program—the transportation of alleged Islamic terrorists for their interrogation. The airplane that landed in the Yucatán Peninsula had already been employed previously for a secret drug operation. U.S.

intelligence learned that *The Turk* was looking for a large airplane. Through intermediaries that would not raise any suspicions, he was made aware of the fact that a DC-9 was available for lease in Florida. When the deal was reached, the drug cartel declined the offer to also hire pilots, as it preferred to employ its own crew. The CIA and the DEA had bugged the airplane with hidden microphones and signal-emitting devices that allowed the U.S. agencies to monitor what the narco-traffickers were up to. It was not determined whether the plane was delivered with programmed mechanical malfunctions that would disrupt its flight.

Despite the charges that were formally brought against Makled, U.S. authorities kept their indictment secret until the drug lord was arrested in Colombia, near the Venezuelan border, in a joint opera-tion between Colombia and the DEA. In its November 2010 indict-ment of Makled, the U.S. Attorney's Office for the Southern District of New York accused him of having "controlled and operated run-ways located in Venezuela." He used the "runways to enable the multiple shipments of tons of cocaine from Venezuela to Central America and Mexico by numerous drug trafficking groups, knowing that a part of the drug load was bound for the United States." He was described as the "king among kingpins," and "among the biggest global narcotics traffickers." The indictment went on to assert that, were he to be tried and sentenced in the United States, he could face up to sixty years in jail.

The U.S. federal attorney's office indictment rattled Venezuela because Makled could disclose damaging information if the Colom-bians handed him over to Washington. "I paid off fifteen Venezuelan generals," the trafficker himself stated. "If I am arrested over a DC-9 loaded with drugs that took off from Simón Bolívar airport in Cara-cas, General Hugo Carvajal, director of Venezuela's military intelli-gence; General Henry Rangel Silva, head of internal intelligence; General Luis Motta Domínguez, commander of the National Guard; and General Néstor Reverol, head of the Anti-Drug Office, should go to jail for the same reason." According to reports compiled by the private intelligence agency Stratfor unveiled by Wikileaks, Venezuelan military officers exerted a lot of pressure on President Chávez so he would act quickly to avoid Makled's extradition to the United States.

The Obama administration's handling of the Makled case raised eyebrows. The DEA had gathered a significant amount of evidence against Makled and the U.S. Embassy in Bogota informed the Ministry of Foreign Affairs of Colombia that it would request his extradition if he were found and arrested. When matters came to a head, the U.S. State Department took its time in requesting the extradition. Republican Senator Marco Rubio of Florida called Obama's chief of staff to urge the U.S. president to back the extradition request, but everything unfolded very slowly, allowing Venezuela to strike an agreement with its neighboring country. Chávez secured the extradition by promising Colombian President Juan Manuel Santos that he would settle the debt of $800 million Venezuela owned to Colombian exporters, a debt the Colombians had been demanding be paid to no avail, which had led them to stage a commercial strike. Makled arrived in Caracas in May 2011. But in order to let matters cool, the trial did not begin until a year later, and when it did it barely got off the ground.

Narco-General Promoted to Defense Minister

Makled's arrest upset the tenuous balance of power within the chavista underworld. The drug lord turned out to have a judicial license which had allegedly been provided by Judge Eladio Aponte. Despite the judge's denial, Makled insisted that Aponte was on his payroll. This was the justification the government used to oust Aponte from the Supreme Tribunal of Justice. The government was trying to sever as many of its ties to drug trafficking—which the public was learning about—as it could.

Several criminal groups also began to settle scores. On the day that Aponte arrived in the United States to be debriefed by the DEA, General Wilmer Moreno, who had been the head of the military region that included the state of Táchira, was killed in a hail of gunfire.

Two weeks earlier Jesús Aguilarte, a retired captain and former governor of the state of Apure, died of gunshot wounds he sustained in an attack. Táchira and Apure states border Colombia and are the usual gateway for drugs into Venezuela, and both victims—General Moreno and Captain Aguilarte—had been involved in the drug trafficking business.

To fall from grace due to a change of tide in narco-trafficking was not a new development within Chavismo. General Raúl Isaías Baduel was serving a jail sentence, in part for his denunciation of the increasing involvement of high-ranking military officers in the drug trade. Baduel had been a member of Chávez's inner circle. Indeed, Baduel freed the president from his arrest at La Orchila when Chávez was transferred to the island after his brief overthrow in 2002. Baduel was named Defense minister in June 2006. In January 2007, he wrote a letter to the president accusing Brigadier General Henry Rangel of narco-trafficking, specifically in the aforementioned Maggino case. Rangel headed the Venezuelan intelligence and counterintelligence services.

After addressing the letter to "citizen" Chávez, a requirement of the Bolivarian revolution, the letter quickly got to the point. "There is sufficient evidence that links Brigadier General (Army) Henry de Jesús Rangel Silva," Baduel wrote with the customary Venezuelan practice of using all of a person's names and last names, "with the investigation and trial launched by the Attorney General's Office" of those indicted for the drug stash stored overnight in the barracks of the border town of La Fría. Baduel added that the driver of the vehicle that transported the cocaine shipment was a cousin of the general, "with whom he was in telephone contact." Baduel did not furnish additional details, but it was obvious that he knew them given the risky step he was taking. "I very respectfully suggest that a thorough investigation and audit be opened into the assets of citizen Brigadier General (Army) Henry de Jesús Rangel Silva, and that he be placed on leave until his implication in the aforementioned events can be ruled out. This communication I submit to you for your knowledge and other considerations."

The evidence against Rangel must have been conclusive and overwhelming, since calling for the firing of the head of intelligence was not within the minister of Defense's remit. Therefore Chávez's ensuing decisions were not only a cover up, but also a personal authorization of all of the actions that were taken. Baduel left the Ministry of Defense a few months later. He was arrested in 2009 and sentenced in 2010 to eight years in jail for misuse of funds during his short ministerial stint. Chávez and Baduel's growing estrangement had removed the latter from the Miraflores Palace inner circle and turned him into a spokesman of political criticism.

Henry Rangel was appointed Defense minister in 2012. At the time, his collusion in drug trafficking was no longer a secret; neither was his key role in the criminal conspiracy that the Venezuelan state engaged in with the Colombian guerrillas.

The FARC on the General's Harley

Pictures of the FARC guerrillas' leader Iván Márquez riding a Harley Davidson quickly circulated in the Internet after they were published in the influential Colombian magazine *Semana*. Iván Márquez was an elusive figure who had been rarely photographed. In addition to being a journalistic scoop, the report generated a lot of interest because it showed up a contrast between two opposing symbols: an *anti-imperialist*, who had called for an uprising by the poor, riding a U.S. icon. With a price tag of $15,000, the Harley was a luxury that most of his fellow Colombians could not afford. A former guerrilla commander, Alexander García, nicknamed *Caracho*, contended to Colombian media that the pictures had "caused discomfort and been badly received among the guerrillas' rank-and-file because they displayed the respective differences and privileges."

Semana published the pictures in February 2013, but the pictures themselves had apparently been taken in 2007. The Harley Davidson's chromed body reflected the façade of the building in front of which Márquez and his colleagues had posed for pictures that had already made the rounds after they were found in computers seized from the guerrillas. These pictures, where the Colombian Senator Piedad Córdoba appeared with a bouquet of flowers next to the FARC commanders Iván Márquez, Jesús Santrich, and Rodrigo Granda, had been taken in Venezuela during negotiations formally convened to deal with the liberation of persons held by the guerrillas. Although the talks were supposedly called because of humanitarian reasons, the flowers and body language underscored the FARC's proximity to Chavismo, especially when the Colombian government of Alvaro Uribe had gathered plenty of evidence regarding the logistical support Chávez was providing to his neighbor's rebels.

The entire collection of pictures was taken at Fuerte Tiuna, a military compound in Caracas. This had already been assumed, because in the emails found in the computers belonging to Raúl Reyes and Mono Jojoy, in 2008 and 2010, respectively, there were messages in which Márquez gave an account of his meetings in Caracas. "We gathered in our bunker at Fuerte Tiuna with Gabino and Antonio in a relaxed and fraternal atmosphere," Márquez wrote, referring to the ELN's two leaders. Now sources who are familiar with Fuerte Tiuna confirm the location and point out that the Harley Davidson which Márquez mounted probably belonged to General Clíver Alcalá, head of the Armored Division.

The Venezuelan government's ties to the leadership of the FARC and ELN were very close. This exhibition of comradeship probably took place in November 2007, months after the secret contacts between Chávez and the narco-terrorists that were described at the beginning of this book. At the meetings at Fuerte Tiuna and Miraflores Palace, where the Bolivarian leader publicly welcomed Márquez, the Colombian insurgents held talks with the heads of intelligence, generals Rangel Silva and Hugo Carvajal (of the national intelligence agency and military intelligence, respectively), and with generals Wilmer Moreno and Clíver Alcalá, who were commanders in the drug trafficking regions. They also conferred with Ramón Rodríguez Chacín, a retired navy captain, who became Chávez's main emissary with the Colombian guerrillas; two months later he was appointed minister of Interior and Justice.

"Ties with the Army are at a level close to what the Strategic Plan calls for. We are befriended and have empathy with five generals. Moreover, Chávez ordered in my presence that locations for rest and medical attention for the guerrillas along the border be set up, and he assigned a kind of Joint Chiefs for these ties," Márquez reported at the time to the rest of the narco-guerrilla leadership. Another important achievement of the FARC's strategic plan was international recognition of its status as a *belligerent* (not terrorist, as it was classified in many countries), which Chávez promoted at the Venezuelan National Assembly in January 2008. The plan also called for a larger amount of drugs to be dispatched through Venezuela. In order to fulfill this objective, an increased involvement by the Army was agreed upon.

The groundwork for the direct and intense cooperation between the FARC and Chavismo had been paved in the previous years by General Rangel Silva. As head of the Venezuelan national intelligence service, the general had toured the FARC terrorist camps, also on Colombian soil, obviously unbeknownst to Bogota. "We arranged for Rangel to come over. To come here and to see Iván," wrote Timoshenco, the nickname of the man who soon would become the commander-in-chief of the organization, in one of the emails that was later found. "After Timo's visit, we welcomed general Rangel Silva... He proclaimed that his visit was appropriately authorized by Chávez," Iván Márquez wrote up in another email. These messages were written in 2006. At the meeting in Caracas in 2007, Márquez again referred to Silva: "On our way over here we spoke to general Rangel Silva..., a great friend of Timo's, whom he wants to visit after December 2. He took part in the lunch attended by Chávez, the elenos [the leadership of the ELN], and the FARC. He is in charge of security for the elenos."

A year later, the United States took action against Rangel Silva and two of his colleagues. They were placed in the Treasury Department's Foreign Assets Control (OFAC) list, thereby freezing any assets they might have on U.S. soil and banning any financial transactions with them. In its decision of 2008, the U.S. Treasury established that it had been proven that Rangel had "materially assisted" the FARC's narco-trafficking activities and had "fostered a greater cooperation between the Colombian terrorists and the government of Venezuela."

The U.S. Treasury also charged General Hugo Carvajal of "assisting" the guerrillas, which included "sheltering the shipments of drugs from the anti-narcotics Venezuelan institutions and supplying weapons to the FARC, allowing them to hold on to a prized haven in the department of Arauca." After underscoring that coca was grown and cocaine was produced in the Colombian region of Arauca, the accusation also implicated *The Chicken* Carvajal in the "provision to the FARC of government identification documents which enable FARC members to travel to and from Venezuela with ease." Finally, Rodríguez Chacín was held accountable as the main "weapons liaison officer" between Chávez's government and the Colombian guerrillas, who use the proceeds from the sale of drugs to purchase weapons from the Venezuelan government." In this regard, it was underlined that at a meeting in Caracas in 2007, Rodríguez Chacín had been designated as the manager of a loan of $300 million to the FARC.

Venezuela officially justified its public meetings with the Colombian guerrillas, among them a reception of some of their chieftains at the Miraflores Palace, as an attempt to mediate in the negotiations to secure the release of prisoners held by the FARC. These kind of meetings between the government of a country and an armed group from another are not unusual. During Carlos Andrés Pérez's second term, such discussions were held, and France itself was interested in Chávez's involvement to secure the freedom of Ingrid Betancourt, the Franco-Colombian leader who would be rescued by the Colombian Army in July 2008. Chávez also sought to get Spain involved in the process. However, an international mediation never takes place with secret agreements behind the back of the democratic country targeted by the armed groups. And international mediation efforts most certainly do not occur while secret economic, logistical, and weapons support is being funneled to the guerrillas who combat the constitutional order of a neighboring country which has been legitimately formed as an expression of the population's will.

Transfer of Business Due to Decease

The military officers in charge of these activities were proven and staunch Chávez loyalists. He knew many of them from the time they spent together at the Military Academy. Several had also taken part in the failed coup of February 4, 1992. There was a brotherhood among them that lasted during Chávez's entire presidency. To fore-stall a possible postponement after his foreseeable death, Chávez ensured that several of them ran for the office of governor in the 2012 regional elections, which actually took place in December of that year while the president was on his deathbed in Cuba. This was the case with the former ministers of Defense Henry Rangel Silva, Carlos Mata Figueroa, and Ramón Carrizález, and former Interior and Justice Minister Ramón Rodríguez Chacín, who were elected governors of the states of Trujillo, Nueva Esparta, Apure, and Co-jedes, respectively.

These four veteran leaders were instrumental to the cartel of the Suns, which also prominently featured Adán Chávez, the revolution-ary leader's brother and governor of Barinas state, as well as Tareck el Aissami, governor of Aragua. El Aissami also conducted the coor-dination with Hezbollah, which was also involved in the drug traf-ficking. In the cartel, Hugo *The Chicken* Carvajal was assigned the duties similar to a chief operation officer (COO) in a company, while José David Cabello, the superintendent of the National Integrated Service for the Administration of Customs Duties and Taxes (SE-NIAT), served in a role akin to that of a chief finance officer (CFO) as head of finances and logistics; his brother Diosdado was at the helm of the enterprise, with the powers granted to a chief executive officer (CEO).

This is the kind of structure which Leamsy Salazar described in January 2015 when the former personal assistant to Diosdado Cabel-lo arrived in Washington, to testify against his former boss. Salazar's

216

arrival and his main accusations were known through a piece I wrote then in my newspaper. Cabello later sued some of the Venezuelan media that reproduced my article—*El Nacional, TalCual*, and *La Patilla*—and harassed their owners. In May 2015, *The Wall Street Journal* published its own investigation, titled "Drug Probe Eyes Venezuela Elite." It quoted a source in the U.S. Justice Department saying that "there is extensive evidence to justify that Cabello is one of the heads, if not the head, of the cartel."

Within the conspiracy, PDVSA was instrumental for the laundering of money for the illicit business. But there were other means to launder the drug revenue. As Industry minister, a position he held along with that of chief of the SENIAT, José David Cabello held sway over MINERVEN, the public gold mining company. Precisely one of the bunkers filled with cash that Salazar connected to the president of the National Assembly was located in Bolívar, the state with the longest tradition of gold mining and where MINERVEN's headquarters were located. Control of the mines was conducted by organized criminal groups that sometimes clashed violently. In March 2016, almost twenty miners went missing. Their mangled bodies were later recovered after being viciously killed in a settlement of scores between mafia groups. The illegally-mined gold was usually shipped to the Dutch islands of Aruba and Curaçao for sale as jewelry to tourists.

The Cabello brothers' cooperation in narco-trafficking had taken on many forms. In another case, while José David was president of the Maiquetía airport, they would order that a Boeing 727 be stripped of its seats and filled with drugs in order to fly it to Mexico on a weekly basis, as another witness cooperating with U.S. authorities had recounted.

During his time in office, Chávez held the reins of this effort, most likely acting as a non-executive chairman, although he intervened often to chart the course. "All accuse Chávez of the great narcotics trafficking that went on in Venezuela. They confirm over and over that he was the boss, that he oversaw the operation at each step of the way, although Chávez's control was more conceptual than operative. He left the details regarding the execution of operations to others," explains someone who has stayed in touch with members of the criminal undertaking with a view to cooperating with the United States. What about Maduro? Did he inherit the position as president of the board of the narco-state? "All of those involved accepted Chavez's authority. This was the way to maintain control over a business which is inherently anarchical and prone to betrayals. Maduro is also aware of the situation and at times has sought to intervene in day-to-day operations, but this unleashed tensions, and Cabello got more autonomy," the source asserts.

With his father's authorization, in any case, Nicolasito Maduro would have sought to profit from drug trafficking, as Salazar's testimony unveiled. Apparently the president's son worked closely with his stepbrother Walter Jacob Gaviria Flores, a lower court judge in criminal matters and the son of the *first combatant*, Cilia Flores.

Narco-Nephews

They were not the only members of the president's family involved in drug trafficking. Two other young men, who were cousins as well, were apprehended in November 2015 after arriving in Haiti on a small plane that carried a shipment of almost eighteen hundred pounds of cocaine bound for the United States. Efraín Campos Flores and Francisco Flores de Freites were escorted during the flight to Haiti by two members of the presidential guard, and two active-duty officers—one a lieutenant colonel—piloted the plane. The plane took off from Maiquetía, Caracas international airport, specifically from the terminal reserved for the Venezuelan president and his ministers. The arrest was possible because an undercover DEA agent had been monitoring the operation for some time. The agent suggested flying the drugs into Port-au-Prince with the intent of bringing the two cousins into a country where they could be arrested and turned over to U.S. authorities. Haiti has an extradition agreement with the United States that allows the immediate handover to the U.S. of a detained individual.

The DEA did not notify the State Department about the identity of the men until they were in handcuffs on board a plane headed for New York, according to the confidential source quoted above. This lack of communication can be explained as a means to prevent a hypothetical political decision from the White House that might thwart the process in light of the personal blow it would deal to the Venezuelan president. The two young men were nephews of Maduro's wife. One of them, Efraín Campos Flores, was raised since childhood in the Maduro family home, and the Venezuelan president had adopted him as a stepson. At their trial in New York on charges of conspiring to import cocaine into the United States, the two initially pled not guilty. But they later decided to cooperate with U.S. officials by furnishing information in order to avoid a possible sentence of life in jail. One of the persons they would have accused was another of Cilia Flores' nephews, Carlos Erick Malpica Flores. As PDVSA's finance director and Venezuela's national treasurer, he could arrange for the laundering of the money from the drug trafficking operations undertaken by his cousins. In light of these allegations, Malpica Flores stepped down from both of his posts.

This youthful cooperation followed in the trail of the one between Chávez's son, Huguito, and that of the Cuban Ambassador Germán Sánchez Otero, who was in charge of the Cuban Embassy in Caracas for fifteen years and was very close to the Bolivarian leader. The cocaine shipments, with the knowledge of Sánchez Otero and other Cuban officials, were generally carried out with small PDVSA airplanes that flew from Venezuela to Cuba and whose cargo was then sent to the Unite States by a network on the island, according to Leamsy Salazar. In 2009, when the extent of these operations became public, the ambassador's son was arrested while flying alone, while his partner was forced to undergo rehabilitation. Cuba dismissed Sánchez Otero as his continuity was embarrassing.

It is difficult to gauge the degree of complicity of the Castros with the chavista narco-state. Given the dictatorial nature of the regime and taking into account its substantial control over Venezuela, Cuba, at a minimum, protected the Venezuelan drug business. But there are examples that indicate Cuban collaboration and profiting. "The administration of the governorship of Apure, the state with the most permeable border with the FARC, is controlled by the Cubans. The Cuban intelligence service finances itself with drug trafficking operations," a person familiar with the situation assures.

All in all, alliances were shifting as Chavismo transitioned to survival mode. Maduro moved General Hugo Carvajal around from one position to another. Ironically, he named him president of the National Office Against Organized Crime, and later appointed him to his old position as head of the Directorate of Military Intelligence. In January 2014, he named him consul of Venezuela to the small Caribbean island of Aruba, a Dutch territory located off the Venezuelan coast, where Carvajal could continue his involvement in drug trafficking.

The DEA seized on this last appointment as an opportunity to cage *The Chicken*. The agency wanted to take advantage of the time period which elapses between an appointment for a diplomatic position abroad and the official acceptance by the country of destination. Until the host country formally accepts the appointee there is no diplomatic immunity. Thanks to a tip-off at the Aruba airport, the DEA controlled the military officer's movements and found out about his arrival at the beginning of July 2014. Washington liaised with Dutch authorities, which were initially willing to proceed to arrest and extradite Carvajal, but the narco-general slipped out of Aruba in a yacht before he could be detained. On July 23, Carvajal again landed in Aruba after flying in on a jet owned by Roberto Rincón, who was later charged by a judge in Texas with bribery in his business with PDVSA. On this occasion Carvajal was arrested.

The United States formally charged Carvajal with having "coordinated" the delivery in 2006 of 5.6 tons of cocaine from Venezuela to Mexico, a shipment that later crossed into the United States, according to the charges contained in respective indictments by two federal prosecutor offices—the Southern District of New York and the Southern District of Florida—which had been filed some time back but had remained sealed. Carvajal was also accused of having maintained close ties for several years with drug traffickers and "of harboring them so they could evade arrest, furnishing them with information about the activities of military and police personnel, and investing in stashes of cocaine exported from Venezuela." The U.S. federal prosecutors' charges also admonished that "other officers of high rank, both civilian and military" had taken part in the cover up of the narcotics trade.

It appeared that a trial would be held in the United States, with Carvajal as the main defendant and the expectation that he would implicate the rest of the chavista hierarchy. But the enormous pressure brought to bear by Caracas on the authorities of Aruba and the Netherlands yielded significant results. Although the island's judge and prosecutor took it as certain that the extradition to the United States would go ahead, the Netherlands backtracked and, contradicting its usual practice, asserted that Carvajal did enjoy diplomatic immunity. An airplane swiftly dispatched by Maduro picked up the general, who was given a hero's welcome upon his return to Caracas. What caused the Netherlands' about-face? Did it fear collateral damage in the oil industry? Was it intimidated by the Venezuelan military maneuvers close to Aruba?

Someone who took part in the operation to nab *The Chicken* is more inclined to think that the government of the Netherlands lost interest in doing the United States a favor. The Dutch government was disappointed by president Obama's aloof reaction to the shooting down of a civilian airliner by rebels in eastern Ukraine. Obama's initial focus on the only U.S. victim—there were 298 fatalities, 193 of them from the Netherlands—and Washington's inefficient pressure on Russia so it would grant access to the plane's wreckage site might have dissuaded the Netherlands from standing up to Caracas on the United States' behalf in the Carvajal case.

In addition to *The Chicken*, other generals involved in drug trafficking have been formally charged by U.S. authorities. News leaked at the beginning of 2016 that federal prosecutors from the Eastern District of New York had brought charges against several of them in an indictment that was sealed in order not to tip them off and enable their arrest should they leave Venezuela. According to sources familiar with the investigation, the most high-ranking official among those charged was General Néstor Reverol, a former director of the National Drug Office, who now was the commander of the National Guard, the branch of Venezuela's military that oversees its borders. The charges were as well against ten other high-ranking Venezuelan military officers, mainly from the National Guard.

The DEA's Maps

Venezuela's enhanced role in narco-trafficking—it shipped almost three hundred tons of drugs in 2014, an average of five a week—are depicted no better than on the DEA's maps. The agency draws up maps with the location of drug operations and shipments based on monitoring of drug traffickers' flight routes by the U.S. Southern Command's long-range radars. The maps designed by U.S. authorities highlight in red the itinerary of each of the illegal flights—the main transport mode in the Caribbean—displaying the most common points of origin and destination for the shipments, as well as the routes.

Until 2000, most of these flights originated in Colombia. On the 2005 map, one can discern the effects of the pressure from the joint U.S.-Colombia anti-trafficking plan (Plan Colombia) which forced the FARC to reroute some of their shipments through Venezuela. The change in trend is most obvious in the 2012 map, which showed a single red stain: almost all of the suspected flights left the region of Apure, one of the Venezuelan states which border Colombia, flew north into the Caribbean, and took a ninety degree turn west to avoid the radar installed in Colombia and land in Honduras. The U.S. State Department estimated that almost 80 percent of the flights laden with drugs from South America arrived in Honduras, where they were later sent to Mexico by sea or land before making it into the United States.

Most of the shipments were transported aboard small Cessna airplanes, which made up to ten daily flights with between seven hundred and nine hundred pounds of cocaine. Some of the drugs were flown on King 300 planes, which are somewhat bigger, and whose load could reach fifteen hundred or eighteen hundred pounds. Usually half of the interior of the airplane was stacked with drugs, and the other half was arranged to fit a fuel tank: the weight carried was determined by the distance that would be flown. The six hours of flying time between Venezuela and Honduras could be eased with a layover in Punto Fijo (Falcón state) before departing Venezuelan territory.

The narco-planes were operated by a pilot and copilot, who could earn as much as $50,000 per mission given the risk of flying planes used continuously, with minimal maintenance, and which suffered occasional accidents due to mechanical malfunctions. In case the plane was seriously damaged because it was forced to land on inadequate terrain, it was set on fire after removing the freight to avoid leaving behind any traces. The profits easily covered the purchase of a new plane: the drugs could fetch up to $10,000 per kilogram of cocaine in the market. Each flight could thus generate between $3 and $4 million in revenue.

In a continually evolving situation—there is a reference to the balloon effect, whereby applying pressure at one point displaces the traffic to another one—the air route to Honduras had lost its almost absolute preeminence in 2014, due to the pressure also exerted on the Central American country. But with a long coast along the Caribbean, Venezuela maintained its status as a leading distributor of drugs. The flights to Central America were cut by a third and the shipments that arrived in the United States through the Caribbean islands, especially the Dominican Republic, increased to 16 percent. The maritime routes had stopovers in Aruba and also used the Bahamas as a staging area; from the archipelago many loads were dumped in the sea equipped with GPS, so that they could be retrieved by fishing or recreational boats operating out of U.S. ports.

With regard to the Colombian cocaine sent to Europe, the majority is dispatched in fishing boats that sail from the Venezuelan ports of Puerto Cabello and Maracaibo. The drugs grown in Peru and Bolivia also reach Europe. By 2012 both countries, with a production of almost three hundred tons each, had surpassed Colombia's supply. In 2014 cocaine production had risen again in Colombia, which had become the second largest producer, following only Peru, according to data from the White House Office of National Drug Control Policy. The shipments that originated in Peru and Bolivia were distributed mainly through southern South America.

The cocaine's main point of entry into Europe is Spain, on whose Atlantic coast the shipments landed directly in the 1980s. Greater surveillance forced the cartels to look to western Africa as a beachhead, so that, before reaching Spain or other European destinations, the shipments first arrive in Mauritania, Senegal, Guinea Bissau, Sierra Leone, or Ivory Coast.

Because of greater maritime monitoring, the amount of drugs dispatched by air has increased. They are sent on flights that depart Venezuelan cities such as Barcelona or Valencia. A Bombardier jet with 1.2 tons of cocaine took off from Valencia in August of 2012 and landed on the island of Gran Canaria—nine national guards involved in the flight were arrested in Venezuela. Red flags were raised in November of 2009 when the remains of a Boeing 727 were located in the desert in Mali. The use of a big airplane meant that operations were being scaled up; it had been set ablaze after transporting a shipment of cocaine, probably of several tons.

Another episode that caused an uproar was the smuggling in September 2013 of 1.3 tons of cocaine in an Air France jetliner that covered the Caracas-Paris route. The drugs were stashed in thirty suitcases. How was it possible to evade controls at Maiquetía and detection in Paris? At the point of origin the implication of high-ranking airport security officials was certain, and the ease with which the drugs were transported suggests that the French authorities purposely arranged for a controlled delivery. Given the international outcry, Venezuelan authorities had to conduct several arrests, which included those of Colonel Ernesto Mora, head of security at Maiquetía, as well as of other National Guard military officers from his outfit.

Maduro's reaction revealed the reluctant nature of the arrests. Instead of welcoming the detection of the vulnerability at Caracas' international airport in order to address it, he lashed out against foreign agents. "The DEA's hand had better not be involved in this. We are investigating," he stated, attributing to the United States the intent of fabricating evidence to accuse Venezuela of being a narco-state. The truth is that Washington already had plenty of evidence to prove that and to link Maduro to other dubious activities.

7

NICOLAS IN HEZBOLLAH'S LAIR
Ties to Islamic Extremism

G et on a plane, we are going to Iran." Hugo Chavez's voice on the phone sounded as when he gave out orders during the failed coup of February 4, 1992. Rafael Isea, who was only twenty-three years old at the time, had that day etched into his memory as it linked his fate to that of Chávez, and included him in the future president's inner circle. Isea had the recollection of everything that happened thereafter when he flew from the Dominican Republic to Washington, in September 2013. It was a one-way trip undertaken in order to cooperate with ongoing investigations in the United States. But in 2007, when Chávez summoned Isea to include him in his entourage for the official visit to Iran—that order of getting on the plane—there was no time for recollections, as he had to immediately prepare for the intense work of the following days. As deputy minister of Finance and president of the Economic and Social Development Bank (BANDES), he had to update data that he would share during the stay in Tehran. But he was not ready for a surprise that awaited him.

Isea was going to join the official delegation directly in the Iranian capital. He was given a plane ticket with a stopover in Damascus.

This was the route covered on alternate weeks by the Venezuelan flagship airline Conviasa and Iran Air. The flight, inaugurated in March 2007, was not launched because of a real demand for it, but rather because it facilitated the swift transport of people and cargo between Chávez's Venezuela and Iran's Ahmadinejad without having to rely on third countries. The presidents of Venezuela and Iran struck an agreement to operate the flight at their meeting in Caracas in January 2007. This encounter paved the way for the mysterious trip to Iran we are describing as well as the deal between Argentina and Iran which we will recount later.

At first the Caracas-Tehran flight included a layover in Madrid. As Spanish authorities insisted on inspecting the cargo in accordance with European Union regulations, the Venezuelan and Iranian carriers switched to longer-range aircraft to avoid the refueling stopovers. The direct link with the Middle East put the Caribbean more easily within Hezbollah's reach and enabled the flow of cocaine and weapons. As is known, Hezbollah is a Shia Lebanese militia financed by Iran, supported and trained by the Iranian Revolutionary Guards, and endorsed as well by Syria. As the relationship between Venezuela and Iran intensified, and both countries developed other ways of frequent contact, the regular flight was no so needed and was suspended in 2010. By then its real mission had become obvious to everyone— the flight was known as *Airterror*—and both Conviasa and Iran Air could be subjected to international sanctions.

One of the military officers who would later seek refuge in the United States also revealed secrets about the trips to Iran. In a testimony that I obtain he described how, on a flight from Damascus to Caracas operated by Iran Air, his wife took too many pictures. She was enthralled by the Iran Air stewardesses and the veils they wore. After a few seconds and before the cabin crew had closed the plane's doors, a security guard took the camera and made sure that all of the pictures were deleted. This was not the trip's only mishap. Ten minutes after taking off, the captain announced that he was returning to Damascus because of a mechanical problem. After the plane landed, the Venezuelan military officer noticed that members of the ground crew were attaching boxes to the plane that had broken loose. He quickly determined that the boxes were filled with weapons, probably grenades, as he could read the codes on the boxes' cover. The merchandise that the plane was transporting did not alarm any technician on the runway. This was, after all, a military base's airfield and not the civilian airport in Damascus. But the Venezuelan military officer's wife was unable to sleep during the flight to Caracas. She was haunted by the thought that the military cargo could blow up at any time as they flew over the Atlantic back to Caracas.

Rafael Isea was also in for a shock in Damascus. When his plane landed at the military base to refuel, a Syrian security official boarded the plane and asked Isea to follow him. "You have to get off the plane right now and attend a meeting; an official from your country is waiting for you," he told him. He sought to get more information in vain. He was driven in an official Syrian government car to a hotel where security measures were extraordinary. After taking the elevator and making his way to the room he had been instructed to stay, the deputy minister received a phone call. It was Nicolás Maduro, who at the time served as Foreign Affairs minister, who asked him to proceed to a specific room. "What is Nicolás doing here? How strange!" Isea told himself. When he knocked on the door and then entered the room to which he was summoned, he was struck to see Maduro alongside Hassan Nasrallah, Hezbollah's secretary general and one of the United States' most wanted men. A translator was also present. The day after that unexpected meeting, Maduro and Isea flew on a private PDVSA plane to Tehran, where they joined Chávez.

What was discussed in the hotel room has never been revealed. But sources point to an agreement to give Hezbollah a role in Venezuela, particularly in narco-trafficking. Venezuelan officials also promised to ship weapons to Hezbollah in Lebanon, as well as to issue passports so Hezbollah militants could have a greater freedom of movement. Isea offered details of the dealings to U.S. authorities. If they were interested in him as witness, it was precisely for this kind of hot information.

The links between the chavista government and Hezbollah had been denounced on many occasions. However, the lack of terrorist attacks planned or executed by Hezbollah cells located in Venezuela, or in the rest of Latin America, detracted attention from the links between Hezbollah and the Venezuelan state's security structure. One would have to go back to the 1992 and 1994 massacres in Buenos Aires to find instances of effective Islamic terrorist attacks south of the Rio Grande. But the absence of terrorist attacks did not negate the risk that they might take place. In fact, Iranian agents had been behind several actions that were thwarted in the United States and Mexico. The ascent of Hezbollah's networks through Central America from its base in Venezuela prompted Washington to pay closer attention to the threat. When the security of the United States' own borders is at stake, its agencies rush to cooperate in order to respond to the threat.

I was able to examine documents that confirm that on August 22, 2010, a small summit of Islamic extremist leaders took place. Communications between embassies and plane tickets from the Middle East-Caracas route operated by Conviasa provided evidence regarding the summit. Leaders of Hezbollah, Hamas, and other agents of jihad met at the headquarters of Venezuelan military intelligence. The ambassadors of Venezuela and Iran to Damascus, Imán Saab Saab and Ahmad Mousavi, respectively, were involved in the summit. As a matter of fact, the chavista second-highest diplomat in Syria, a Lebanese naturalized Venezuelan named Ghazi Nassereddine (also written Nasr al-Dine), was Hezbollah's point man in Venezuela. Nassereddine was very close to Tareck el Aissami, who served as Venezuela's Interior minister between 2008 and 2012.

Prosecutors in the United States singled out Nassereddine and El Aissami as Chávez's main emissaries with Hezbollah. Nassereddine was thought to be in charge of financing terrorist operations, and El Aissami of securing passports for Hezbollah's activists and handing them out through Nassereddine. In a study titled *Iran's Strategic Penetration of Latin America* (2014), its author Joseph Humire counted up to 173 individuals linked to Hezbollah and Iran's Revolutionary Guards who used Venezuelan passports on trips to other countries, including Canada.

The Nassereddines, Visas from Beirut

To check the Internet in order to know at what time he was supposed to lie down and pray was "an unnecessary risk that Oday Nassereddine should never have incurred voluntarily," according to an informer who is the source of the following revelations and who closely tracked Nassereddine and other members of his family. Oday was very cautious in terms of where and when he used his cell phone to avoid being tracked on certain missions. He did not realize, however, that when he inputted his location on a website in Venezuela to find out the exact times for sunrise and sunset, he was giving away his whereabouts. His digits, tracked at a distance, left behind a trail. Hence, the U.S. Drug Enforcement Administration (DEA) found out that he lived in Barquisimeto, a town located only sixteen miles from Hezbollah's training camp in Yaritagua, in the neighboring state of Yaracuy. The camp was under the command of Oday Nassereddine himself. Guerrilla training was carried out in an estate that was confiscated from Eduardo Gómez Sigala, a member of parliament from the opposition.

Satellite location eventually closed the noose around Ghazi Nassereddine, Oday's brother and deemed to be Hezbollah's point man in Venezuela. A trip they undertook together to Cancun at the beginning of 2013 tipped off the DEA, enabling different agencies in Washington, including the CIA, to work together. During the trip to Mexico, the Nassereddine brothers contacted the drug mafia in the Yucatán Peninsula. They worked out a mutually beneficial deal: logistical help for Hezbollah cells so they could reach and breach the border with the United States in exchange for part of the drug money that the Shia terrorist group handled in Venezuela.

Ghazi's connection to Venezuela started with his brother Abdalah, who at the beginning of the 1980s emigrated from Lebanon to the Caribbean and settled in Margarita Island. Part of the family followed in Abdalah's footsteps, so that several brothers eventually wound up permanently residing in Venezuela. Ghazi made frequent trips between Venezuela and Lebanon, with long stays in Venezuela that entitled him to apply for and obtain dual citizenship—his Venezuelan identity card was issued in July 1998. Hugo Chávez's victory in the presidential election at the end of that year elevated the family's status. Abdalah, who financed Chávez's campaign in Margarita through his money laundering businesses, was elected to a seat in the Constituent Assembly the following year. Ghazi then joined the Venezuelan Foreign Affairs Ministry—knowing Arab and Farsi, among other languages, was helpful to open a lot of doors that Chavismo wanted to knock at.

Recruited in his youth by Hezbollah, Ghazi Nassereddine was very skillful at taking advantage of his new diplomatic position to build up his power base. An array of internal communications that I accessed through a leak—we can refer to them as the *Nassereddine cables*—highlight his role in the issuing of Venezuelan visas and passports to members of Hezbollah. In 2005, for example, when he served as minister councilor at the Venezuelan Embassy in Damascus, Nassereddine moved at ease between Syria and Lebanon, where he meddled in the internal affairs of Venezuela's Embassy in Beirut. Confidential complaints filed with the Venezuelan Ministry of Foreign Affairs in Caracas about Nassereddine described how he had showed up at the Venezuelan Embassy in Beirut in order "to undertake an evaluation of its operations" despite the fact that he had no position at the embassy, as Venezuelan diplomats would attest. On one occasion, Nassereddine sought to review the applications for visas that had been filed, and "proceeded to analyze, examine, and decide" about whether to issue them or not, a competency that only the authorities in Caracas could exercise. During the ensuing two years, Venezuela's Embassy in Beirut "was subject to the continuous presence of numerous Lebanese citizens who claimed to have been recommended" by Nassereddine, who appeared to act as a plenipotentiary, "so they would immediately be issued a visa without having to fulfill the necessary requirements."

Nassereddine later accused the Venezuelan ambassador in Beirut, Zoed Karam, of passing on the compromising secret complaints to the CIA and, working with the U.S. agency, of thwarting his next appointment. In 2007, months after Nicolás Maduro took over as Foreign Affairs minister, he sought to place the controversial diplomat where he would be of most use, and named him minister councilor in Beirut. Maduro had just held his face-to-face meeting with Hassan Nasrallah, Hezbolla's secretary general, and Nassereddine was a key piece of the evolving relationship. But, not prone to follow formalities, neither Maduro nor his protégé realized that, as a Lebanese citizen, Nassereddine could not hold a high-ranking diplomatic position in Lebanon. Lebanese authorities rejected Nassereddine's appointment after they were made aware of it. Nassereddine would later claim to have evidence that it was the Ambassador Zoed Karam herself who disclosed the circumstances to the Lebanese. Karam complained to Maduro about a process that had flouted the rules and betrayed a strange sense of urgency—the new minister councilor was already in Beirut before he was officially informed about his appointment. After receiving official notification by fax, Nassereddine showed up at the Embassy in Beirut before the authorities in Caracas reported it to anybody at the diplomatic mission.

Nassereddine did not take his rejection well and demanded reprisals against Karam. But he was forced to return to the Venezuelan Embassy in Syria, although he continued to travel to Lebanon. In 2012 he was still pleading his case: "I suggest that I be allowed to renounce my Lebanese citizenship immediately and to be appointed minister councilor in Lebanon, and thereafter Venezuelan ambassador to Lebanon after the traitor [Karam] is removed," he wrote to the Ministry of Foreign Affairs. The appointment as ambassador to Beirut appeared to be part of the plan originally agreed upon between Maduro and Nassereddine. If the arrangement could not be carried out, he requested the right to live in Beirut, maintaining diplomatic immunity for himself as well as for his wife and children, as his activities had put him on the "damned empire's" radar. He boasted about having "put together several social organizations with a revolutionary character" and "maintained close fraternal ties with all of the progressive and anti-imperialist political forces" in the Middle East. Without a posting but with a diplomatic passport, his stays in Venezuela became longer. He settled down in the Alba Hotel in Caracas, which was renamed after Chavismo nationalized it from the Hilton chain. After the civil war broke out in Syria, he labeled his Twitter account "Syria resists," accompanied by a picture of him with Syrian president Bashar al-Assad and Chávez.

Margarita Island and Money Laundering

The Nassereddine brothers' activities transformed Margarita Island, located fourteen miles northeast of the Venezuelan mainland, into a haven for money laundering and drug trafficking. As a significant tourist destination and duty-free zone, the island is ideally suited for the flow of luxury goods and wealthy non-residents. Its population numbers over 400,000 in an area of almost four hundred square miles. The island had traditionally been home to one of the few Islamic communities in Venezuela, which was mainly Palestinian and Sunni. It was not numerous, as Arab immigrants into Venezuela had spread out around the country and were predominantly Christians from Syria and Lebanon.

Among the Muslim population of the island, popularly known as the *Turks*, were many small business-owners willing to support the Palestine Liberation Organization (PLO) with funding and money laundering. This financing was small scale given their businesses' limited turnover. The United States estimated that the yearly remittances sent by the businessmen from Margarita to the PLO did not exceed $100,000. But U.S. intelligence continued to monitor developments in this part of the Caribbean as it was almost the only place in Venezuela were the CIA had manpower in the field.

The international dynamics that Hugo Chávez set in motion transformed the island. A new wave of Muslim immigrants from Syria and Lebanon raised the profile of Shias. They became involved in the sale of white goods, appliances, automobiles, financial services… and drugs, which turned into the main funding tool for Hezbollah. The money laundering structure that existed up to that point in Margarita was only able to handle amounts under four figures. Ghazi Nassereddine made a name for himself with money laundering operations that easily topped $40 million, as the documents that the New York Attorney's Office used to justify its allegations. The drugs were shipped first to Africa, and then to Europe in order for Hezbollah cells to distribute them. Global operations also involved smuggling and arms sales.

The U.S. Treasury Department's Office of Foreign Assets Control (OFAC) included Nassereddine on its 2008 black list of facilitators of terrorism. The FBI included him in 2015 on its list of wanted persons. "It is extremely troubling to see the government of Venezuela employing and providing safe harbor to Hezbollah facilitators and fundraisers," an OFAC statement from 2008 read. The statement went on to specify that Nassereddine "has counseled Hezbollah donors on fundraising efforts and has provided donors with specific information on bank accounts where the donors' deposits would go directly to Hezbollah." The investigation also highlighted that the Venezuelan diplomat had met with high-ranking Hezbollah officials in Lebanon in order to discuss "operational issues" and had "facilitated the travel of Hezbollah members to and from Venezuela." On one of those trips, made in 2005, according to the U.S. Treasury, he went to Iran to participate in a training course. The following year Nassereddine organized a visit to Caracas by two Hezbollah members of the Lebanese parliament to solicit money and coordinate the opening of a community center and office funded by Hezbollah.

These trips were managed from Caracas by Mustafá Kanaan's travel agencies. Kanaan was also placed on the U.S. Treasury Department's list of designated enablers of terrorism. According to OFAC, Kanaan "met with senior Hezbollah officials in Lebanon in order to discuss operational issues, including possible kidnappings and terrorist attacks," and even "traveled with two other Hezbollah members to Iran to receive training." Kanaan was the owner of the Hilal and Biblos travel agencies, both of which were located in the same building in the center of Caracas. He denied the Treasury's accusations. The reader should nonetheless bear in mind that when the U.S. Treasury designates a person as an enabler or participant in terrorist or other criminal activities, thereby freezing whatever assets that person may hold in the United States and banning its citizens from any business transactions with the said person, OFAC has diligently reviewed its evidence. It would otherwise be risking a lawsuit for harming the affected person's estate.

The fact that Hezbollah has two distinct dimensions has blurred its perception as a terrorist organization. On the one hand, it operates as a political party and provides services to the communities where it operates in Lebanon. These political and social operations endow it with some legitimacy in the eyes of some. But Hezbollah also wields its military power and militia to carry out terrorist attacks, wage wars against Israel or fight on behalf of Bashar al-Assad's regime in Syria. The United States had been designating Hezbollah as a terrorist organization for many years, but the European Union did not follow suit until 2013, and even then did so grudgingly, wary of tarnishing all of its operations. As Matthew Levitt concludes in *Hezbollah. The Global Footprint of Lebanon's Party of God* (2013), the organization cannot be analyzed without examining its political, social, and military activities in Lebanon, but "its operations outside of Lebanon are equally significant, and include criminal enterprises and terrorist networks." Levitt confirms that Hezbollah's undercover international operations wing, entrusted with soliciting funds and logistics as well as executing terrorist attacks, is under the authority of its Shura Council, as are its other wings.

It is not a U.S. obsession to demonize all sympathizers of radical Middle East movements. The chavista regime's inner circle was well aware of the risks of embracing Hezbollah. "Chávez was no fool. He might play with fire, but he took precautions," assures a source who saw a list of approximately three hundred Hezbollah operatives residing in Venezuela, whose personal data was well registered: postal addresses, identity cards, telephone numbers, and email addresses. A dozen Hezbollah members in Venezuela were specifically deemed to be terrorists. Most were from Lebanon, but there were also Syrians among the group. This list was strictly kept under wraps. Its value is underlined by the fact that Diosdado Cabello offered to turn it over to U.S. authorities in his failed dealings with Washington that sought to cast him as an alternative to Maduro at the beginning of his presidency. Chávez had agreed that Hezbollah could widen its network in Venezuela, but he also monitored the group—he assigned Venezuelan intelligence agents to track them and listen in on their conversations. A unit of the government's civilian intelligence service, then called Directorate of Intelligence and Prevention Services (DISIP), watched them around the clock. Chávez handed over to Hezbollah part of the drug trafficking business and gave them free rein to launder money. But he always kept an eye on them, ensuring that they did not try to play a bigger role than he would allow or that they would carry out a terrorist action that was not on his agenda.

Beaches for the Mossad and Al-Qaeda

The Mossad knows the Venezuelan islands' white beaches well. When the Israeli intelligence service wanted to reward its agents with some rest and recuperation (R&R), it would send them to Los Roques, an archipelago in the Lower Antilles that belongs to Venezuela and which is even more beautiful than Margarita. The choice of Los Roques owed to its natural beauty, but there was also a practical reason. On Los Roques merchants only accepted payment in cash. It was a big inconvenience for tourists that credit cards were not accepted but a blessing for the agents, who therefore left behind no trail of their stay—they became as transparent as the waters that washed up on Los Roques. The marvelous vacations that the Israeli agents enjoyed on Los Roques ended with Chávez's rise to power. They could no longer take chances and lie on the beaches' fine sand oblivious to the revolutionary changes sweeping Venezuela.

Although it was no longer safe for R&R, the Caribbean nonetheless continued to be a theater of operations for the Mossad. And Israeli agents were especially bewildered, as a former agent explains, by the "degree of cooperation between Hamas and Hezbollah, something we were not accustomed to." It was not frequent for Sunni and Shia extremism to collaborate, but in some places in Venezuela, particularly Margarita, both communities lived alongside one another. When the second wave of Islamic immigration into Venezuela occurred (basically from Lebanon and Syria), its members settled where Muslims of Palestinian origin already lived, partly because they did not speak Spanish. Chávez's overture to Iran would be the glue between both groups. "The agents of the Iranian Revolutionary Guard were the ones who set order. They told both [Hamas and Hezbollah followers] that there was plenty of money to be made with the illegal business they were involved in," the former agent assures.

Individuals of a third Islamist group would find shelter as well in Margarita—Al-Qaeda's terrorists or activists linked to its cells visited the place. But they only transited through the island or remained there briefly to freeze their identities. They never employed the island as an operational base from which to launch future terrorist attacks. The most well-known case was that of Mustafa Setmariam Nasar, also known as Abu Musab al-Suri, a Syrian from Aleppo who holds Spanish citizenship. His numerous writings on strategic issues (including the sixteen hundred page book *The Global Islamic Resistance Call*) and experience in guerrilla warfare turned him into a lecturer an unofficial advisor to a wide range of jihadi groups. He is regarded as a mastermind of the Madrid terrorist attack of March 11, 2004, which killed 191 persons after terrorists set off ten almost simultaneous explosions on four trains, as well as of the London bombings of July 7, 2005. He is also linked to the 1985 bombing of the restaurant El Descanso near Madrid, frequented by U.S. servicemen stationed in the nearby military base of Torrejón de Ardoz, which claimed the lives of eighteen people.

Nasar's presence in Venezuela in September 2005 was denounced by Johan Peña, a former commissioner of the Venezuelan intelligence service who was living in exile in Miami. But the announcement of Nasar's arrest weeks later in Pakistan seemed to dispel the Caribbean connection. Files managed by the FBI do confirm

Nasar's stopover in Venezuela. Bob Levinson, a former FBI agent who worked as a consultant for both the FBI and the CIA, revived Nasar's trail within the U.S. intelligence community. Levinson was kidnapped in Iran in 2007, an action that authorities in Washington blamed on the Iranian intelligence services.

According to a copy of the investigation undertaken by several FBI collaborators, which I obtained, Mustafa Setmariam Nasar arrived in Venezuela on June 9, 2004, with the alias Hartinger Luis Gunter Santamaría and identity card number 82.187.492. This was probably an identity that had been employed by different persons on several occasions until it got *burnt*. Nasar was monitored in Caracas and Puerto Ordaz, where he was seen boarding a ship registered under a Liberian flag on several occasions. He then vanished until his arrest was announced. The information arrived to the FBI suggested that Nasar's disappearance was prompted by Johan Peña's public tip-off, who along with former DISIP agents might have been seeking a reward for delivering him to U.S. authorities. Nasar was captured in the Pakistani city of Quetta in October 2005 and turned over to U.S. officials in that country a month later. But at a later date he was rendered to Syria, where he was also wanted. Despite rumors to the contrary, in April 2014 Al-Qaeda leader Ayman al-Zawahiri confirmed that Nasar was still in prison.

Another Al-Qaeda militant was Hakim Mohamed Ali Diab Fattah, a Venezuelan who took flying lessons at two of the New Jersey flight academies also attended by Hani Hanjour, one of the 9/11 suicide pilots. Hanjour was at the command of the American Airlines jetliner which crashed into the Pentagon. Fattah was arrested in the United States a month after 9/11, on October 18, 2001, when he sought to extend his expired U.S. visa at an immigration office in Milwaukee. U.S. authorities seized multiple identity documents with different names from him.

The investigation into 9/11 in the United States initially began amid a certain degree of chaos and urgency. At the time, the different U.S. agencies' databases were not linked. A judge ordered Fattah's deportation from the country. The FBI turned him over to Venezuelan authorities with the understanding that he would be kept under arrest and that they would seek to determine his real identity. Venezuelan officials were also supposed to return Fattah to the United States for further questioning after the investigation into 9/11 had progressed. According to the cable sent by U.S. authorities to the Venezuelan Ministry of Interior and Justice, "while he attended the flight academy in the New Jersey area, Fattah threatened to blow up an Israeli airliner." The cable also added that Fattah "had undergone medical treatment and was under medication for psychological problems."

Fattah arrived at the Maiquetía airport near Caracas on March 8, 2002, on a Delta flight. "A DISIP team, which had been advised of Fattah's deportation, boarded the plane but never left the airport premises through the passenger exits, so that the appropriate procedures were never followed," Brigadier General Marco Ferreira Torres would later disclose in his blog. Ferreira Torres had served as director of the Administrative Service of Identification and Migration Affairs (SAIME), and left Venezuela just after Fattah's arrival. The FBI was informed, as was presumably confirmed by one of the DISIP agents in charge of whisking Fattah away, that he was driven immediately to Margarita Island following orders issued by Venezuela's leading government officials. Fattah was "frozen and protected" at Margarita by Venezuelan intelligence agents. FBI informants located and photographed Fattah on the island. The government of Venezuela officially declared that he had never arrived in Venezuela, thus ignoring Washington's request that he be returned to U.S. custody for further interrogation as had been agreed upon initially.

Fattah surfaced in 2015 in Jordan, where he was arrested for allegedly financing terrorist groups. Jordanian intelligence concluded that he was using two passports, one Venezuelan and the other Palestinian, as Misael López Soto, counselor of the Embassy of Venezuela in Iraq, was able to establish. López Soto was relieved of his duties for accusing fellow Venezuelan officials of issuing Venezuelan passports to Islamic extremists. The former Venezuelan diplomat gathered evidence about several cases, such as that of El Tamimy, born in

Basra according to his Iraqi passport and in Maracaibo according to his Venezuelan identity. El Tamimy had tried to board the suspicious flight between Caracas and Damascus with a suitcase packed with almost fifty pounds of cocaine.

Narco-Terrorism

Fattah worked on Margarita Island as the collector for a group of residents who described themselves as part of Hezbollah and whom the FBI had designated as persons of interest for their alleged involvement in money laundering, especially via Panama and Curaçao, and for illegally smuggling people into the country. Some of the members of this group included Abdalah Nassereddine (Ghazi Nassereddine's brother), Fatthi Mohammed Awada, Hussein Kassine Yassine, and Nasser Mohammed al-Din.

Abdalah Nassereddine, according to a FBI informant, organized the illegal entry into Venezuela of a long list of Arabs with the assistance of the regional director of Identification and Migration Affairs. One of the persons apparently smuggled into the country was Hasan Izz-al-Din, a Hezbollah terrorist of Lebanese citizenship sought by U.S. authorities for his alleged involvement in the hijacking of TWA flight 847 in June 1985, during which the attackers assassinated U.S. Navy diver Robert Stethem. He was also linked to the hijacking of Kuwait Airways flight 422, which lasted for sixteen days and thus became one of the longest skyjackings in history. During the siege, the hijackers—whom Kuwaiti authorities suspected as belonging to Hezbollah—killed two hostages in cold blood. Hasan Izz-al-Din was included in the FBI's list of twenty-two most wanted terrorists disclosed after 9/11. He was apparently spotted around 2004 in Porlamar, the capital of Margarita, at the home of Nasser Mohammed al-Din, one of the aforementioned persons on FBI's radar. He reached Margarita before making his way to Ticoporo, a national park in the state of Barinas. Several FARC members also attended a meeting held in the forest reserve. It was hosted by Ramón Rodríguez Chacín, former Venezuelan minister of Interior and Justice.

Hezbollah's ties to the FARC and especially to the Venezuelan narco-state provided the Lebanese organization with a safe haven and a source of funds through drug trafficking. This enabled Hezbollah to extend its activities in Latin America. Until Hugo Chávez's election as president, radical Islam's operational area in South America was the so-called Triple Border, which is the area were the borders of Paraguay, Brazil, and Argentina meet. This spot was chosen for several reasons. The borders were porous and poorly guarded. It is close to the successful free-trade zone of Ciudad del Este (Paraguay), which is the world's third-biggest after Miami and Hong Kong. Moreover, Ciudad del Este is part of a sprawling urban area that encompasses two neighboring cities, Foz do Iguaçu (Brazil) and Puerto Iguazú (Argentina). This turned it into an ideal enclave to evade security agencies and to launder money.

The Triple Border was the place where the material preparations for the big terrorist attacks against Jewish interests in 1992 and 1994 in Buenos Aires were conducted, as the Argentinian justice system concluded. Chávez opened the way for radical Shiism to extend its activities beyond the Triple Border, as several heads of the U.S. Southern Command testified before Congress. SOUTHCOM monitors Central and South America, with a special focus on the Panama canal. In 2003, the then head of SOUTHCOM, General James Hill, warned that Islamic groups were operating beyond the Triple Border, in places such as Margarita. These organizations, according to General Hill, were raising "hundreds of millions of dollars through drug trafficking and arms smuggling carried out in association with narco-terrorist groups."

With the passage of time General Hill's warnings became an understatement. The head of SOUTHCOM had limited the term narco-terrorism to local groups such as the FARC. But researcher Matthew Levitt has no qualms about applying it to Hezbollah: they are not terrorists who engage in drug trafficking as an additional activity, Hezbollah has turned the drug business into the center of its operations as a global terrorist group. Moreover, its cells would have reached the U.S. border itself with the assistance of Mexican cartels.

This was the surprise that awaited a former member of Mossad who was invited to teach a course to the police force of a U.S. county that borders Mexico. According to the agent, he was shown a pouch left behind by an illegal immigrant who had managed to enter the United States. Several coats of arms had been sewn into the haversack. The agent recognized them as being those of several Hezbollah units. In 2010, the Kuwaiti newspaper *Al Siyasah* published an article about the arrest of a resident of Tijuana, Jameel Nasr, by Mexican authorities. Nasr, an alleged Hezbollah militant, had been attempting to develop "a logistical infrastructure made up of Mexican citizens of Shia Lebanese descent in order to set up an operational base." Among Nasr's suspected movements was a two-month stay in Venezuela in 2008.

Venezuela appeared time and again in drug and arms trafficking operations attributed to Hezbollah. In 2009, almost nine hundred pounds of cocaine were transported on board the strategic flight operated by the airline Conviasa which covered the route Caracas-Damascus-Tehran. It was difficult to rule out official collusion: the origin was especially monitored by Venezuelan authorities, and the stopover in Damascus was at a military base. The cargo was transported from Syria by land to the Lebanese border, where two Venezuelan citizens and two Lebanese were arrested. The botched drug smuggling operation stirred unease at the Venezuelan Embassy in Beirut, as diplomatic sources attested.

There was another moment of concern in 2009 for the Venezuelan ambassador to Beirut, Zoed Karam, although the information that implicated Chávez's government would not surface for some time. Forty containers with more than three hundred tons of weapons were seized by Israeli authorities near Cyprus from a ship named Francop which was registered in Antigua. It was later revealed that the cargo had been shipped from Venezuela to the Iranian port of Bandar Abbas, whence it was transported to Damietta, in Egypt, the port from which the Francop sailed. Its destination was Hezbollah, with the delivery scheduled to take place at a Lebanese or Syrian port. The load featured thousands of Katyusha rockets, mortar projectiles, shells, and other munitions from Russia. The freight had inscriptions in Spanish and was transported in containers marked with Iranian codes.

Hezbollah's criminal activity in Venezuela and the rest of Latin America was not of a great scale, nor was it always attributable to the organization itself. The group often garnered funds through Lebanese citizens who were not affiliated with Hezbollah and whose financial contributions were due to an ideological affinity or to the pressure exerted by their environment. There was no single financing model, as Matthew Levitt's study describes, quoting official DEA sources. "Some fund Hezbollah because of family links to the organization, others because it embodies the cause of resistance against Israel and the West. Part of the drug trafficking is Hezbollah actively implicated as a group, and part is simply Lebanese Shias dealing with drugs who happen to be Hezbollah sympathizers."

In Venezuela's case, without obviously criminalizing the majority of its Muslim population of Middle East origin, the funding for Hezbollah and Hamas terrorism was often provided by residents with business activities in the main areas of Muslim settlement. This was the case with the neighborhood of the city of Maracaibo known as Las Playitas, which had managed to attract part of the trading activity that traditionally had taken place in the nearby Maicao, a Colombian town located on the other side of the border. Maicao, which features the biggest mosque in the Caribbean, was often officially singled out as a smuggling area. The stalls of Maicao and Las Playitas, which were tightly linked, were run by Muslim Arabs.

The money laundering that occurred at these locations paled in comparison to the operations allegedly run on Margarita, which always raised more suspicions among U.S. authorities.

Training Camps

"There is a Lebanese bank here with which all traders do business as it provides good terms. The DEA came and investigated the bank during three months. They looked into all of the accounts, client by client, and uncovered nothing," assured Mohamad Abdul Hadi, a Venezuelan of Lebanese descent who was vice president of the Islamic Community of Margarita, in an interview in 2006 with Antonio Salas, the pen name of a Spanish writer who has published several books after infiltrating different groups. In *El Palestino* (2010), Salas recounted his immersion as a fake Palestinian into the realm of Islamic extremism, which included several stays in Venezuela. Hadi added in his interview with Salas: "They [U.S. agencies] left without finding any incriminating information. But they continued to talk about terrorists, terrorist training camps in Macanao... Macanao is a desert, there is nothing there other than rabbits and a few Lebanese traders who go hunting on Sundays. Did they get the rabbits mixed up with the terrorists?"

Hadi was rebutting two of the main accusations leveled from Washington. However, despite Hadi's conclusions in the interview, the DEA did not close its investigation into the banking operations from Margarita and continued to track developments, especially after the U.S. government filed a lawsuit in 2011 against Lebanese Canadian Bank for its participation in a scheme to launder drug trafficking money and other funds for terrorists. Although the Beirut-based bank's transactions had appeared completely legal in the past, in 2011 a DEA and U.S. Treasury investigation unveiled money laundering operations of $329 million over five years. Lebanese Canadian Bank settled the lawsuit with U.S. authorities by paying a fine of $102 million. As *The New York Times* chronicled, the laundered money originated mainly from drug production in Colombia, which reached overseas markets via Venezuela, and whose revenue flowed to bank accounts linked to Hezbollah.

It is very likely that Hadi was right about the inexistence of a terrorist training camp on Margarita Island in the years that followed 9/11 and which would have trained Al-Qaeda members for the jihad. U.S. authorities had never explicitly made such an accusation. When the *Palestinian* and Hadi spoke, increased cooperation between Venezuela and Iran was still being worked on, which is ultimately what afforded the strategic framework for the spread of Islamic radicalism in Venezuela and Latin America. Thus in 2010 took place the afore mentioned terrorist summit in Caracas with the attendance of high-ranking Hezbollah and Hamas officials. The same year, two Iranian advisors, one of whom had obtained a Venezuelan identity card, were driven by a member of the Venezuelan Directorate of Military Intelligence (DIM) to the Macanao Peninsula on the western part of Margarita, where classes on urban terrorism techniques were conducted, according to testimony before the U.S. Congress.

In a tourist destination like Margarita it is easier for outsiders to go unnoticed due to the high number of visitors. But, on the other hand, it is harder to cover up activities from foreign surveillance. In any case, Macanao is located on the opposite side of the island from the capital Porlamar, where the tourists congregate. Macanao has a small population, beaches that have not been developed, and a big central arid area that is unpopulated and lacks paved roads. The evidence seems to indicate that this was the area where courses in street violence were taught on an occasional basis.

More permanent guerrilla training courses took place in other parts of Venezuela. The Hezbollah camp at Yaritagua, which was run by Oday Nassereddine, has already been referred to. The *Palestinian* pointed out that of Guaira, where he underwent training, as well as those of Santa Teresa, Santa Lucía, and Filas de Mariche, all of which were located in Caracas' metropolitan area. Chavismo had developed them to train its irregular strike forces in the theory and practice of asymmetrical warfare, with the participation of Army members and the cooperation of the Ministry of Interior. There were also installations managed by the FARC in its havens of western Venezuela.

The indoctrination camps in Venezuela have received thousands of youths from all of Latin America. In his testimony in 2013 before the U.S. House of Representatives' Committee on Homeland Security, Douglas Farah—an expert from the Center for Strategic and International Studies (CSIS) in Washington—assured having spoken to students who had been recruited and trained in Venezuela, in some cases as a first step in a more intense program pursued in Qom (Iran).

Farah's contacts were mainly from El Salvador, but similar testimony from Mexican youths and those of other countries, compiled in various studies, prove that there was a permanent flow of enthusiasts, as well as a constant model of recruitment. The recruitment frequently materialized in mosques or Islamic cultural centers through individuals associated with the Bolivarian governments of the ALBA countries.

As a first step, the youths were offered the opportunity to attend courses in Venezuela, with the added incentive of getting to know other Latin American youths similarly attracted by the revolutionary epic. These gatherings were akin to transnational revolutionary festivals whose travel costs were paid by the Venezuelan authorities. After assembling in Venezuela, according to Farah, a chosen group was invited to travel to Iran to undergo additional training, accompanied by Venezuelan instructors. The training lasted between one and three months, and featured lectures on intelligence and counterintelligence, control of masses, and incitement to violence in street protests. There was also a component of Shiite indoctrination, which portrayed the United States as the great Satan and justified the destruction of Israel. The youths returned from Iran to Venezuela. This meant that their native countries had no record of their travel to Iran, only of their trips to and from Caracas.

"What is the potential threat?" Farah asked rhetorically before the members of the U.S. House of Representatives. "That Iran is creating small groups of sleeper cells throughout the region. These cells are made up of individuals who have received specialized training and are not Iranian citizens. They are therefore subject to much less scrutiny by their governments and by U.S. authorities should they seek to travel to the United States." Farah estimated that since 2007 hundreds of recruits had been sent for training every year to Iran.

Cyberattack Plan with Hidden Camera

Moshen Rabbani was the host of the visitors in Qom, Shiism's holy city. Rabbani was regarded as one of the main sponsors of Islamic radicalism in Latin America. He served as international affairs advisor in a Qom-based educational institution committed to the spread of Islamic Shiism around the world. In reports presented before the two chambers of the U.S. Congress, former Assistant Secretary of State for Western Hemisphere Affairs Roger Noriega designated Rabbani as the head of Hezbollah's other big network in Venezuela, alongside the one that was coordinated by Ghazi Nassereddine. Noriega identified "at least two parallel terrorist networks that cooperate with one another": the one run by the Iranian Revolutionary Guard's Quds Force, which operated in all of the American continent and which apparently was mainly directed by Rabbani, and the one described in the preceding pages more restricted to Venezuela and mainly linked to Nassereddine. There were other possible interventions, some of which functioned autonomously, and others were directed from Beirut. In any case, Iran was deemed to play a coordinating role over all of the Shia extremist forces.

Rabbani was linked to the terrorist attack carried out against the Israeli Embassy in Buenos Aires in 1992 which claimed the lives of twenty-nine people, and especially to a second bombing in 1994, also in Buenos Aires, that demolished the building of the Argentine Israelite Mutual Association (AMIA) and killed eighty-five people. Both attacks wounded hundreds and deeply shocked the 200,000-strong Jewish community in Argentina, the largest in Latin America and sixth in the world outside of Israel. The AMIA attack was the deadliest bombing in Argentinian history. The Organization for the Islamic Jihad claimed responsibility for the suicide car bomb against the Israeli Embassy. It was a fundamentalist Shiite group financed and trained partly by Iran, which was especially active during the 1980s in Lebanon. Some experts consider that it was part of the framework from which Hezbollah eventually emerged. The investigations into the material authors of the 1992 attack were not conclusive—the trail disappeared in the Triple Border.

The outcome of the investigation into the 1994 bombing was no different. No group claimed responsibility for the attack. The investigation was plagued by irregularities from the outset and the judge in charge of the case was impeached and removed in 2005. In 2006, prosecutors Alberto Nisman and Marcelo Martínez Burgos announced the conclusion of their inquiries: "We have determined that the decision to attack AMIA was made in August 2003 at the highest level of the Iranian government, which outsourced the organization and execution of the attack to Hezbollah." According to the prosecution, the Iranian government orchestrated the attacks as retaliation after Buenos Aires decided to suspend a nuclear technology transfer contract with Iran. This has been disputed because the contract was never finalized, and Iran and Argentina were negotiating the restoration of full cooperation on all agreements from early 1992 until 1994.

In November 2007 Interpol published the names of the six individuals accused of plotting and executing the AMIA bombing, and inserted them into its red notice list. The accused were five Iranians and one Lebanese citizen: Moshen Rabbani, cultural attaché at the Iranian Embassy in Buenos Aires at the time of the attack; Ahmad Reza Asghari, third secretary at the Embassy; Ahmad Vahidi and Moshen Rezai, officers of Iran's Revolutionary Guard; Ali Fallahian, Iran's Minister of Intelligence; and Imad Fayed Moughnieh, a Hezbollah agent. According to Nisman, Rabbani had acted as a liaison between Hezbollah and the so-called *local connection*. Rabbani steadfastly denied his involvement. Nisman rejected a 2013 memorandum of understanding signed with Iran to investigate the attack. The case made it back into the headlines in January 2015 after Nisman's death. He was possibly assassinated, just hours before he was about to publicly denounce President Cristina Fernández de Kirchner, Foreign Minister Héctor Timerman, and other Argentine politicians in parliament for allegedly trying to cover up the Iranian connection. Nisman had published a 288-page report on the case just six days before he was found dead in his apartment.

As we shall see later, the name of Rabbani appeared in a Univision documentary that aired in December 2011 which set off alarm bells among U.S. legislators. The documentary, which focused on other suspects, was based on the work carried out with hidden cameras by several infiltrated Mexican students. The broadcast highlighted the possible use by Iran, with a certain degree of collaboration from Venezuelan and Cuba, of native Latin American cells to conduct hypothetical attacks against the United States. The recordings were undertaken between 2007 and 2010 by Juan Carlos Muñoz, a student at the Autonomous University of Mexico (UAM) and expert in databases and computer systems. He started recording them when he realized that his collaboration on a project with UAM professor Francisco Guerrero Lutteroth was going too far. Lutteroth, whom some sources would later identify as a possible Cuban agent, had put Muñoz in touch with the Iranian, Venezuelan, and Cuban embassies in Mexico City in order to finalize an IT project that evolved into a possible cyberattack. Muñoz created a team among his friends and acquaintances to go with the flow and hence be in a position to incriminate his contacts. Lutteroth requested a list of targets in the United States, such as nuclear power plants and military installations. In the recordings, Muñoz discussed these targets with the then Iranian ambassador in Mexico, Mohammad Hassan Ghadiri, as well as with Livia Acosta, who served as cultural attaché at the Venezuelan Embassy.

It is difficult to ascertain whether the plan was hatched in Iran or Ghadiri simply observed the Mexican students, as he would later declare to Univision from Iran, to determine the outcome of the project. It is indisputable, in any case, that the Iranian ambassador in Mexico was formally entangling himself in the preparation of a possible attack against the United States whose objective was not just destruction in the virtual world, but also in the physical one. When Acosta was informed about the plan, she requested all of the details so she could send them to Chávez. She was sure the president would be very pleased to know them.

A Wikileaks cable published in 2009 disclosed that the Mexican intelligence services were closely monitoring Ghadiri. His intention to open a consulate in Tijuana, on the border with the United States, had rung alarm bells in Washington. U.S. agencies took the Univision allegations very seriously, even if they might turn out to be a terrorist pipe dream. When they were made public, the Iranian diplomat had already returned to Tehran, but Acosta was within Washington's reach, as she was serving as consul in Miami. In January 2012, she was expelled from the United States. Chávez retaliated by closing the consulate. Professor Lutteroth, in the meantime, had died of cancer.

Crossing the Rio Grande

The Obama administration's decision to expel the Venezuelan consul was very swift. At other times, the administration had taken its time in responding to aggressive language or measures adopted by Chávez's government. On this occasion, the quick reaction was a product of a state of heightened alert in Washington. U.S. agencies were very wary about even the perception of Shiite terrorism making its way across the border with Mexico. Two months before the Univision broadcast, it was announced that officials from the Quds Force, the Iranian Revolutionary Guard's special operations unit, had planned to assassinate the Saudi ambassador in Washington. The Quds Force plot also included a U.S. citizen of Iranian descent and the assistance of a Mexican cartel. This cocktail changed a lot of assumptions. On October 11, 2011, U.S. Attorney General Eric Holder and FBI Director Robert Mueller accused an Iranian with U.S. citizenship, Manssor Arbabsiar, and his liaison in the Quds Force, Gholam Shakuri, of plotting to plant a bomb in a restaurant where the Saudi Ambassador Adel al-Jubeir frequently dined.

The plan was conceived during Arbabsiar's visits to Iran, which were followed up by telephone conversations. It envisioned that the smuggling of explosives into the United States and the execution of the attack would be carried out by several members of a Mexican cartel, as was detailed in the charges. As Arbabsiar's contact in Mexico was a DEA source, the material preparations for the attack never got off the ground. But several wire transfers from Iran proved its willingness to fund the assassination of the ambassador and cause mayhem in the capital of the United States. In the final stretch, Arbabsiar was arrested in New York on September 28, 2011. He admitted the plan and, in a telephone conversation monitored by the FBI, discussed the final orders with Shakuri, who had always remained in Iran. In May 2013 Arbabsiar was sentenced to twenty-five years in jail.

Despite the evidence presented at the trial, experts were baffled by the plot. First, because there had been several instances of improvisation during the entire process. This ran counter to the meticulous professionalism attributed to the Quds Force: Arbabsiar worked as a car salesman in Texas and his only original association to the Iranian security apparatus was a cousin whom he thought held a high-ranking position within the Force. Second, because in its "covert operations abroad, including terrorist attacks, assassinations, and kidnappings," as the U.S. government described it, the Quds Force resorted to radical Islamist individuals or groups, especially the Shiite organization Hezbollah. It did not employ alien agents such as members of a Mexican cartel. Attorney General Holder and FBI Director Mueller insisted nonetheless that such an attack would have required the express authorization of the Iranian supreme leader, Ayatollah Ali Khamenei, and the head of the Quds Force, General Qasem Soleimani. But most people found it odd that those at the helm in Tehran would seek to deal such a devastating blow in the heart of Washington, precisely at a time when the Iranian economy was reeling under the weight of international sanctions. The quick riposte to such objections was that the attack could have been planned by elements within the Iranian regime's security structure who were acting on their own.

There was, however, another and more worrying interpretation for the United States: the possibility that radical Shiism, after its northward ascent into Mexico by way of Hezbollah's penetration of global narco-trafficking, was seeking partners south of the Rio Grande in order to cross the border. This was an element common to both the plot against the Saudi ambassador and the one conceived at the Iranian Embassy in Mexico to launch cyberattacks against sensitive U.S. installations. Both seemed to follow the same pattern: representatives of the Iranian regime allowed initiatives developed by others to take shape. These plots were devised by unusual suspects—a car salesman, Mexican students—without leaving any trail that could point to Tehran. Was this the new normal? Maybe. Alarm bells sounded again in Washington when Ghazi and Oday Nassereddine were observed by U.S. agencies in Yucatán at the beginning 2013: Hezbollah was negotiating with the Mexican cartels how to share the spoils of the drug trade, and thereby getting closer to the U.S. border.

Rabbani Again

"Died under strange circumstances," was the only explanation proffered when certain sources sought to renew their ties with an Argentinian who had infiltrated Hezbollah and had passed on information about a training course with weapons at the heart of Petrochemical Corporation of Venezuela (PEQUIVEN), the country's biggest petrochemical conglomerate. His widow did not link his death to that mission, but was under no illusions that her husband's activities as a informant of the Brazilian Federal Police had made him many enemies.

In the PEQUIVEN mission, the informant had assured taking part in indoctrination and handling of explosives activities organized for individuals associated with Islamic extremism who had arrived from several Latin American countries. The course was conducted in March 2010 in the Center for the Promotion of the Petroleum Industry, which is part of the PEQUIVEN installations, in the municipality of Morón (Carabobo state). The pupils attended prayers at a small mosque that had been built within the compound for the Iranians who were expected to collaborate on several projects, such as factories for the production of gunpowder and other substances. Such projects were envisioned in the agreements between Iran and the Anonymous Venezuelan Company of Military Industries (CAVIM), which had one of its main sites in the area. The transfer of Iranian foremen to foster these initiatives served as a cover for the terrorist training actions. The biggest disclosure was the visit paid by Moshen Rabbani to the participants in the course.

The former Iranian diplomat would continue to be described by several sources as the person in charge of recruiting and training activists. The aforementioned Univision report of December 2011 accused him directly. José Carlos García, a 19-year-old student at the Autonomous University of Mexico, volunteered to the Iranian ambassador in Mexico City, Mohammad Hassan Ghadiri, to be sent to Iran to attend a course on Islam in Spanish. His real intent was to surreptitiously record the experience. At the beginning of 2011, he flew to Qom to enroll in the lectures. Rabbani was one of his professors. When his recording equipment was discovered, he sought refuge in the Spanish Embassy in Tehran. He was able to return to Mexico and then, fearing reprisals by Iranian agents, applied for political asylum in the United States.

For its documentary, Univision had obtained exclusive footage, provided by the FBI, which incriminated the participants in a plan to attack John F. Kennedy airport in New York. The plan was revealed in 2007, but the footage was never released. The trial against those implicated in the plot, who were predominantly from Guyana, exposed the ties between one of them, Abdul Kadir, and Moshen Rabbani, whom the conspirators planned to lobby with the purpose of obtaining the necessary help to pull off the attack. Between December 2010 and February 2011, judges issued life sentences against Kadir and the head of the group, Russell Defreitas, for conspiracy to commit a terrorist attack. Defreitas, a former employee of JFK, had convinced his partners that they could unleash a massive explosion by blowing up the airport's giant fuel tanks, which were integrated into a network of forty miles of fuel pipelines. One of the conspirators was an FBI confidant, allowing authorities to know the real state of the preparations at all times. This generated some controversy about the real risk the plot had posed. In any event, the Rabbani connection had been uncovered. A convert to Shiism, Kadir had contacts among extremist groups in Venezuela and Iran. He was arrested as he boarded an Aeropostal plane in Trinidad and Tobago. The Venezuelan airliner was bound for Caracas, where Kadir was supposed to gather a visa that would allow him to immediately fly off to Tehran.

He was planning to attend an Islamic conference where he would meet with Rabbani.

Despite being on Interpol's red list for his role in the attack against AMIA in Buenos Aires, Rabbani pursued his travels without being arrested, possibly because he was using false documents. In addition to having been spotted in Venezuela in the Morón training course, some sources assured that he occasionally flew to Curitiva, a Brazilian city where his brother lived. Mohammad Baquer Rabbani Razavi was the founder of the Iranian Association of Brazil. Rabbani also had ties to imams who were his disciples and were in charge of mosques in Brazil and Argentina. The excellent relations between Iran and Venezuela sheltered many contacts and movements.

8

CHAVEZ-IRAN, LOVE AT FIRST SIGHT

Deal to Elude International Sanctions

I t was what we could term love at first sight. There is no question that the two men hit it off after their first encounter. It took place in Tehran in one of Hugo Chávez's first trips to Iran. Mahmoud Ahmadinejad was at the time the mayor of the Iranian capital, and Chávez inaugurated a monument to Simón Bolívar. "I feel I have met a brother and a comrade-in-arms," the Iranian leader would later say about Chávez. The brotherhood was sealed with Ahmadinejad's ascent to the presidency in August 2005. Since then, their respective mandates overlapped. It was eight straight years of intense collaboration, during which Ahmadinejad traveled to Venezuela six times, while Chávez undertook a dozen trips to Iran if we include his prior visits. "If the U.S. empire is successful in consolidating its hegemony, then humanity will have no future. We must therefore save humanity and put an end to the U.S. empire," Chávez said during one of his visits in an accurate description of the aim of the alliance between Iran and Venezuela.

The relationship between Venezuela and Iran did not start from scratch. The founding of the Organization of the Petroleum Exporting Countries (OPEC) in 1960, an initiative fostered especially by Venezuela and Saudi Arabia, created a framework for regular contacts between Caracas and Tehran. In 1970, the two countries exchanged ambassadors; five years later the Shah was in the Caribbean nation, and in 1977 Venezuelan President Carlos Andrés Pérez returned the visit. Relations between the two countries cooled as a result of the 1979 Islamic revolution, but were revived after Chávez came to power. The new Venezuelan president was a vocal proponent of a change of policy within OPEC that called for an increase in oil prices. This was in stark contrast to the pressure that Saudi Arabia had traditionally exerted within OPEC and whose tactic was to guarantee a certain level of revenue by increasing production. In his advocacy of a maximum rise in oil prices, Chávez found an ally in Iran, the natural counterweight to Saudi Arabia in the Middle East.

As a means of laying the groundwork for the OPEC summit in 2000, which was held in Caracas and ratified the change in policy, the previous year Chavez visited Libya, Iran, and Iraq, three regimes that were ostracized by most of the international community. This was the moment of the famous picture of Saddam Hussein at the wheel of his Mercedes Benz driving Chávez. Due to the no-fly area decreed over Iraq, the Venezuelan president flew by helicopter from Tehran to the Iraqi border, where his host came to pick him up in his car. During this tour, a round of conversations was launched between the Bolivarian leader and the Iranian president at the time, Mohammad Khatami. They set the stage for a schedule of visits and a range of agreements fostered after Ahmadinejad's ascent to the presidency. The first strategic alliance between both countries, in the oil sector, paved the way for a broader communion of interests: countering the United States' influence, regarded as a brake on their respective governments' influence on the world stage, and doing so by building up a front of nations.

"The main and possibly only real area of agreement between Ahmadinejad and Chávez in forging their ties," according to Douglas Farah, an expert on Iranian activity in Latin America, "is that both leaders openly stated their hostility to the United States." "Indeed, the common desire to build a power structure free from U.S. dominance is one of the few reasons that populist, self-styled revolutionary, and profoundly secular Latin American regimes made common cause with a reactionary and theocratic Islamic state." Farah's view, expressed at a Woodrow Wilson Center event on Iran's relations with Latin American countries, was summed up in a expressive verdict made at the event organized by this Washington-based think-tank: the Venezuela-Iran bond was basically the result of a mutual desire to make the White House as nervous as possible on as many issues as possible. The growing Iranian contacts with the members of the Bolivarian Alliance for the Peoples of Our America (ALBA) proved that the Persian country took advantage of any opportunity to showcase that it was not isolated and to challenge Washington's influence in its backyard.

Ahmadinejad referred to his pact with Chávez as a tool aimed at "bringing about three elements: tractors, influence, and fear." Given the low degree of fulfillment of the trade and investment agreements signed by Iran with Venezuela and other ALBA countries, we can conclude that Iran's main interest was not the first of the aforementioned three elements, but rather the other two. The reference to tractors alluded to one of the initial tangible products of economic relations between Caracas and Tehran: a factory for the assembly of Iranian agricultural machinery on Venezuelan soil. It was one of the approximately two hundred agreements negotiated between Ahmadinejad and Chávez during their years of cooperation; the deals were estimated to be worth $30 billion.

Iran's trade flows with other ALBA members also skyrocketed. The ALBA countries all probably envisioned the productive gains stemming from maintaining close ties with the more developed Iran, as well as welcoming the opportunity to diminish their dependence on U.S. goods and capital. However, many of the projects were executed in a haphazard way or ran into obstacles shortly after getting off the ground; quite a few were never finished, and the list of planned projects that were never carried out is long. Despite the increase in trade volumes between Iran and the ALBA members, the relative positions in their respective trade accounts were not significantly altered.

Hence, despite the much-touted *special relationship* between Iran and Venezuela, trade between the two countries only accounted for 0.02 percent of Venezuela's total trade volume in 2010, a year when the Chávez-Ahmadinejad partnership was in full swing. Iran was Venezuela's forty-eighth trade partner. For its part, the Latin American countries that conducted the most trade with Iran were ranked eighteenth (Brazil) and thirty-fourth (Argentina) among Iranian partners. None of the ALBA members placed in the top fifty. The United States kept being the leading trade partner for all countries in Latin America. Since then China has displaced the United States from this leadership position vis-à-vis several countries in the region, but Iran remained always at a far lower level. Tehran nonetheless benefited financially from the attention and time it lavished on Venezuela. Ahmadinejad may or may not have been shedding crocodile tears at Chávez's burial, but Iran's Treasury mourned his passing and feared a change of fortune.

The Iranian Rip-Off

Iran greatly benefited from its business transactions with Venezuela. China and Cuba also took advantage of Venezuela at different levels, but the Iranian case was the first to be denounced to president Chávez. A member of his economic team drew attention to the situation, but the Venezuelan president did nothing to prevent the ongoing racket. Rafael Isea, who was appointed to the position of deputy minister of Finance in 2006 and was promoted to minister in 2008, had reviewed the numbers. He was taken aback by the volume of dollars that Iran repatriated with the Venezuelan Central Bank's consent. The flow of dollars out of Venezuela was not in accordance with the magnitude of the business transactions carried out by the Iranians. Suspicious of these transactions, Isea called several currency operators to figure out who was exchanging so much hard currency. His inquiries uncovered the Iranian scheme.

With the payments it received for building thousands of housing units in Venezuela, an Iranian construction company, for example, could access the black market exchange rate. If it had originally received $80 million, the exchange operation could net it more than 400 million bolivars. The company would approach the official currency exchange operators and would obtain $180 million in return, more than doubling its original sum in dollars. It would request permission from the Venezuelan Central Bank to repatriate the latter sum, in accordance with the special agreement on free repatriation signed between both countries. The Iranians had quickly caught on to what others were doing. When minister Isea submitted the case to Chávez, the president did not look surprised and declined to raise the matter with Ahmadinejad.

–"Mr. President, they are bleeding us dry.
–Rafael, we have to preserve our strategic partnerships.
–Yes, Mr. President, but at what cost?"

Venezuela was being drained of its hard currency reserves at a fast pace. The losses accrued by Venezuela objectively revealed how much damage was inflicted by Chávez's attempts to forge strategic partnerships. Chávez managed to stand out on the international stage, but Venezuela and its citizens paid the bill. The deals with Iran were not a matter of choice, the result of an innocuous ideological preference, or a justifiable bet on South-South cooperation when it came to choosing a trading partner. The alliance took a big toll on Venezuela's finances through the swindle on the dollar reserves that enabled the Iranians to overcharge on their execution of projects, and it tarnished Venezuela's prestige and credibility on the world stage since helping Iran evade sanctions ran against the consensus reached at the United Nations, and not just pushed by the United States. The partnership also undermined the security of Venezuelans by way of the infiltration of Shia radicalism, especially by Hezbollah.

Iran had never paid much interest to Latin America. In an attempt to diversify their partners, both of the presidents that preceded Ahmadinejad (Hashemi Rafsanjani and Mohammad Khatami, who each served one seven-year term between 1989 until 2005) had cast their nets wider and carried out several trips to Africa with multiple layovers. The pivot to Latin America, which was geographically further away from the Iranian sphere of influence, was caused by two factors. In first place, many countries in Latin America lurched to the left at the end of the 1990s and especially in the first years of this century. They came to be governed by parties which, in the post-communist international order, could more easily align themselves with partners with differing ideologies but with a common opposition to a *Pax Americana.* Those countries were fertile ground for Iranian diplomacy. In second place, the United States' effort beginning in 1995 to diplomatically isolate Tehran spawned a need by the ayatollahs to actively search for and exploit the opportunities for economic and political cooperation with third countries in other regions of the world.

Ahmadinejad stepped up both processes during his term. His presidency overlapped chronologically with the development of a left-wing populist front in Latin America embodied by ALBA. He also felt the pressure of Iran's international isolation given the alarm about its nuclear weapons program and the ensuing application of sanctions. Ahmadinejad stepped up the enrichment of uranium and he also challenged the United States in its traditional sphere of influence. But Iran's new foothold in Latin America was prompted by a change of circumstances in the continent itself. It was Chávez who opened the door of Latin America to Iran, first to Venezuela and then to the ALBA countries, over which he exerted influence. Many cooperation projects were first agreed upon between Chávez and Ahmadinejad, and then extended to Ecuador, Bolivia, or Nicaragua. It was a play that required Chávez to place himself at the vertex of a power triangle, as he was the one who could ensure the maintenance of the flows.

Iran's meddling in Central and South America was viewed with suspiciousness in the United States. The House of Representatives approved in 2007 a resolution which expressed "concern" about the threat posed to the United States by the deepening economic and security ties between Iran and "like-minded regimes in the Western Hemisphere, including Venezuela." The main fear was that the Iranian presence could hatch cells of Hezbollah, the Lebanese terrorist group financed by Iran. Assistant Secretary of State for Western Hemisphere Affairs Thomas Shannon warned that "past is prologue," a reminder of the terrorist attacks committed in Buenos Aires at the beginning of the 1990s, and which were attributed to Hezbollah. As Barack Obama succeeded George W. Bush as president, the tone of the alarm bells emanating from the U.S. administration diminished. But the Iranian threat continued to be addressed in the same terms on Capitol Hill during testimony delivered by experts and in formal declarations.

Threat or Fiasco?

In December 2012 the Countering Iran in the Western Hemisphere Act was approved by both chambers of the U.S. Congress. It stated that Iran "is pursuing cooperation with Latin American countries by signing economic and security agreements in order to create a network of diplomatic and economic relationships to lessen the blow of international sanctions and oppose Western attempts to restrict its ambitions." The law urged the U.S. administration to work with allies and partners to "mutually deter threats to United States' interests." The act highlighted the symbiotic relationship between the Islamic Iranian Revolutionary Guard Corp's (IRGC) Quds Force and Hezbollah, and warned that their increased coordination could take place in Iranian embassies, cultural centers, and charities around the world. It also underlined the increase "in Iranian diplomatic missions to Venezuela, Bolivia, Nicaragua, Ecuador, Argentina, and Brazil. Iran has built seventeen cultural centers in Latin America, and it currently maintains eleven embassies, up from six in 2005."

Iran's aspiration to maintain a strong economic presence and an ability to exert direct political influence in the United States' backyard was regarded as a real danger in Washington. But it gradually descended into a fiasco. The U.S. government was right to be on high alert with regard to Hezbollah, which was strengthened by its greater access to drug trafficking. But the trade and production cooperation agreements between Iran and its Latin American partners did not go very far. They were never really a priority for the parties involved. Tehran's aim was: first, to break its isolation, underscoring its political alliance with other countries, and second, to evade economic and financial barriers applied by the United Nations sanctions. The partnership with ALBA rewarded Iran with some relief regarding the former and certainly on the latter front. It must be acknowledged that Ahmadinejad and Chávez's accord enabled them to weave a business and banking net that facilitated murky financial flows that sought to loosen the stranglehold of international sanctions on Iran.

The latter objective was stated in an internal document drafted during the exchange of visits carried out by both leaders in 2009. Chávez traveled to Tehran in September, and Ahmadinejad flew to Caracas in November. The document is a part of minutes of meetings between both countries that someone in the presidential circle leaked and we spell out. "The sanctions have made it difficult for the Iranian government and companies to access hard currency," the document admitted. It was therefore paramount to "create mechanisms within the cooperative bilateral relations to allay the impact of the sanctions and enhance financial flows." The fact that at the end of the day so many projects announced with great fanfare were not completed was probably not a matter of grave concern for its main sponsors, as the cover they had designed fulfilled their wishes.

As Douglas Farah explained before a U.S. House of Representatives committee, it was a "mistake to think that the economic agreements were designed with the aim of seeing them through. They were really forged to allow the ALBA countries and Iran to conduct mutually beneficial state-to-state transactions, including trafficking in illicit substances, purchase and transportation of significant mineral resources and dual-use technology, and the frequent free flow of persons." Farah spelled out the relationship's three aims: first, to design tools that enabled Iran to cushion the impact of international sanctions; second, to foster Iran's nuclear ambitions and ease the potential flow of components for weapons of mass destruction, including dual-use technology; and third, to place personnel and networks throughout Latin America, both to help spread Iran's revolutionary vision as well as to carry out attacks against objectives in the United States and Israel, particularly as a reprisal should Iranian nuclear facilities come under attack.

Tractors, Nuclear Bicycles, and Yellowcake

By now, Iranian tractors should be dotted about the Latin American countryside. Veniran Tractor, a joint company assigned to put together parts imported from Iran, was the first joint venture executed by Iran and Venezuela. It officially started work in March 2005 in the Ciudad Bolívar industrial zone. Its aim was for its assembly line to annually manufacture three thousand tractors, in addition to several agricultural tools. By the middle of 2012, the company said it had built 7,500 units, a third of its ultimate goal. Problems in starting up the factory, delays in supplies, a lack of operational understanding between the Iranian management and the one hundred Venezuelan employees, as well as Iranian logistical limitations caused by the embargo lowered the initial expectations. At the beginning of 2012, Chávez's enthusiasm for Veniran vanished and he became enamored with Veneminsk, an assembly of tractors in a joint venture with Belarus, whose inauguration he announced for a few months later.

Veniran Tractor's initial low level of activity was odd. Whoever approached the installations witnessed little labor movement. It was not what one would expect given the declared production volume in a facility with three buildings—no bustle at the entrance or exits by shifts, nor grouping of employees at the canteen at lunchtime. The factory's only labor union denounced in 2008 that production had plummeted to forty tractors per month, and that neither employees nor the community were informed of the company's accounts. The National Guard's presence outside the factory and the double security fence helped feed suspicions about an alternative and not publicized use of the installations. The existence of an entry zone accessible only to the Iranians, who slept at a nearby military base, contributed to the mystery. The hypothesis that seemed to make the most sense bore the name of a chemical element: uranium.

The possibility that Iran could be extracting uranium in Venezuela was widely discussed in policy circles. There had to be a reason for the appearance of Iranian factories in unusual locations, with a very low level of activity, and built according projects whose calculations made little sense. This was the case of the cement factory Cerro Azul, in El Pinto (Monagas state), an initiative that foresaw the investment of the exaggerated sum of approximately $750 million. The fact that overflight of the factory was banned, apparently because of a strategic installation, and that it was still unfinished after years of construction bred distrust. Venezuela's political opposition also was suspicious of Fanabi, a bicycle factory opened in Tinaquillo (Cojedes state). Inaugurated in 2008, by 2011 it had only assembled twenty-five thousand units, one fourth of the total planned for its first year. The deceit seemed to lie in the fact that these installations for the production of tractors, bicycles, or cement were located not very far away from mineral basins, and could therefore be linked to the extraction of uranium.

That Iranians had searched for uranium in Venezuela was in the public domain. The Geological Institute of Industry and Mines sealed an agreement with Iran in 2007 to perform a geological survey with the purpose of determining the country's mineral wealth. Given Venezuela's tradition as a producer of minerals, the location of its gold, diamond, and bauxite deposits was already well-known. The survey's main aim was to estimate the reserves of yellowcake, the name given to uranium concentrate powder. Minister of Basic Industries and Mining Rodolfo Sanz openly admitted in 2009 that Iranian specialists were developing geophysical tests and surveillance flights. "Our geological prospections indicate that we may possess substantial uranium reserves," Sanz stated. His words were scrutinized by the U.S. Embassy in Caracas, as a cable from Wikileaks revealed. The cable highlighted that a few days later "a journalist reported that

Chávez reprimanded Sanz for his comments about Iran, ordering him not to interfere in matters about which he had no knowledge—Note: the time of Sanz's comments coincided with news accounts that Iran was building a secret nuclear installation in Venezuela."

The Iranian geological survey concluded that the most attractive areas for investments in the extraction of uranium were in the states of Mérida and Táchira. Curiously, in the area with the most uranium deposits, located in the state of Bolívar, Iran was planning to extract gold. Was it a ruse to divert attention from its real intentions? The Iranian company that was awarded the contract, Impasco, did not appear later on the list of companies that extracted gold in Venezuela, nor did it appear in any international registry of companies from the sector. Impasco's mineral activities were linked to the Iranian nuclear program. The same Iranian officials who in November 2008 signed the Impasco contract reached a separate agreement days later with Ecuador for the performance of a topographical and cartographical analysis, which would enable Iran to extract "strategic minerals."

"The Iranians Were the Biggest Bluff"

The search for uranium could also be conceived as an attempt to develop a nuclear energy program in Venezuela and Bolivia. In 2010, Evo Morales announced during Ahmadinejad's visit that Iran was going to help Bolivia build a nuclear power plant in exchange for a share of the Andean country's uranium. Chávez, who was likely cannier, did not disclose anything publicly, but in November 2008 leading Iranian and Venezuelan officials inked a secret cooperation treaty "in the nuclear technology domain," as the minutes of the meeting stated. Chávez presented the agreement as a deal with Russia, which was less controversial for public opinion. Atomstroyexport, the Russian company that was building a reactor at Bushehr in Iran, would be in charge of the Venezuelan project. Nobody questioned the right of Venezuela or Bolivia to pursue a civilian nuclear energy program, but to do so in close cooperation with Iran was not authorized by the International Atomic Energy Agency.

The deals amounted to a tempest in a teapot, and they wound up going nowhere. The studies for the construction of a nuclear power plant were discontinued at a very preliminary phase. Chávez announced their suspension after an magnitude 9.0 earthquake and subsequent tsunami heavily damaged the Japanese Fukushima Daiichi nuclear power plant in March 2011 in the worst civilian nuclear disaster since Chernobyl. Iran was also not in a position to fulfill the agreements. Its inability to successfully set up in Venezuela the cement factory Cerro Azul, for example, prompted the dismissal of executives. The chain of Iranian subcontracted companies allowed the main contractor of the factory, Edhass Sanat, to place the blame for the failure with the Iranian companies it resorted to for certain operations.

"The Iranians were the biggest bluff," asserts a Venezuelan ministerial source who was assigned the thankless task of managing the Cerro Azul fiasco. "It was not only that the factory employed old equipment, but that for many projects we received technology from former Soviet republics." Here the Latin American habit of improvising and the renowned Middle Eastern practice of bargaining were combined. The resulting ineptitude burst the bubble of suspicions of any danger for the world. Chávez responded to criticism about the projects by resorting to humor. When Fanabi factory came under the spotlight, the Venezuelan president labeled the bicycles assembled there as "atomic," and that is how the Chavist media began to refer to them.

But the issue was not entirely a laughing matter. Foreign intelligence over time determined that no uranium was handled at Veniran Tractor, but also concluded that a strange mix of substances was taking place there. According to someone involved in his selection, an agent managed to secretly make his way into the factory with a small camera and a small container. He pretended that he had been instructed to carry out an inspection of the electrical service or the water pipes. The National Guard, which was in charge of surveillance at the compound, did not facilitate matters. But he finally convinced the uniformed men to allow him to discharge his supposed obligation. Once inside, the agent opened one of the sewers and got down to work. With a spatula, he poured into the container the black mash which had accumulated in the plughole. As the water flowed, different substances had settled in the drainage. The hidden camera he carried with him proved that he was following the steps of the entrusted task, without any possibility for deceit because the container was air-tight. When the material was analyzed in a laboratory outside of Venezuela, an immediate conclusion was reached: there was no trace of uranium, but it did contain the chemical elements necessary for the fabrication of explosives.

These substances could also be employed in the production of certain metal products, but the suspicion of an intent to manufacture explosives dovetailed with the seizure in Turkey at the end of 2008 of twenty-two containers that Iran sent to Venezuela. Transported on trucks to the Turkish port of Mersin, they were about to shipped to Veniran Tractor. The travel documents indicated that the containers were transporting "tractor parts." After opening the containers for inspection, barrels of nitrates and sulfates were found inside. These are chemical substances commonly used to manufacture explosives. There was as well "enough equipment to set up an explosives laboratory," as Turkish authorities would later disclose. The containers were not externally marked to signal the presence of dangerous materials despite the real cargo they were transporting. They were withheld for some time in Turkey before being returned to Iran.

This was not the only shipment of containers of a deceitful nature. Venirauto, a joint venture company for manufacturing cars established in 2006 by Iran and Venezuela in Maracay (Aragua state), also received bizarre shipments, as we shall later explain. It was another initiative whose real output fell well short of its initial projections. In the middle of 2012, the number of finished units was twelve thousand, only 15 percent of the envisioned total. It manufactured the Centauro model (the Iranian Samand) and then produced the Turpial (Saipa 141). The Venezuelan opposition chastised the government for striking the deals, and advised that they should have been negotiated with countries with higher levels of technological development and more reliability in the stages of execution, such as France, Germany, or the United States. Western countries may not have been the appropriate partners for the development of an home-grown industry, with a *creole* stamp, as the Venirauto advertisement trumpeted. But the deal with Iran was just as *colonialist*: the models to be assembled in Venezuela were spin-offs of the ones manufactured by the Iranian companies Khodro and Saipa, which in turn were based on antiquated versions of the KIA and Peugeot models; in addition, 97 percent of the parts came from the Islamic republic. Moreover, problems with the assembly line translated into long waiting periods for buyers. Chavismo's ideological stubbornness was again harming the lower class in Venezuela, while the Iranians managed to repatriate their profits. And cooperation in the civilian domain was not the only one that flopped.

Creole Drones

Chávez had big ambitions. "We are going to turn Venezuela into an industrial powerhouse." It was June 2012, and the president had just unveiled the Arpía, an unmanned aerial vehicle (UAV) purchased from Iran, to television cameras. The Bolivarian leader dreamt of producing UAVs in order to export them to neighboring countries. It had been two days since I had written an article which for the first time published pictures of one of the Arpías (the Iranian Mojaher-2) owned by the Venezuelan armed forces. The *comandante* was thus forced to show it off in public to the Venezuelans, and to Washington. "Now, let the United States say that they have to monitor Venezuela. Don't waste your time. They may soon claim that the airplanes carry a nuclear warhead in their nose cone," he suggested with scorn, underlining the fact that they were designed for aerial surveillance and were not capable of launching any attack.

The U.S. State Department nonetheless remained vigilant. "We will track ongoing developments in Venezuela," State Department Spokeswoman Victoria Nuland admonished in a press conference. The United States expressed its "concern" about the possible violation by Venezuela of any of the sanctions imposed by the international community on Iran. The issue at hand was not whether Venezuela acquired drones—which many countries already boasted in their arsenals—or developed its military industry, but whether it did so in partnership with Iran, thus eluding the international embargo applied on the Islamic republic because of its alleged pursuit of nuclear weapons. But Chávez glossed over the nuance, which was no trivial matter, and indulged in patriotic tirades: "The international media reported that an investigation is being conducted in New York because there is a gunpowder factory in Venezuela. Of course we are building one, as well as one to manufacture drones. We would not have these factories if we were a colony. But we are a free and independent country. This country is ruled by the Venezuelan people and not by lackeys, dummies, or little Yankees."

By the time Chávez uttered these words, the factory to build unmanned aerial vehicles *made* in Venezuela was already a doomed idea. The five-year plan for the Venezuelan armed forces for 2011-2015, named Victory Mission, foresaw that in the second half of 2011 thirty drones would be built. But instead of working at full capacity, the premises were employed as a warehouse for household appliances assembled for the social program My Well-Equipped Home. In fact, when Chávez made his television appearance from the Ministry of Defense and connected live with several military facilities, the Arpía was showcased not in the supposed factory, but rather in a contiguous factory of Russian AK-103 rifles. This was proof that, despite the propaganda, the project was in trouble. Of the dozen drones that arrived from Iran, several were rendered inoperative after they crashed on their first test flights in Venezuela. This was a further source of disappointment in the relationship with the Iranian friend.

The strong ties between the Venezuelan Military Industries Company (CAVIM) and several Iranian weapons companies targeted by the international sanctions were investigated by the Manhattan District Attorney's Office, which claims universal jurisdiction to investigate and prosecute any illegal transaction carried out in dollars. With these operations, Iran obtained hard currency, opened up financial flows for its banking system, and obtained some military spare parts. Venezuela thus acquired some technologies and dabbled in certain military programs, stirring unease among U.S. officials.

The United States followed the trail as closely as it could. A telegram in March 2009 from the State Department to the U.S. Embassy in Ankara, which was shared with the U.S. Embassy in Caracas, alerted to the imminent shipment from Iran to Venezuela of Unmanned Aerial Vehicle technology. "The United States believes that this cargo is made up of armaments and materials that Iran is banned from transferring in accordance with U.N. Security Council resolution 1747," read the statement which was later revealed by Wikileaks. The cable also pointed out that the materials had been produced by Quds Aeronautics Industries, an Iranian company subject to sanctions. Washington alerted the U.S. Embassy in Ankara because there was proof that prior shipments from Iran to Venezuela had transited through Turkey. It was the case already mentioned about the seizure of the containers in the port of Mersin in late 2008 that transported materials usually employed to produce explosives had highlighted.

The investigations turned up irregularities regarding the aforementioned UAV factory, located within the confines of CAVIM's main site in Maracay (Aragua state). Working in collaboration with Russia, Belarus, and Iran, Venezuela developed installations on a mountainside which was separated by a highway from an adjoining Venezuelan Air Force Base. From two large hangars, Chávez planned to export the *creole* drones. As the preparations for the flights were finalized, Venezuelan officials became acquainted with Iranian technology. In November 2011, the Air Force displayed one of the first drones purchased from Iran, a small model named ANT-1X, and indicated that it also had bought another unspecified model. It was actually the Arpía, the Venezuelan denomination for the Iranian Mojaher, which Tehran also sold to Hezbollah.

The Arpía did not pose a direct threat to the United States. This drone, which was 9.5 feet long and twelve feet wide, could not reach the Florida coastline from Venezuela because its operational range was sixty-two miles. It flew at a speed of 124 miles per hour and an altitude of eleven thousand feet, and had a resistance of ninety minutes. The Arpía (the Iranian Mohajer-2) was designed for surveillance, although it might also be able to direct laser-guided munitions to their target.

A way to evade the United States' surveillance on this program to transfer technology, known internally as Project M2 (Mohajer 2), was the suspicious air link between Caracas and Tehran, with a layover in Damascus, serviced by Iran Air and Conviasa, the Venezuelan flagship carrier. One of the invoices examined by the Manhattan District Attorney's Office referred to a delivery made to CAVIM on a Conviasa flight by the company Kimia Sanaat, which was involved in the development of UAVs and included in the United Nations' black list for its alleged link to weapons of mass destruction programs. The company was a division of the conglomerate Aviation Industries Organization (AIO) of the Iranian armed forces. AIO and CAVIM were jointly undertaking Project M2.

Confidential financial documents hinted at the program's possible secret aims. The construction of what amounted to a drone factory (two hangars and a surveillance building) was reserved for AIO, which subcontracted the execution—under Iranian foremen—to a local company that Venezuelan military officers often hired as a contractor. The construction was finished in 2010 and the local contractor received $2.4 million, which were transferred to its account in a branch of Banco Santander in Valparaíso (Chile). Santander authorized the transaction despite the fact that it had been notified about the identity of the remittent (subject to European Union sanctions) and the project's military nature. The low cost of the installations and the drones stood in contrast to the $28 million which CAVIM paid to AIO in a transfer executed via Commerzbank in Frankfurt. The payment was in dollars that later were exchanged into euros, in an operation designed to circumvent banking supervisors. Of the total amount, more than half was earmarked to cover generic expenses such as "technical assistance" and "technical documents."

Ramin Keshavarz, an engineer in Iran's Revolutionary Guard, was in charge of the project. He had previously worked in the Iranian missile program. While Kashavarz oversaw the construction of the buildings related to the drone production, he forced the Venezuelan contractor to turn over construction material to build other adjacent installations which only Iranian personnel could access. U.S. intelligence and security agencies focused on this secretive operation. They did not reach the conclusion they expected.

Missiles on the Shopping List

The United States paid special attention to CAVIM's fields in Maracay. Satellite photographs showed strange excavations in the installation's annex, located on the mountainside beside a highway. This was next to the drone factory where the Iranians had been working secretly, and which was off limits to Venezuelan technicians. The pictures appeared to show the entrance of a tunnel that connected that area with the interior of the mountain. Suspicions were also raised by the route for a rail line that was being built parallel to a highway. At the location of the CAVIM factory, the rail line no longer ran parallel to the highway but took a detour to cross the interior of the mountain.

How could one not surmise that the tunnel, abnormally detoured from its otherwise route parallel to the highway, was connected inside the mountain to the tunnel supposedly located nearby and linked to Iranian activity? If Venezuela harbored Iranian missiles, or was planning to do so, these underground galleries with rail infrastructure and adjoining a military base would be very suitable. U.S. intelligence spent months trying to crack this enigma.

Another element that raised eyebrows was that the satellite pictures revealed the presence of up to seventy large containers in a nearby field. A transportation document related to one of the containers indicated a weight of eleven tons. It had been sent to Venirauto, the Venezuelan-Iranian car joint venture, which coincidentally was located in an industrial park adjacent to the military compound at Maracay. The *modus operandi* between both countries called for the creation of bogus civilian companies with misleading official missions. Informants on the ground assured that they had seen large structures which could be missiles, but no corroboration for these accounts was ever found.

For some time, a hypothetical installation for medium or even long-range missiles in Venezuela was monitored by Western intelligence agencies. In May 2011, the German newspaper *Die Welt*, drawing on German intelligence sources, raised the possibility that such a project was being carried out in the Paraguaná Peninsula. A visit to the site by Iranian Revolutionary Guard engineers in prior months had generated speculation. From the Paraguaná salient, Venezuela's northernmost point, the missiles could not reach Florida, but could threaten traffic through the Panama canal.

Nobody believed that Chávez was foolish enough to challenge Washington in such a direct fashion, based on an mistaken risk assessment. In an environment of confrontation between Iran and the United States, however, it was not absurd to speculate that the Iranians might have considered—as a theoretical exercise—a repeat of the 1962 missile crisis, when the Soviet Union and the United States came to the brink of war after Moscow deployed nuclear missiles on Cuban soil. What if Iran, in another cold war, was again using the Caribbean platform to deter the United States from any possible military attack that infringed on its sovereignty? This was consistent with a public warning issued in March 2012 by Masud Jazayeri, a general in the Revolutionary Guards and deputy chairman of the Iranian joint chiefs of staff. Jazayeri assured that any U.S. attack on its territory would unleash reprisals, and not only in the Middle East. "No part of the United States would be secure," he warned.

Fortunately, the world was not dragged into another dangerous missiles crisis. Venezuela did discuss with Iran the feasibility of developing a medium-range missile system, as Rafael Isea confirmed. As Finance minister and close advisor to Chávez during the period when the bond between the Venezuelan president and Ahmadinejad deepened, Isea was privy to the discussions about the missiles. But he assures that they never yielded a credible negotiation process.

What the Venezuelan government was developing in the Paraguaná Peninsula, in the municipality of Los Taques (Falcón state), was a base designed to host the Russian-built surface-to-air S-125 Pechora missile system. Venezuela had purchased eleven units of the S-125 in 2011 and received twelve more in 2014. These missiles have a shorter range as they possess a defensive nature, and therefore pose no military challenge.

In all likelihood, there was another reason for the presence of the Iranian engineers detected on the Paraguaná Peninsula. Iran had several docks there—seized by Chávez from their owners—which it could freely employ, allowing it to smuggle containers into Venezuela without having to clear customs. Although there is also the possibility that, to lay the groundwork for a project that never materialized, Iranian agents inspected the area assigned to host the missile base or had planned to build storage silos in Maracay.

In order to *reach* the Florida coastline, Iran did not need missiles. Ramin Keshavarz, the Iranian in charge of the drone factory at the CAVIM-Maracay facilities, ordered goods from a supply warehouse in the Miami area, as invoices that I examined revealed. The items ordered did not include anything suspicious, but the FBI would have broken up the purchase if it had known that Keshavarz's name was on the invoice. The Tehran-Caracas connection may not have directly threatened the Florida coastline, but the *enemy* had the nerve to brazenly purchase from U.S. warehouses the equipment it needed.

Of F-16 and Other Spare Parts

The military cooperation encompassed more chapters, such as the delivery to the Islamic republic of an F-16 fighter plane in 2006 that was colorfully described by a high-ranking Venezuelan military officer who had knowledge of the operation. The following paragraph draws on his account.

"Boys, this is a very important mission. You cannot let us down. The country is counting on you. Do not disappoint me,"

Major General Roger Cordero Lara admonished the pilots of the Boeing 707-6949, without providing more details. The freight being transported was presumably a disassembled F-16 bound for Tehran. Before taking off, the Air Force general boarded the plane and motivated the crew that would be commanding the cargo-tanker on a long flight. The pilots would later recount to their colleagues their conviction—based on certain details—that they were transporting an F-16, although they were not able to see the inside of the sealed containers that were not marked and which had been entrusted to them. They were ordered to fly a special route, with layovers in Brazil and Algeria. "Nobody in the crew knew the content of the cargo. As soon as they landed in Tehran, the airplane was seized by Iranian agents and military officers. The Venezuelan crew was escorted off the plane and driven to a hotel, where they remained under watch until the next day. They never saw the unloading of the cargo. They were driven to the airport the next day, where their plane had been readied for the return flight."

Why would the Iranians want an F-16 if the U.S.-built fighter was not in its military fleet and since they would be without spare parts? The answer proffered by sources close to the Mossad is that Iran possibly wanted to use the F-16 to fine-tune its radars and acquaint itself with the features of the fighter to prepare for a hypothetical attack by Israel or the United States. Analysts believed that, in case an attack was launched against Iran's nuclear facilities, the brunt would be borne by fleets of Israeli F-15s because the McDonnell Douglas (now Boeing) built F-15 Eagle has a longer range. But the F-15s could also be supported by a wave of F-16s, especially if they could take off from a base in a country bordering Iran, such as Azerbaijan or Turkey. The United States also had F-16 squadrons based in the Persian Gulf.

Venezuela purchased F-16s from the United States before Hugo Chávez's rise to power. Of the twenty-four units bought in 1983, three were rendered inoperative because of accidents. Analysts estimated that, after two decades, less than a dozen F-16s were in service in Venezuela. Chávez replaced them with a fleet of twenty-four Russian-built Sukhoi fighters. Chávez signaled his willingness to sell some of the F-16s to third countries, including Iran, without the United States' authorization, which violated the clauses of the 1983 sale. No such transaction was officially carried out. But Caracas and Tehran negotiated a technological transfer agreement. In addition to the alleged shipment of one F-16 in the aforementioned account from 2006, three years later both countries expanded the deal to include more F-16 aircrafts. A confidential document dated in Tehran in August 2009 indicated that "the Venezuelan side commits itself to speeding up the feasibility studies submitted by AIO regarding the F-16s." The minute of the meeting was signed by the then president of CAVIM, General Eduardo Richani, and the deputy minister for logistics at the Iranian Defense Ministry, General Mohammad Beig Mohammad Lu.

At that meeting in Tehran both officials reviewed the implementation status of the agreements already signed, which indicated that an intense cooperation in military matters was ongoing. For example, the Iranians had almost finished the inspection and upgrades of fourteen J-85 engines, used in the Venezuelan F-5s, that had been shipped to Tehran. The project to build a gunpowder factory and a detonator factory in Venezuela with Iranian expertise and materials was also examined, as well as progress with regard to the unmanned aerial vehicles (UAVs) systems. Iran's Defense Industry Organization (DIO) also submitted proposals "for the construction of 60-millimeter mortars and munitions, RPG-7 rocket launchers, and complete the fulminant lines."

As with all confidential documents I analyzed, the most sensitive issues had been omitted. This was done not only because the cooperation could encompass dual-use technology, which was best left unnamed, but also because there was an intent to keep matters secret. The confidential document implicitly acknowledged that international rules were being violated: "To facilitate the transportation of equipment to Venezuela, DIO requests that the acronyms DIO and

CAVIM be modified or replaced by others. The required documents shall be prepared accordingly."

Iran was obviously interested in using Venezuela as a source to procure spare parts for those weapons purchased from the United States before the 1979 Islamic revolution. The collaboration between Chávez and Ahmadinejad envisioned "T-56 engines and 707 airplanes," probably a reference to spare parts for Iranian aircrafts such as the Hercules C-130 and the Boeing 707. Moreover, it is possible to singled out Karim Lezama, a retired Venezuelan lieutenant colonel, as a key player involved in the purchase of spare parts for both countries.

In one of his trips to the United States to deal with weapons traffickers, in 2009, Lezama "revealed that he was working alongside Major General Angel Colina, who was in charge of Venezuela's Aerial Defense Command. Colina wanted to bypass the Spanish company Geci-Levante, a well-known supplier to Venezuela and to Muslim countries," according to an informant. "The company is on very good terms with the Iranian Embassy in Caracas due to a contact, *Puria*, who officially works as a translator but who really is in charge of acquisitions for the Iranian government. In that meeting, Lezama also disclosed that he was in charge of procuring logistical supplies (spare parts and weapons) for the F-14 Tomcats operated by Iran, and a very specific list of tools to be employed in the UAV project undertaken by Venezuela and Iran." The informant certified that in the ensuing years Lezama, as well as General Colina and the retired General Luis Reyes Reyes, who served in the cabinet-rank position of President's Office minister, were in close contact with *Puria*, the Iranian Embassy contact in Caracas in charge of illegally acquiring military material.

The embassy also oversaw other operations. In Morón (Carabobo state), where CAVIM has another facility and where the Venezuelan Petrochemical Corporation (PEQUIVEN) is also located, the Iranians started up a gunpowder factory as well as one for explosives. They also took the lead in a project to revive a nitroglycerine plant and another to upgrade a nitrocellulose factory. The company involved in all of these initiatives was Parchin Chemical Industries, which had been sanctioned by the U.N. Security Council for exporting chemical products for possible use in ballistic missiles. Due to these and other ties, the United States applied sanctions on CAVIM on several occasions. In 2008, the U.S. State Department, pursuant to the Iran, North Korea, and Syria Nonproliferation Act, imposed sanctions on CA-VIM for allegedly violating a ban on transferring to or cooperating with Iran on technology that could assist in the development of weapons systems. The sanctions, which prohibit any U.S. procurement or collaboration with CAVIM, have been extended twice since 2010 for two-year periods. With so many international limitations on trade flows and financial transactions, how could Venezuela and Iran continue to do business with one another?

Eluding Banking Supervision

When Tahmasb Mazaheri, former Iranian minister of Economy and Finance (2001-2004) and president of the Iranian Central Bank (2007-2008), was detained in Germany in January 2013 some points became clear. He carrying a check for 300 million bolivars, which amounted to $70 million. As the press described the incident, Mazaheri was arrested at Düsseldorf airport after landing on a flight from Turkey which had originated in Iran. When he tried to clear German customs, Mazaheri declared that he was carrying less than €10,000. When German customs officials searched his luggage, they found the check for the extraordinary amount. Mazaheri was unable to provide a convincing explanation regarding the source of the check. The explanation the Iranian Embassy in Caracas later proffered was that, as a consultant to the Iranian company Kayson, which was in charge of building twenty thousand housing units for the Great Bolivarian Housing Mission of Venezuela, Mazaheri was taking the money to the Bolivarian republic for the payment of its employees' salaries. The check was apparently signed by Kayson of Venezuela and was written out to the same company. There were compelling indications that the German police had searched

Mazaheri after being tipped off by another country's authorities. The evidence was probably not as strong as law-enforcement expected, for Mazaheri was released. But the episode hinted at the business and financial network that kept Iran afloat during the years of international sanctions.

A more compelling piece of evidence is the cooperation provided by some Venezuelan banks to abet Iranian capital flows. Mazaheri's check was for money deposited in the Bank of Venezuela, an institution that was renationalized in 2009. This indicated that Iranian interests had spilled over to the Venezuelan banking system, probably due to the fact that the International Development Bank (IDB) had been subjected to international sanctions. The IDB was a state-owned Iranian bank and had its headquarters in Caracas. It was the main executing arm of operations between Venezuela and Iran.

The *contamination* of other banks was also uncovered in a letter from April 2011 written by Iranian Ambassador Abdolreza Mesri to Nicolás Maduro, who then was Foreign Affairs minister. The letter was part of a bundle of undisclosed documents, in this case linked to the Iranian IDB, which I was able to examine. Under the usual heading "in the name of Allah," the ambassador referred to a deposit the IDB had in the Federal Bank. This Venezuelan institution had been nationalized and Mesri requested the chavista government's help to obtain the reimbursement, with interest, of the account's 22.5 million bolivars.

"This letter is important because it proves that the IDB had funds in other banks. Given the international sanctions against the IDB, it would have to carry out its transactions through other banks," as Adam Kaufmann points out. He headed the investigative unit of the Manhattan District Attorney's Office until 2012. Kaufmann knew the score, as he had extracted big fines from banks such as Lloyds, Credit Suisse, Barclays, and HSBC for covering up transfers in dollars to Iran from other countries. Kaufmann had worked for Robert Morgenthau, who shortly before retiring in 2009 as head of the Manhattan District Attorney's Office publicly alerted the Washington political establishment that the Iranian IDB allowed Iran "to exploit the Venezuelan banking system" and provided it with the means to bust the sanctions regime.

The name International Development Bank can be misleading as its acronym is the same as that of the Inter-American Development Bank. The latter was founded in 1959 and has been the leading multilateral bank in terms of fostering development and reducing poverty in Latin America and the Caribbean. It is headquartered in Washington.

The creation of the Iranian IDB was agreed upon in September 2007 by Chávez and Ahmadinejad, and it started operating in Caracas in January 2008. Its president was precisely Tahmasb Mazaheri, the carrier of the check detained in Düsseldorf. He was sent to Venezuela to preside over the IDB after stepping down from the presidency of the Iranian Central Bank, a fact that underscored the high expectations that Tehran held out for the IDB. The Iranian IDB had already been on the United States' and European Union's blacklists for some time, as was its holding company, the bank Toseyeh Saderat Iran, also known as the Export Development Bank of Iran (EDBI), which the U.S Treasury had designated as a proliferator for providing finance to the Iranian Ministry of Defense and the Iranian Armed Forces Logistics.

The U.S. Treasury also imposed sanctions against the Iranian-Venezuelan Bi-National Bank (IVBB) for acting as a financial representative of EDBI, in whose name it processed funds. When Chávez inaugurated the Bi-National in Tehran in 2009, he heralded it as "part of a strategy to develop a new financial architecture between us, independent of the international financial system."

As IDB's own managers admitted in confidential letters to the Venezuelan Ministry of Finance, the entity's mission was to finance trade flows between Venezuela and Iran, included trade based on defense agreements. Additionally it was supposed to "overcome the limitations on currency operations" and also "some of Iran's international problems, linked to the current economic sanctions." Among the confidential documents were directives from the IDB to transfer funds from Venezuela to Iran, eluding the international supervision.

Hence, the dollar remittances from a Venezuelan bank had to be converted into euros using the European-Iranian Trade Bank, headquartered in Hamburg. This institution would later also come under the European Union's sanctions regime. "There is no need to mention the beneficiary in Iran in your message to the correspondent bank," the directive recommended in order to ensure secrecy. The possibilities for these operations grew exponentially when in June 2012 Chávez authorized the opening of accounts in dollars in Venezuelan banks. Previous cables between the IDB and the Ministry of Finance highlighted Iran's unease about the slow pace of resorting to the National Center for Foreign Commerce of Venezuela to obtain authorization for the transactions.

Diesel for Assad and Rouhani's Arrival

The civil war in Syria offered new opportunities for cooperation between Venezuela and Iran. From the beginning Iran was keen on propping up Bashar al-Assad as president of Syria in the face of the moderate and jihadist forces fighting his regime because of his traditional alliance with Tehran and sponsorship of Shia groups such as Hezbollah. Moreover, the survival of the authoritarian Syrian regime became a casus belli for the hybrid regimes in their struggle against traditional democracy. Venezuela sided with its partners: Russia stepped up its involvement in the war to support the Syrian regime, and China was not hindering Damascus' actions.

Between 2011 and 2012, as international news agencies reported, Venezuela sent several shipments of diesel fuel to Syria in defiance of the sanctions applied by the United States and the European Union against several Syrian oil companies, such as state-owned Sytrol. Among other goals, the sanctions sought to prevent the supply of diesel to Syria, as it could fuel its army's tanks and thus bolster Bashar al-Assad's military power. "As many shipments as necessary shall be sent. We are strong friends and cooperate intensely with Syria," countered PDVSA President Rafael Ramírez against those who objected to the deals. On the return trip to Venezuela, some tankers transported naphtha, a refined petroleum product that can be used to obtain gasoline.

Naphtha was not the only product that was shipped from Syrian ports. Tankers presumably belonging to the fleet of Venezuelan businessman Wilmer Ruperti transported Iranian oil, subject to international sanctions, to refineries in India. Sources with inside knowledge of the operation assured me that Iranian oil was being mixed with Venezuelan to increase its density in order to be sold as produced in Venezuela. This would explain the strange appearance in PDVSA's accounts of growing sales to India. Given its remoteness from the Caribbean, it makes no sense for India to purchase Venezuela's oil. This scheme created an outlet for Iranian oil, subjected to international sanctions, into some markets. Most of Iran's traditional clients had been forced to cut their purchases as they joined the international effort to halt Iran's nuclear power program with the imposition of sanctions. Venezuela tried to dodge the embargo often. In 2011, the United States slapped PDVSA with sanctions because of its supplies to the National Iranian Oil Company. Washington had tracked down two deliveries worth $50 million of an additive used in gasoline.

The oil cooperation, however, did not flourish as Chávez and Ahmadinejad had expected. In a 2006 meeting they announced the creation of a large oil corporation which would foster collaboration between their respective state-owned giants. The new joint venture was named VENIROGC, a name derived from Venezuelan-Iranian Oil & Gas Co. It sought to become "another" Chevron, Shell or Eni, as one of its Iranian executives asserted the following day in a press conference. It was to be a global firm, with operations in several countries, and involved in all stages of the business, from drilling to gas stations. The officials speculated about locating the headquarters in Spain, but the company never got off the ground. In 2011, in its purported office in Madrid, only the company name appeared on the outside of the locked front door, behind which all was still.

It is possible that, at the outset, VENIROGC might have been conceived as a front company to justify movements of capital. Its very name suggests it had not been envisioned as a commercial brand to be used in all over the world. In any case, it was another of many projects launched by Chávez and Ahmadinejad which languished. If this happened while the relationship was at its peak, what could one expect after Chávez and Ahmadinejad's departure? The Iranian president left office in August 2013, five months after the burial of his Venezuelan counterpart. Nicolás Maduro had to focus on internal matters to build up his power. Hassan Rouhani, the new Iranian president, embarked on a conciliatory course towards the West to attain a normalization of Iran's international status. Given these developments, the Iran-Venezuela relationship began to fizzle.

According to Douglas Farah, a specialist on Shiite activity in Latin America, Chávez's disengagement as a result of his illness led to Iran strengthening its ties to other countries in the region it was already dealing with, thereby diminishing Venezuela's standing as Tehran's paramount partner. Faced with the Venezuelan president's terminal cancer, the Iranians tried to make their contacts more institutional so that commitments would be honored, regardless of Chávez's fate. They also stepped up their interactions with other ALBA countries without Venezuela's mediation. In Farah's words, "the Iranians realized that Venezuela was beginning to stagger and started to diversify their interests." The new chavista leadership was not about to cut the ties with Tehran, but it didn't have the same room to maneuver as Chávez had in order to forge ambitious alliances with countries like Iran. Under this realignment Ecuador took on a bigger role as a base for banking operations, distribution of fake passports, and meddling by Iranian intelligence, according to the expert's research.

It was foreseeable that Tehran would keep its relations with its Latin American partners, and that it would do so without Ahmadinejad's confrontational approach as Iran reengaged with the United States. Even in the thaw regarding the Iranian nuclear program, following the lifting of sanctions, the Persians would maintain their foothold in this new sphere of influence. Latin America was certainly not the most important region for Tehran from a geopolitical standpoint, but it played a role in the globalization of its strategy. As long as someone opens the door to Iran in Latin America, why would it not seek to make inroads in the United States' backyard?

9

SCHIZOPHRENIA WITH THE EMPIRE

The Cost of Insulting and Lobbying in the U.S.

J oseph P. Kennedy II is familiar with Venezuelan funeral
marches. The eldest son of Robert F. Kennedy was present at
Hugo Chávez's funeral rites, just as he had attended the funeral of former President Rómulo Betancourt in 1981. These two commitments were born of gratitude. In 1980, Joe Kennedy launched his initiative Citizens Energy, which sought to supply home heating oil to low-income families in Boston. To this effect he signed an agreement to purchase Venezuelan oil at market prices. When Hugo Chávez became president he realized the potential of having an ally such as Joe Kennedy at the heart of the *Empire*, and he began to massively subsidize the oil earmarked for Citizens Energy.

But honoring Betancourt, the founder of Venezuela's democracy, was not akin to becoming the main stalwart in the United States of someone who was violating some of his countrymen's main civil rights. Joe's partnership with Chávez's Venezuela increasingly isolated John F. Kennedy's nephew and wound up sowing discord within his own family. Defending Chávez north of the Caribbean was politically toxic, but the *comandante* always found those who cheered him on. This was a role that was played especially by Citgo, the brand of Petróleos de Venezuela (PDVSA) in the United States.

For a long time few in the United States were cognizant of the fact that Citgo, which owned the second biggest network of gas stations in the country, had been purchased by PDVSA. The Venezuelan oil company bought 50 percent of Citgo's shares in 1986 and the remainder four years later. Most Americans continue to perceive Citgo as a U.S. brand and view its gas stations as part of the national landscape. On September 11, 2001, and the days that followed that day's heinous terrorist attacks, journalists and military officers queued up at Citgo's gas station at the entrance to the Pentagon. They drove there to buy groceries as the wreckage of the plane flown into the Pentagon still smoldered. For decades, a big neon Citgo sign has stood in Boston near Fenway Park, the Red Sox's stadium. It appears in all of the televised sports broadcasts and is part of the city's skyline by day and night. The Citgo orange and red symbol is almost a local emblem. "See It Go," locals paraphrase as they cheer on the runs scored by the Red Sox.

Maintaining Citgo's U.S. presence was one of PDVSA's priorities when it bought the company. In the context of an internationalization process undertaken by PDVSA at the beginning of the 1980s, a cornerstone of the company's policy had been to create joint ventures in the refining business with local companies. This was the case with acquisitions in Germany and Sweden, as well as two others in the United States. Negotiations were first conducted to buy half of the stock in Champlin Refining, owned by Union Pacific, and then in Citgo Petroleum, owned by Southland Corporation, which also operates the well-known 7-Eleven convenience stores across the United States. Both partners then sold their respective halves and PDVSA executed its preferred purchase option, although winding up with the totality of the shares was not what it had originally intended. In 1990 PDVSA merged both companies under the brand name Citgo.

"That is how you end up riding a monster company that has the third or fourth refinancing system in the United States, with a 12 percent share of the market in refined products and the second biggest network of gas stations operated as franchises," according to Pedro Mario Burelli, who at the time was employed at JP Morgan and who was involved in providing consultancy services to the operations. Burelli had previously been an executive at PDVSA and he returned to the state-owned oil company at a later stage as member of its board. Chavismo's consolidation prompted Burelli to leave Venezuela and settle in Washington, as an analyst and consultant.

One of the main strategic advantages of joint ventures is that the foreign company teams up with a local partner who is in charge of dealing with the country's government and thus maintains the perception that operations are being run nationally. When PDVSA took a 100 percent stake in Citgo, "it went to great lengths to hide Venezuela's involvement, as it did not benefit us." "Indeed," Burelli proceeds, "the more American the company appeared in consumers' eyes, the better. We wanted Citgo to be perceived as a U.S. corporation headquartered in Tulsa, Oklahoma, in order not to be the target of a public campaign rejecting products not made in America."

Chávez's Gas Stations

Venezuela's ownership of Citgo raised concerns. No country with which Washington has been at loggerheads with has owned such a strategically important business in the United States. Due to legal limitations for new refineries, on environmental grounds, the country's capacity to refine oil is limited. A company such as PDVSA controlling 12 percent of oil refining in the United States is therefore a very important player. What would happen if, as a result of an escalation in the confrontation between the two countries, Venezuela decided not to deliver more fuel to its subsidiary Citgo? Would the supply to U.S. gas stations with the triangle logo be halted? Would the U.S. government in such a scenario force Citgo to cut off its ties to PDVSA and make it refine oil from another supplier in order to meet national demand? These were the questions on everyone's minds.

The irony regarding the case, Burelli asserts, is that after purchasing all of Citgo's shares, PDVSA believed it could compensate for the lack of a U.S. partner, which shielded it from Washington's scrutiny, by hiring attorneys that disguised Citgo within a structure of holding companies that distanced it from Venezuela. This made it possible to keep the holding company beyond the grasp of the United States' Internal Revenue Service and claim the company's private-sector status if Venezuela's public ownership in such a strategic sector were questioned. "Nobody could have foreseen that PDVSA would fall into the hands of a group of unhinged characters who chose to engage U.S. authorities in a confrontational way," Burelli regrets.

In fact, PDVSA's investments in the U.S. were affected by Chavismo's sharp tongue. Hugo Chávez was in the mood to change the strategic gears at Citgo after years of having the company maintain a low profile. Chávez ranted that Citgo was not just Venezuelan but also Bolivarian. The new strategy's effects were soon on display: almost half of the franchises sought a new partner after their contracts expired. The number of Citgo gas stations dropped from almost sixteen thousand to six thousand.

"The gas at the pump is NOT from Citgo," read the signs placed in 2006 at the gas pumps located at 7-Eleven. The signs were in response to Chávez's outburst a few days earlier before the United Nation's General Assembly. On September 20, the Venezuelan president had uttered one of his most infamous sentences from the U.N.'s podium. "The devil was here yesterday," he snapped in reference to President George W. Bush, who had addressed the delegates the day before from the same place. The memorable episode and Chávez's "sulfur smell" remark had immediate consequences. A week later, 7-Eleven announced it would not renew its contract with Citgo after a partnership that had lasted twenty years. "Leaving politics aside, we sympathize with the worry expressed by many U.S. citizens regarding the disparaging statements about our country and its leadership recently voiced by the president of Venezuela. Mr. Chávez's stance and assertions during the past year do not encourage a continuation of the partnership with Citgo," read the 7-Eleven press statement.

Chávez's diatribes in the preceding year had been particularly abrasive. "You are a jackass, Mr. Danger. Coward, assassin, genocidal. You are a drunkard. Immoral, sick. You are killing children who are not at fault for your complexes, man," he had lashed out at Bush from Venezuelan television in the context of the Iraq war. Chávez also lambasted Bush after the disaster unleashed by hurricane Katrina at the end of August 2005. "That man, the king of vacations, said nothing at his ranch, only that people should flee, and that cowboy did not explain how. Many ran into the hurricane's path," Chávez chastised. "The world's superpower, so involved in Iraq, leaves its own people to fend for themselves."

Chávez had won his first election in 1998 expressing distrust towards PDVSA, wariness towards multinationals operating in Venezuela's oil sector, and opposition to the internationalization of the public holding company. He rejected owning refineries abroad, because instead of generating jobs in other countries they should be created in greater numbers in Venezuela. "Why are we giving the *gringos* our jobs?" he asked PDVSA's managers at the time. They explained to him that it was profitable to refine close to the markets where PDVSA was operating, and that the refineries themselves do not employ a lot of people. But Chávez paid more attention to those advisors who opposed the oil company's internationalization and preached an ideology of oil sovereignty. Bernard Mommer was among the latter group. He was a European with Venezuelan citizenship who was Chávez's main advisor on fossil fuels during a certain time period.

Chávez finally decided to *nationalize* Citgo instead of selling it. Citgo was presented as an embodiment of Bolivarian ideals, even on U.S. television commercials. The highest-ranking executive positions, which had previously been reserved for U.S. professionals, were filled by Venezuelans, among them an active duty general who was appointed CEO. This appointment generated a situation whereby a high-ranking military officer from a country at odds with the United States was placed at the helm of a foreign company that was influential in the strategic energy sector.

Chávez had already blasted the United States during his run for the presidency and continued to do so from the Miraflores Palace after being sworn into office in February 1999. The invasion of Afghanistan in 2001 and Washington's undisguised glee over Chávez's short-lived overthrow in 2002 ratcheted up the tension between the two governments. But the opportunity to use Citgo as a political tool in the United States came in 2005 after the havoc wreaked by hurricane Katrina. George W. Bush was taking a beating among public opinion over his clumsy reaction to the emergency situation caused by the catastrophe. This enabled Chávez to portray himself as the savior of the victims. He offered to send to New Orleans thousands of soldiers, firemen, and volunteers, and he promised $5 million in aid and fuel from Citgo's plant in Louisiana. U.S. authorities deemed the human resources unnecessary, and Chávez barely made good on his financial commitment. But he nevertheless had managed to find a way to publicly humiliate the White House.

From 2005 until the Bolivarian leader's funeral in March 2013, Citgo invested more than $400 million in energy assistance in some of the more vulnerable regions of the United States. In 2012, the last full year of Chávez's presidency, Citgo's accounts showed that the Texas-based corporation (it moved its headquarters there from Oklahoma) donated $60 million worth of heating fuel. From 2005 until 2014 Citgo's largesse funded the donation of 235 million gallons of heating oil to 1.8 million people (individuals or families living below the poverty line and native Americans). Some of this assistance was funneled through Joe Kennedy's Citizens Energy.

Joe Kennedy stated the foundational idea in 1979 in the inauguration of John F. Kennedy—his uncle—presidential library. He had just turned twenty-seven. In the midst of the oil shock of the 1970s, Joe dreamt up the idea of creating a company that would purchase oil from OPEC members and could provide heating fuel at a significant lower price for low-income families from Boston. Joe's idea was a rebuke to the abuse of generating capital gains during the process that started with crude flowing from a well to the delivery of gas at a pump or heating from a furnace.

Joe's youthful enthusiasm was stymied almost everywhere. The Venezuelans were the only ones who were willing to lend a sympathetic ear, and they did so because of his last name. Given his nephew's inability to implement the project, Ted Kennedy got involved. The man who would go on to be known as the Lion of the Senate remembered that Pedro Mario Burelli had been an intern in his office when his father was serving as Venezuela's ambassador in Washington (Miguel Angel Burelli later served as the last Venezuelan Foreign Affairs minister before Chavismo). Senator Kennedy, the family's patriarch asked the young Burelli, who was twenty-one at the time, to lend a hand in order to arrange meetings for his nephew in Caracas.

The Young Kennedy's Odd Urgencies

Pedro Mario Burelli recalls two specific highlights of Joe Kennedy's trip to Caracas, the first of which seemed to pave the way for an agreement, and a second that appeared to squash any hope. In the first meeting Energy Minister Humberto Calderón Berti remarked to Burelli while Joe was in the men's room: "Look, Pedro, Kennedy is not requesting anything out of the ordinary. He wants us to sell him five thousand barrels of oil at the official price. This is a small amount. We would obviously be making an exception because he is not our typical client. The deal he is trying to arrange is a good idea. Namely, that without achieving economies of scale, it is possible to purchase oil, ship it to Puerto Rico to refine it, sell the gasoline, and transport the fuel oil to Boston harbor, where it can be sold without a loss at half the price that multinationals charge. We can thus show that it is not OPEC that is ripping off the consumer, but rather that it is the multinationals that impoverish people because of their excessive profit margins." "Moreover," Burelli recalls that Calderón added, mentioning something that probably Chávez would later think as well, "it is in our interests to have a good relationship with the Kennedy family." When Joe returned from the men's room, Minister Calderón—in the presence of the two young men—rang up the president of PDVSA, General Rafael Alfonzo Ravard, so that he would meet with them.

General Alfonzo took advantage of another break in the conversation the following day prompted by another trip to the men's room by Joe Kennedy to level with Burelli: "Do you know, Pedro, which were the two happiest days of my life? The day they shot this guy's father and the day they shot his uncle; they were communists." The remark was obviously an exaggeration which owed a lot to the general's military nature, but it underscored the lack of sympathy he felt for this other Kennedy and for his proposal.

It must have been bravado on Alfonzo's part, or the Energy minister exerted a lot of pressure, because in February 1980 the first shipment of fuel bought, refined and chartered by Joe Kennedy's recently-created non-profit company, Citizens Energy Corporation, arrived in Boston. Given Citizens' non-profit nature, PDVSA initially urged that part of the profits be reinvested in development projects in the Caribbean.

Joe Kennedy's social activism helped to propel him into the U.S. Congress. In the 1986 mid-term elections, he won a seat representing Massachusetts' eighth district, which included a part of Boston, and was subsequently re-elected every two years until 1999. His brother Michael managed Citizens Energy during Joe's tenure as a congressman. After Michael's death due to a skiing accident, Joe retired from Congress and went back to the company's helm.

After his return, Joe Kennedy revived the corporation's non-profit activities, which had been a sideshow to more lucrative operations during his absence. They were given a boost when, in the wake of hurricane Katrina, Chávez played the propaganda card afforded to him by the provision of subsidized fuel to the United States. It was no longer PDVSA that sold the barrels directly to Citizens Energy, but rather Citgo that took care of the refining and transportation and delivered to Kennedy fuel ready for distribution to consumers.

His dealings with Chavismo subjected Joe Kennedy to political criticism and forced him to justify his actions publicly. "If we were to consume oil only from those countries with which we agree morally, we would wind up with a very short list," Kennedy asserted in one of his public statements before the local press in Boston. He added that, if it was unacceptable for poor people to benefit from subsidized Venezuelan oil, what about the "cars, yachts, jets, and heating furnaces of the rich that use fuel from the same source at the market price?" "Why censure a small amount of oil that helps older people and those that face economic hardship" while overlooking the millions of barrels of Venezuelan oil consumed in the United States every year?

The answer to this questions was provided on several occasions by Burelli himself, whose initial friendship with Joe Kennedy eventually soured. Among other considerations, he argued that chavista Venezuela could afford to give away fuel because of the profit margin it obtained from an officially overpriced barrel of oil that Chávez had brought about. At the 2000 OPEC summit in Caracas, the Venezuelan president fostered a policy of not exceeding the cartel quotas in order the market price to rise. At the time, with a barrel of crude priced at $20, Chávez trumpeted that a fair price should be close to $100.

Burelli estimates that of the total amount that a barrel of oil cost for several years, consumers were paying between $7 and $10 because of the Venezuelan president. He termed this the *Chávez Premium*. Hence, "while forty-five thousand families in the Boston area could benefit from reduced prices for three weeks in the wintertime, every family in the United States was paying a lot more every day for gas, diesel, heating fuel, and lubricants due to Hugo Chávez's recklessness."

"Defending the poor is never easy," as Joe Kennedy II averred in a letter to "His Excellency" President Chávez in January 2012. "As you know," he proceeded in the letter, "it draws vicious attacks, but there are millions of U.S. citizens who appreciate that Venezuela is ruled by someone with a high degree of empathy towards the neediest in society." It was not easy to champion the Bolivarian leader in the United States, but it was well rewarded. Although Citizens Energy was a non-profit, the distribution of fuel was performed by a for-profit company, Citizens Enterprises. The latter company paid Kennedy and his wife the lion's share of their respective salaries of

$400,000 a month, as the portal HumanEvents.com revealed in a study whose findings were not called into question.

Baseball on Moby Dick's Island

At a certain time it appeared that relations between Venezuela and the United States could even surpass normality. In the summer of 2003, on Nantucket Island in Massachusetts, facing Cape Cod, members of congress from both countries squared off against one another in a baseball game. Nicolás Maduro was the captain of one of the teams. At the time he was the head of the Movement Fifth Republic, as Hugo Chávez's party was then called, in the Venezuelan National Assembly. Chavista and opposition members of Venezuela's parliament and Democrats and Republicans played on mixed teams during a sunny outing that was also attended by then Senator John Kerry of Massachusetts. This event of batters and pitchers on the island that inspired scenes of *Moby Dick* was described by Roger Santodomingo in his biography about Chávez's successor *De verde a Maduro* (2013) [the title is a play on words: an inexpert Maduro became a mature politician, as a green or unripe fruit becomes ripe—in Spanish *maduro* means both mature and ripe].

This was the experience of the so-called Group of Boston. It involved a binational inter-parliamentary forum made up of members of congress from both sides of the ideological divide in Venezuela's National Assembly as well as the U.S. Congress. Its main goal was to provide a laid-back setting to enable political dialogue in Venezuela at a time of heightened internal confrontation. Chávez's brief overthrow from the presidency in April 2002 and the strikes that preceded and followed it had cut off discussion through official channels. The Group of Boston thus sought to foster meetings in a different and informal setting, where Venezuelan parliamentarians could frankly debate matters and draw conclusions from the congressional cooperation that took place in a mature democracy such as the United States. The U.S. ambassador in Caracas, Charles Shapiro, launched the initiative, which was given special momentum by representatives Cass Ballenger, a Republican from North Carolina, and William Delahunt, a Democrat from Massachusetts.

The preparatory sessions were held in Boston, which is where the group got its name from. The first meeting took place in September 2002 in the remote village of Brewster, also in the state of Massachusetts, and the second was the already referenced one on Nantucket Island. The gatherings went on for five days and were attended by between twenty and thirty parliamentarians from both countries. They were followed up by trips to Caracas by the U.S. congressmen.

One of the men who circled the bases that day was Leopoldo Martínez, who was playing on Maduro's team, something which underscored the tentative harmony they had achieved. Martínez had been appointed minister of Economy during Pedro Carmona's very brief presidency in April 2002, an event that was still fresh on everyone's minds. But since they were in Massachusetts to mend fences, it was precisely this kind of confrontation which they had to overcome. "Partisanship in Venezuela had worsened and internal dialogue was very difficult. Moreover, Chávez developed a narrative whereby the United States was behind the 2002 coup and any negative development that unfolded, from a blackout to anything that broke down. Relations between Venezuela and the United States reached a very low keel," explains Martínez, currently the president of the Center for Democracy and Development in the Americas, headquartered in Washington. The Group of Boston's objective was two-fold: "Internally, to furnish a channel for dialogue between Chavismo and the opposition; and in foreign policy to smooth over the tensions that had built up in the bilateral relationship."

Leopoldo Martínez's assessment is that the initiative yielded "positive results as well as setbacks." Among the former he cites laws which the opposition rejected and which the government accepted delaying until the 2004 recall referendum on Chávez's presidency. Among the latter, an agreement to create a television channel aimed at covering the National Assembly's activity, but which wound up becoming another chavista mouthpiece. But Martínez's biggest regret is that the Group of Boston's lifespan was abruptly terminated by the Venezuelan president. "Chávez began to recognize that something was taking shape and was developing a life of its own. And that was the crux of the matter. It was about the National Assembly turning into a forum for the meeting of ideas and persons; that the chavista parliamentarians could realize that their positions could be a springboard for political leadership positions. Chávez was already stifling any possible successors from emerging from within his movement and would crack down even harder over time. Chávez banned his members of the National Assembly from attending the meetings and thus ended the Group of Boston, despite some attempts to revive it."

The short experiment came to an end, but Chavismo had realized that it had friends in the United States, especially the members of the Group of Boston who were more understanding of Chávez, such as the Democratic representatives William Delahunt and Gregory Meeks. Years later, when he reached the presidency, Maduro tried to rekindle some of the chemistry with John Kerry, who by then had become U.S. secretary of State, but the Nantucket days were a distant memory.

Lobbyists on Venezuela's Payroll

Bernardo Alvarez was a key player in the development of a network of benefactors in Washington. Chávez appointed him ambassador to the United States in January 2003. He had been a member of the Venezuelan parliament for five years, where he had served on the Committee for Energy and Mines. After Chávez's rise to power, Alvarez was appointed deputy minister of Energy. At the time of his appointment as ambassador, Alvarez had already garnered many contacts in the oil business and was very savvy in leveraging Venezuela's main resource in the United States. One of Alvarez's missions as ambassador was to tighten the political grip on Citgo in the same manner that Chávez had done with its holding company, PDVSA. Alvarez was instrumental in bringing about the partnership between Joe Kennedy and Citgo, and he employed the social programs to finance the electoral campaigns of the more liberal politicians within the Democratic Party such as William Delahunt and Gregory Meeks. He also strengthened Venezuela's ties to Chevron, one of the world's biggest oil companies, and which he had already dealt with in Caracas given the U.S. multinational's substantial investments in Venezuela. The partnership with Chevron was justified on the grounds that "we have to get married with one of the United States' oil giants."

Bernardo Alvarez forged alliances with members of the U.S. Congress, whom he needed as friendly voices that would defend the Chávez regime. He employed the same approach with them as Chávez had with Caribbean countries in order to obtain their vote within the Organization of American States: the supply of discounted oil. Alvarez enabled the delivery of Citgo fuel to dozens of homes in the electoral districts of as many U.S. congressmen as were willing to praise Chavismo's success. Citgo's documents indicated its goal of "fostering ties to key players, including elected officials."

Over the course of Chavismo Venezuela's biggest ally on Capitol Hill was William Delahunt, a member of the U.S. House of Representatives who represented a district contiguous to that of Joe Kennedy II. They served together in Congress in 1997 and 1998. Delahunt retired from Congress in 2011 and established his own lobbying firm, Delahunt Group. In 2005 he offered to broker an agreement with Chávez to politically sponsor the delivery of Citgo fuel to seven states in the northeast of the United States which went beyond the scope of Kennedy's *Joe4oil* program. This initiative was questioned by Republicans in the House's Commerce Committee. They alleged that it would violate federal antitrust laws as Citgo—a state-owned company—was the only corporation which had submitted a tender for a project to assist poorer people in the wintertime. By 2013 the program encompassed twenty-five states and the District of Columbia.

Delahunt visited Chávez on several occasions in Caracas. He also attended his funeral as part of the low-level delegation sent by the Obama administration. The delegation also included James Derham, chargé d'affaires at the U.S. Embassy in Caracas (since 2010 both countries had withdrawn their respective ambassadors) and Representative Gregory Meeks. Joe Kennedy II, the actor Sean Penn, and the reverend Jesse Jackson also traveled to Caracas for the funeral in a private capacity.

Gregory Meeks owed his presence at the funeral to the defense of Chavismo he had undertaken among African-American members of the U.S. Congress—the Congressional Black Caucus—, where his colleague Charles Rangel had also promoted the same agenda. Born to a Puerto Rican father in Harlem, Rangel had been a member of the House since 1971—he was dean of New York's congressional delegation—and had for so long represented the Bronx as congressman for different electoral districts. In some of them had been replaced by José Serrano, another Puerto Rican Democrat.

It was precisely in New York's Bronx where Citgo undertook its most trumpeted assistance program. Chávez even traveled there in 2006 in order to personally endorse it. It was the same trip during which the Venezuelan president spoke from the United Nations' General Assembly podium a day after President George W. Bush had done so. Chávez referred to Bush as the "devil," and histrionically claimed to smell the sulfur left behind by the occupant of the White House during a long diatribe against U.S. foreign policy and imperialism. Part of the delegates at the General Assembly received the speech with applause, but it was roundly condemned by Democrats as well as Republicans in the United States.

Emboldened by his partial success, the Bolivarian leader displayed his wit and fiery rhetoric again when he delivered another speech at Mount Olivet Baptist Church in Harlem. He was, after all, on friendly terrain, that of representatives Charles Rangel and José Serrano, which had been generously doused with Venezuelan oil. But whereas the United Nations was an international venue, the Baptist church was a U.S. one. The insults hurled by a foreign president at the president of the United States—Chávez disparaged Bush as a drunkard—were unanimously condemned in a bipartisan manner. Delahunt also distanced himself from Chávez's comments. But despite the incident, everything would remain the same. It was back to business as usual.

At the behest of his nephew, Ted Kennedy joined the group of those who cheered on Chávez from Washington. In 2004, he sent him a congratulatory message after his victory in the August presidential recall vote. The Venezuelan president tried to silence the accusations of fraud in the vote, which he officially carried with 59 percent of voters rejecting the recall. He did so partly by displaying on television the Kennedy patriarch's letter, which included his signature and the U.S. Senate's letterhead.

Ted Kennedy was able to make up for naively playing into Chávez's hands with the 2004 letter two years later by joining a Senate resolution that condemned the closure of the private television channel RCTV, an administrative action that was perceived as a substantive deterioration of freedoms in Venezuela. The resolution was co-sponsored by Hillary Clinton, Barack Obama, John Kerry, and John McCain, thus including all senators with imminent presidential ambitions at the time. It was obvious that none of them wanted to risk losing a single vote by appearing to be too dovish regarding Chavismo.

Chavista Venezuela's need to improve its image in the U.S. capital prompted it to enlist the services of lobbying firms. While Ambassador Bernardo Alvarez was making the rounds in Washington and developing his own network, the task of interacting with the establishment was entrusted at the end of 2003 to Patton Boggs, the biggest lobby on the banks of the Potomac. Special attention was being paid at the time by the media to ties between the government of Venezuela and the FARC, the Colombian guerrillas, with regard to their military as well as their narco-trafficking operations. The report drafted by Patton Boggs, which appeared on the Internet after it was leaked, asserted that such accusations were "sustained by Venezuelan media outlets controlled by the opposition and supported by sympathizers of the political right wing in the United States."

The collaboration with Patton Boggs was short-lived but costly: in slightly over a year, it charged fees of almost $1 million. Venezuela's interests were then transferred from the account of the most established lobbying firm in Washington to that of an individual lobbyist with leftist leanings, the Puerto Rican lawyer Segundo Mercado Llorens. He earned $240,000 between 2005 and 2007 for his work for the Venezuela Information Office (VIO). This office was launched at the end of 2003 by Ambassador Alvarez as the public relations arm of the Chávez government in the U.S. capital. It sought to "portray to the U.S. public a more accurate vision of the current process in Venezuela, develop strategic allies for the people of Venezuela, and prevent the government of the United States from interfering in Venezuela's democratic process," as the documentation submitted to the Federal Register of the Department of Justice stated.

Two people who worked for the Venezuelan Information Office later moved to the Center for Economic and Policy Research (CEPR) after the former's activities languished. CEPR, and especially Mark Weisbrot, its co-director, have been staunch defenders of Chávez and his legacy. Weisbrot's reports were invoked by chavistas when they needed to quote an Anglo-Saxon economist who supported the Venezuelan government's policies. Weisbrot was the co-author of the script for *South of the Border* (2009), a documentary directed by Oliver Stone in order to extol Chávez and the Castros. In their brief CEPR biographies, there was no mention of the fact that Deborah James and Alex Main had previously worked for the Venezuela Information Office (James was its director) and that they had been therefore on Caracas' payroll. This was no involuntary oblivion, but rather done purposely. "Don't you know that saying you work for Chávez is toxic in this town?" Weisbrot admitted when someone alerted him about the omission.

In all, counting the lobbying firms hired by PDVSA or Citgo to influence oil policy, during the Chávez presidency Venezuela resorted to a dozen such companies, according to a calculation by the journalist Casto Ocando. Among the people on Venezuela's payroll was Eva Golinger, a U.S.-born attorney of maternal Venezuelan descent who became a naturalized Venezuelan citizen. Complimented by Chávez as "Venezuela's bride," Golinger set up the Venezuela Solidarity Committee, which was housed in her duplex apartment in Brooklyn. Although she was extolled by Chavismo, her summoning capacity in New York was minimal.

All of this activity allowed Chávez to open some doors in the United States, but at the end of the day the anti-American revolutionary tone always prevailed in the regime's public relations efforts. Not even Barack Obama's historic win, whom Chávez endorsed in 2008 and 2012, brought about a normalization in relations. "The dozens of millions which Venezuela has heretofore spent to pay the most expensive lobbying firms in Washington, and the multimillion dollar contracts signed with the support of powerful families to deliver discounted fuel to poor communities in the United States were no longer working politically for Chávez," Ocando recounts in *Chavistas en el Imperio*. In the lobbying task the problem laid not in the seller but rather in the product. "Chávez always managed to alienate everybody in the United States. For some reason he had infuriated Democrats, Jews, Republicans…," concludes Pedro Mario Burelli. It was a waste of money subjected to the president's changing mood.

The Strange Love for Chevron

"Which government do you want to overthrow, that of Chávez or Bush?" The meeting between the Department of Energy and the Department of State was not proceeding well. With Chávez lambasting George W. Bush on a daily basis, the high-ranking officials at the State Department no longer knew how to bring the Caribbean president down to earth. Somebody therefore suggested that the United States cease to purchase oil from Venezuela, as one of the attendees at the meeting privately recounted. His colleagues from the Department of Energy knew that one could not fool around with the big energy multinationals. Chevron, the second-biggest oil company in the U.S. after ExxonMobil and one of the oil majors of the world, had obvious interests in the Venezuelan wells; part of the crude that flowed from them to the United States, about one million barrels per day, increased the multinational's earnings.

Condoleezza Rice joined the George W. Bush administration's National Security Council in 2001 after working precisely for Chevron. She had chaired Chevron's Public Policy Committee and had been a member of the multinational's board. When Rice was promoted to secretary of State after Bush's re-election in 2004, some officials witnessed telephone calls from Chevron that sought to exert pressure on certain policies regarding Venezuela, according to the aforementioned former official. The fact that Vice President Dick Cheney had served previously as CEO of Halliburton, a multinational of services and equipment for oilfields, meant that two of the most senior government officials with the ability to influence Bush knew the industry's lobbies very well.

The ties between Venezuela and the multinational headquartered in San Ramón, California, went back in time, as companies that would later merge to become Chevron already operated in the Caribbean country in the 1920s. But Chavismo strengthened those bonds. Chávez's arbitrary measures in the oil sector led to a break with other foreign companies. In 2007, the government in Caracas mandated that all foreign companies abandon direct production and create joint ventures with PDVSA, which would hold a majority stake. Some of the oil majors, such as Exxon and Total, rejected what amounted to a nationalization and chose to leave Venezuela instead of turning over their own technology and ongoing investments. ExxonMobil and ConocoPhillips sought compensation before arbitration panels and obtained multi-billion dollar rulings for the expropriations. But Chevron opted to continue to operate its Venezuelan oilfields.

Preparatory backdoor meetings by Ambassador Bernardo Alvarez in Washington and the direct involvement of Ali Moshiri, Chevron's president for Africa and Latin America, had brought about a mutually-beneficial understanding. In 2007, Chevron signed joint venture agreements with PDVSA to operate the corporations Petroindependiente and Petroboscán, which exploited wells in the western Maracaibo area, and PetroPiar, focused mainly in the Orinoco Belt. Moreover, Chevron had a license to extract offshore gas in two blocks on the Deltana platform facing the Orinoco Delta.

Rumors always circulated about members of the chavista government being on Chevron's payroll, as it was odd that leaders with longstanding left-wing credentials who regularly excoriated U.S. multinationals would abstain from criticizing Chevron. But according to John Watson, president and CEO of the California company, there was no more than a relationship founded on many decades of cooperation. "We have been in Venezuela for many years and have a good track record with the Venezuelan government," he answered me when I approached him and questioned him directly about the matter.

Bound by Oil, One More Than the Other

As Venezuela teetered on the edge of collapse at the end of the Chávez era, the shipments of oil and refined products to the United States were a source of vital earnings due to their volume and the hard currency they garnered. They were almost the only supplies sold at market prices. The rest of Venezuela's oil was donated to Cuba, subsidized for national consumption, delivered to the Petrocaribe countries in exchange for partial payments in goods, or charged in advance to China. In order to maintain these commitments and given the drop in production due to the lack of investment and maintenance of the wells, the quota sold to the U.S. had been decreasing.

In 1998, the year before Chávez came to power, Venezuela's exports to the United States reached 1.37 million barrels per day. By 2013 they had plummeted to 700,000, a drop of almost 50 percent, according to the U.S. Energy Information Administration. This reduction did not cause concern at first as it was offset by the increasing price in the global market. But as the market price stabilized and then began to diminish, earnings fell and thus caused hardship for Venezuela's finances.

Venezuela's dependence on the United States to continue earning cash for its oil sales is highlighted by the fact that the Caribbean country was not in a position to find another buyer that could purchase the significant daily shipments exported to the U.S. "No other country has a combination of substantial energy needs and the capability to refine heavy crude that can absorb Venezuela's oil production volume," according to the experts Javier Corrales and Michael Penfold in *Dragon in the Tropics*. "The only market that could conceivably absorb the amount of oil that Venezuela sells to the United States would be China, but that market is unattainable for technical, economical, and political reasons." These reasons refer to the lack of the appropriate refineries in China; the shipping costs, which puts Venezuelan crude at a disadvantage with other exporters located closer to China, and the caution displayed by Beijing in what would amount to breaking into the United States' backyard.

Venezuela certainly has exported substantial amounts of crude to Asia's biggest economy. In 2013, Venezuela's exports to China amounted to 23 percent of its production, with 30.2 percent sold to the United States and 13.1 percent delivered to Caribbean countries. But Venezuela's sales to China materialized within the China Fund framework, an array of loans extended by China and paid for with future production in light of Venezuela's cash-flow needs. The deal made business sense for China because it earned interest on the loans and also obtained contracts for its companies in Venezuela. In the absence of such conditions, China's partnership with PDVSA would not have been profitable. In fact, China was not interested in Venezuelan oil for its internal consumption, but instead for sale in secondary markets without the need to ship it to its ports.

While Venezuela continued to rely on U.S. purchases and consumption of its oil, the United States had decreased its dependence on oil from the Caribbean country. The United States was never strictly dependent on Venezuelan oil, as it could have easily found replacements by raising the quotas it buys from other producers in the event of an emergency or clash with the Bolivarian regime. "Ten years ago there could be the perception in the United States that Venezuela had economic leverage because of its oil exports to the north. Currently the situation is perceived differently," according to Harold Trinkunas, director of the Latin America Initiative at the Brookings Institution.

The United States has made steady progress in its quest for energy independence. The revolution engendered by fracking has turned it into the world's first producer of natural gas and, in 2015, enabled it to surpass Saudi Arabia and Russia as the top global producer of oil. Different studies project that the United States could achieve energy independence around 2035 o even earlier.

Between 1998 and 2013 the amount of oil imported by the United States from Venezuela diminished from 13.5 percent to 9.8 percent of its total purchases, thus losing share to imports from Canada, Mexico, and Saudi Arabia. As Washington's reliance on Venezuelan crude decreased, the Caribbean country became more dependent on its exports to the U.S. In the 1998-2013 period sales of oil to the United States rose from 55 percent to 65 percent of PDVSA's total earnings via exports.

In light of this dependence, it was striking that in 2014 the Venezuelan government announced its intent to sell Citgo, PDVSA's subsidiary in the United States. The urgency of avoiding bankruptcy forced Caracas to carry out capitalization operations, and Citgo was one of its main assets. But even if the sale of Citgo materialized, PDVSA would have for a time to keep supplying oil to Citgo refineries, which are capable of refining 800,000 barrels a day, because they are adapted to Venezuela's extra heavy oil.

If it was in Venezuela's interests to maintain its trade links with the United States, why did the chavista government continue to publicly harass its main oil export market? Harold Trinkunas attributed this attitude as a means of drawing importance to itself and continuing to be perceived as a key player. Taking on the United States rhetorically is useful insofar as it makes Venezuela stand out on the international stage. "It can tell the world: look, we are fighting the world's biggest power, and we are still here. This is a behavior common to all rogue states. They reaffirm their identity as important countries by engaging in verbal warfare with the United States, as they can obviously not seriously contemplate a real confrontation." The historical resentment of Latin American nations towards the imperialist past of their big and rich northern neighbor, a narrative espoused by the continent's left-wing, also explains this obsessive animosity towards the United States.

Yankees Go Home, but We Go to the Shopping Mall

It was a schizophrenia that in resorting to anti-imperialist diatribes masked a fake attitude. Suffice as an example the passion indulged by many leading chavista officials and military officers in visiting Florida regularly to shop in its malls or to purchase real estate, some of it very exclusive, by employing their thick checkbooks. "It is something that I cannot fathom. They seem to live in a contradiction they have become so accustomed to that they no longer question it," comments the journalist Casto Ocando, who has carried out research on the wealth amassed by some of these officials in the United States. "For fifteen years they have broadcast diatribes supporting the poor and against the Empire, which they violate two-fold. They bring their families here, purchase properties, invest, own horses... I am not referring to persons who are fellow-travelers of the regime but rather to the heart and core leadership."

Hence the tag *Yankees go home* sounded often as a chorus required by a script that was repeated without much personal conviction. In the first visit to Washington of his political career, Nicolás Maduro displayed less apprehension towards the United States than could be expected from someone who toed the official line. He even behaved naively. In the autumn of 2001, when he was just a member of the National Assembly, he traveled to the U.S. capital in a delegation with other members of the Venezuelan parliament. The group included Calixto Ortega, Ismael García, Rodrigo Cabezas, Didalco Bolívar, and Cilia Flórez, whom Maduro married in 2013 after years of living together. At the State Department they were welcomed by Thomas Shannon, who at the time was director of Andean Affairs. After the meeting at the State Department, a member of the Venezuelan Embassy assures that he overheard the following conversation among the members of parliament when they were asked about the encounter:

Maduro: –"Much better than I expected. They even served us coffee."
Cabezas: –"Nicolás, you are so gullible. They serve coffee to everyone here. What they have just told us is that the renegade military officers will mount a coup against us."
Maduro: –"Yes, right, but what I mean is that their behavior was not aggressive."

The deferential treatment which the U.S. administration had afforded the delegation was not to serve them with coffee, but to warn them about saber-rattling they monitored among military officers in Venezuela. Chavista propaganda would later accuse Washington of planning what it always deemed a coup in April 2002. In hearings before Congress, the non-partisan State Department's Office of the Inspector General denied the charge. "As opposed to working to foster the overthrow of president Chávez, the United States alerted him about possible coup attempts and credible assassination plots against him," the OIG indicated in July 2002. In addition, the OIG underscored that it had found no evidence that the State Department or the U.S. Embassy in Caracas "planned, took part, assisted, or promoted" the military action against Chávez. The leaking of diplomatic cables published by Wikileaks years later revealed that the internal U.S. communications had merely relayed the information that was in the public domain about tension among the opposition and in the military barracks.

Revolving Ambassadors

By that time, relations between Venezuela and the United States had broken down. Each side could point to a specific event that shattered any illusion it might have harbored about developing a normal interaction. In March 1998, when he was still a candidate for the presidency, Hugo Chávez's application for a visa to travel to the United States was denied by the Clinton administration due to his involvement in the 1992 coup against Venezuela's democratic government. After being elected president, Washington changed its attitude and in 1999 Chávez traveled to the United States both before and after being sworn into office. He did so, however, without having shed the animosity towards the U.S. administration caused by the first visa rejection. Moreover, there would be no time for the new president and the Clinton administration to seek common ground and develop mutual trust, as an abrupt snub from Chávez to the United States would soon deepen the acrimony between the two countries.

At the end of 1999 severe landslides struck Venezuela. Several countries, including the United States, offered emergency assistance. After taking in a first batch of U.S. aid, Chávez initially accepted Washington's offer to send a group of four hundred U.S. Army engineers to help rebuild the damaged infrastructure. But, acting on Fidel Castro's advice, who brainwashed Chávez into suspecting that the engineers could be CIA agents, the Venezuelan president ordered the two U.S. Navy vessels transporting the aid to turn around and sail back, a decision that enormously angered Bill Clinton.

"The Cubans had always been leery of the special relationship that could develop between Caracas and Washington because of the high consumption of Venezuelan oil in the United States," Pedro Mario Burelli argues. "Fidel Castro hence took it upon himself to instill paranoia in Chávez regarding allegedly secret U.S. schemes to overthrow him. Castro became necessary because of his spying reports, and he supplied Chávez with many lies about supposed conspiracies. The barrels of crude that Venezuela began to send to Cuba were a kind of payment for this protection, which in the final analysis turned Chávez into a hostage." The United States then applied the so-called Maisto doctrine, named after John Maisto, who was the U.S. ambassador during the final stretch of Bill Clinton's presidency. Summed up as "mind what he [Chávez] does and not what he says," it called for dealing with the new president of Venezuela on the basis of his deeds and not the demagoguery he might preach.

But it was hard for Washington to stomach the verbal barrage that Chávez unleashed after the 9/11 attacks, less than a year into

George W. Bush's first term. The sympathy that the Bolivarian leader showed towards those Muslims that celebrated Al-Qaeda's terrorist attacks prompted outrage. The White House responded by cheering the forced departure of Chávez from the presidency in April 2002, despite not having been behind the plot. Swords had been drawn on both sides, and the point of no return had been crossed in terms of the bilateral relationship. The Bush administration then came up with a policy that Burelli describes as "ignore the man [Chávez] completely, but investigate his deeds thoroughly." The policy also called for acting as if Chávez did not exist. In fact, Bush never pronounced his name in public nor responded to his provocations, but ordered a thorough investigation into Venezuela's links to Iran and Hezbollah.

Chávez felt quite confident that Barack Obama's election to the presidency would effect a shift in U.S. policy towards Venezuela. Chávez thus saved a last outburst of rage for Bush, expelling the U.S. ambassador to Caracas, Patrick Duddy, by means of a harangue on television in September 2008. "Go to hell, damn Yankees, this is where a dignified nation lives," he exclaimed, expressing his solidarity with Bolivia in a diplomatic confrontation between President Evo Morales and the United States. The Venezuelan president also claimed that Washington and the U.S. Embassy plotting to overthrow him. Washington countered by expelling Venezuelan Ambassador Bernardo Alvarez.

Chávez and Obama met for the first time in April 2009 at the Summit of the Americas in Trinidad and Tobago. The Caribbean leader gave Obama a copy of the book *Las venas abiertas de América Latina* [*Open Veins of Latin America*], which at the time of its publication in 1971 became a must-read for the region's left-wing movements. By then, however, the author himself—the Uruguayan Eduardo Galeano—deemed it pamphlet literature. Obama chose to believe that the diplomatic rifts of the past were caused by the Bush administration's neocon nature. "Venezuelans have Citgo, and their defense budget is six hundred times smaller than ours," Obama pointed out during the summit's closing press conference, thereby suggesting that there was no underlying reason why both countries should not get along well.

Obama preferred that his initiative to restore ties not be debated in the Senate, and in July 2009 he sent the expelled Duddy back to Caracas as the U.S. ambassador. Such an unusual diplomatic move had the benefit of not requiring another confirmation vote for Duddy in the U.S. Senate, and it was completed by the return to Washington of Ambassador Alvarez. The counter of mutual grievances was thus reset to zero. But it was naive to expect that the United States would turn a blind eye to the irregular practices of the chavista government. When Duddy was replaced in 2010, Larry Palmer was nominated as the new ambassador in Caracas. His responses to questions during his nomination hearings in the Senate about restrictions to freedom of expression in Venezuela and chavista leaders' ties to Colombian guerrillas prompted Chávez to reject his appointment. The U.S. responded by revoking Ambassador Alvarez's visa.

The DEA Does Not Sleep

During his re-election campaign in 2012 Barack Obama completely ignored Hugo Chávez. The Republican candidate, Mitt Romney, offered a damning verdict of the Venezuelan president: "Chávez has offered safe haven to drug kingpins, has fostered regional terrorist groups that threaten allies such as Colombia, tightened military links with Iran, assisted Tehran in evading sanctions, and enabled Hezbollah to settle within Venezuela's borders." Obama could have easily ratified such a verdict, but he chose to lower Venezuela's profile in the election campaign: "My impression is that what Mr. Chávez has been doing during the past few years has not directly impacted our national security" (Obama would go on to say the contrary towards the end of his second term).

With a White House reluctant to open more fronts in Latin America, a State Department in charge of applying this policy, and the Central Intelligence Agency (CIA) focused on other regions, the U.S. Drug Enforcement Administration (DEA) was the federal agency that most closely monitored the chavista regime. Reporting to the Department of Justice, the DEA is a law enforcement tool. It operates in order to ensure the laws are followed. It acts according to existing legislation and not the variable priorities or policies of each administration. Although a U.S. president may not show much interest in confronting a foreign country, the DEA cannot ignore its statutory mandate, namely to "enforce the controlled substances laws and regulations of the United States and bring to the criminal and civil justice system of the United States, or any other competent jurisdiction, those organizations and principal members of organizations, involved in the growing, manufacture, or distribution of controlled substances appearing in or destined for illicit traffic in the United States."

Such a broad definition of the DEA's remit allows it to operate beyond U.S. borders in collaboration with numerous countries and turns it into a genuine police force of the Caribbean and Central America, which are the transit areas for U.S. bound narcotics. The DEA's task is greatly facilitated by the U.S. National Security Agency's monitoring through antennas and close attention to the entire region.

At the time of Chávez's passing, the U.S. federal public prosecutor had made much headway in preparing possible indictments of several Venezuelan leaders, among them persons that served or had served in the government, according to sources that have been involved in the process of gathering evidence to prove some of the charges. But it was not known how many indictments had been already finalized, as they could have taken the shape of sealed indictments, formal accusations that remain secret to enable the capture of the defendant or the appropriate timing for their announcement if they implicate high-ranking leaders of foreign countries.

The first announced indictment that affected a key figure in the chavista apparatus was the indictment of General Hugo Carvajal presented in July 2014. It was revealed when *The Chicken* was arrested outside of Venezuela. U.S. authorities also revealed the charges they were bringing against Maduro's two nephews when they were arrested in Haiti in November 2015 with a shipment of almost eighteen hundred pounds of cocaine. Media revealed at the beginning of 2016 that charges were brought against the head of the National Guard, Néstor Reverol, and other generals under his command in a reportedly sealed indictment. But there could also be other ongoing proceedings against persons accused by the U.S. Treasury in the enforcement of the Kingpin Act or the law against drug lords, such as Ramón Rodríguez Chacín and Henry Rangel Silva. The names of even more senior Venezuelan leaders had appeared in the investigations, such as Rafael Ramírez, Adán Chávez, Tareck el Aissami, Diosdado Cabello, and Nicolás Maduro.

The DEA's responsibility is to "investigate and prepare the trial" of narco-traffickers that operate at "interstate or international levels." It provides evidence to convict the accused, but it is the attorney's office that must bring the case before the courts. Moreover, if the entry into the United States of protected witnesses that bolster the prosecution's case is necessary, or the persons must be extradited in order to be tried, the State Department needs to get involved in the process. And if the accused are leading politicians, the White House comes into play.

If so much proof indicated that Chavismo had turned Venezuela into a narco-state, why did Washington not act more swiftly to punish the institutional drug lords who fostered a business that delivered tons of narcotics to the United States? At first there may have been a dearth of witnesses, but Chávez's death and Maduro's political instability emboldened them to step forward and cooperate with U.S. authorities. The delay could also be attributed later to Obama's desire to not undermine the secret negotiations to re-establish diplomatic relations with Cuba and then to preserve this legacy.

This schism between law enforcement and political interests spawned tensions between the DEA and the State Department. The entry into the United States of persons such as Eladio Aponte, Rafael Isea, and Leamsy Salazar because of their value as witnesses for the prosecution was crucial. But on several occasions the issuing of visas for them was more haphazard than what is expected from a power whose prowess in security matters is so impressive in the movies. The State Department's reluctance or sluggishness to grant visas to the aforementioned witnesses was overcome by the pressure exerted from Congress. Such pressure was aroused indirectly by the DEA through some senators or members of the House. Members of Congress then threatened to publicize the administration's lackadaisical pursuit of narcotics, or to request the testimony before committees of administration officials. Such committees would include members of the Hispanic caucus, who would intensify the criticisms. The pressure yielded the intended results and the visas were processed.

On some occasions the maneuvers to circumvent uncooperative agencies designed by the DEA is supported by the CIA, because the federal intelligence services also benefit from the information obtained from debriefing the protected witnesses. But a partnership between those agencies is not always a recipe for success. Sometimes the Federal Bureau of Investigations (FBI) gets in the way. An agreement between several agencies can sometimes be attained but takes some time to be struck.

An End Such As That of Panama's Noriega?

Since the disappearance of Hugo Chávez from public life the contacts of potential defectors from Chavismo's and the government's highest ranks—both civilian and military—with the United States intensified as they sought to reach a deal with authorities in exchange for their testimony. Having an indictment from the United States hanging over your head as a Damocles sword was unnerving. It severely limited movements outside of Venezuela, as they risked arrest by Interpol or the long arm of U.S. agencies. It also vanished any possibility of a retreat should the official fall out of favor or in the event of regime change in Venezuela because very few countries would be willing to offer a safe haven. Hence, as a witness involved in several intermediary processes confidentially recounts, the list of chavistas negotiating entry into their formerly much-maligned Empire began to grow.

Diosdado Cabello, regarded as the regime's number two man, was among the first to seize the initiative to strike an agreement. But in his case he sought not to leave Venezuela or to cooperate with U.S. authorities, but rather to request a non-belligerent attitude from Washington towards him. At the beginning of December 2012, with Chávez about to undergo a surgery from which he would not recover, Cabello discreetly employed the diplomatic track to contact Jim Durham, the chargé d'affaires at the U.S. Embassy in Caracas, in order to convey to his superiors that, should he seize power, he would distance his country from Cuba. The president of the National Assembly probably was privy to the fact that the U.S. Justice system was tracking him for his responsibility in the narco-state. He thus attempted to convince Washington to turn a blind eye towards his illicit activities so his leadership would not be undermined in the case of a power struggle with Nicolás Maduro.

The weekend prior to the announcement of Chávez's death, in March 2013, Cabello reached out via intermediaries to U.S. government agencies, as one of his interlocutors reveals. Cabello portrayed himself as someone willing to sever ties with the Castros and Hezbollah. The negotiations did not go very far. The CIA apparently rejected any meeting with Cabello, such as the one he suggested could take place in Rome during his trip on the occasion of Cardinal Bergoglio's coronation as Pope Francis.

Maduro was also aware of the burden on Chavismo of narco-trafficking activities. To avoid reprisals by the United States at the time of his vulnerable ascent to power, Maduro ramped up the attempts to restore full diplomatic relations with Washington. The idea was that a climate of normality, even if close friendship was not realistic, would restrain the White House from taking measures against the members of the new chavista government.

Michael Braun, former head of operations at the DEA, is convinced that the footage of former Panamanian dictator Manuel Antonio Noriega being arrested often crossed the minds of chavista leaders. Noriega was taken into custody on January 4, 1990, in Miami after his arrest by U.S. troops who had invaded Panama to put an end to drug trafficking sponsored by its government. "A picture as the one of General Noriega being taken to the United States is the last thing that Chávez and his successors wanted," Braun assured. A repeat of the Panama invasion was unimaginable for Venezuela, but precautions nonetheless had to be taken.

Before Chávez's death, a phone call made to Maduro by Assistant Secretary of State for the Western Hemisphere Roberta Jacobson was followed by a confidential meeting between Roy Chaderton, the Venezuelan ambassador to the Organization of American States, and Ricardo Zuñiga, head of Latin American affairs at the National Security Council. Washington was interested in the exchange of ambassadors (the posts were vacant since 2010), for it wanted to have in Caracas a full assortment of diplomatic resources as a period of uncertainty lay ahead for Venezuela. But Zuñiga raised the need to arrange for a visit by the regional DEA director to Caracas to resume cooperation against drug trafficking before the exchange of ambassadors could take place. Zuñiga was requesting a low-profile visit for the DEA, but it was very clear what was of uppermost concern to the United States.

But the diplomatic contacts stopped with Chávez's death. Hours before announcing his death, Maduro resorted to his predecessor's anti-imperialist rhetoric and publicly accused "the historical enemies" of the fatherland—meaning the United States—of having inoculated the Bolivarian leader with cancer. He then ordered the expulsion from Venezuela of two military attachés from the U.S. Embassy, whom he accused of espionage. Washington responded a few days later with a reciprocal measure.

This firm attitude was maintained by the Obama administration in the days that followed the elections of April 14, 2013, whose official results were rejected by the opposition. "There are obviously gigantic irregularities, we will harbor doubts about the feasibility of this government... There should be a recount," Secretary of State John Kerry urged in a hearing before the House of Representatives. But Nicolás Maduro took office as president before the recount could be completed.

After establishing himself as president and settling into Miraflo-res Palace, but needing international recognition, Maduro again fostered a rapprochement with the United States. In June 2013, John Kerry and Elías Jaua, the Venezuelan minister of Foreign Affairs, shook hands at the Organization of American States' General Assembly in Guatemala. But another diplomatic crisis broke out a month later after Venezuela offered to provide asylum to Edward Snowden, the National Security Agency analyst who revealed classified information ranging from U.S. diplomatic cables to electronic communications between U.S. and other citizens which the NSA tracked and stored. In July 2013 Kerry clearly warned that the United States would regard Snowden's transfer from Moscow—where he had fled—to Venezuela as a hostile act. Snowden remained in Russia, but in a public statement Caracas announced "the termination of efforts aimed at a rapprochement with Washington."

Maduro revisited often the matter of the exchange of ambassadors. But he was expressing his wish to build bridges while also accusing the United States of plotting a coup against his regime, as it happened during the massive 2014 street protests. Foreign Minister Jaua disparaged the same John Kerry whose hand he had shaken almost a year earlier as an "assassin of the Venezuelan people."

In the wake of these protests, which resulted in forty-three deaths, almost nine hundred injured and more than 2,500 arrests, the U.S. Congress passed a resolution to deny entry visas to the United States and freeze assets in its territory of those responsible for violating human rights in Venezuela; this was extended to those that engaged in political corruption. The Obama administration was reluctant to apply this sanctions on Venezuela. But after the announcement later that year, on December 17, of the preliminary agreement with Havana to reestablish diplomatic relations, the White House felt more at ease about clamping down on Venezuela's leadership. On the following day, the U.S. president signed the law containing the sanctions against the chavista leadership. In March 2015 Obama issued an executive order that defined the situation in Venezuela as an "unusual and extraordinary threat for the security and foreign policy of the United States." The executive action imposed the sanctions on seven Venezuelan officials.

Obama believed that the thaw with Cuba would shatter the United States' tradition of troubled ties to Latin America. Having reestablished diplomatic relations with the Caribbean island, the other countries in the region would also accept it as a normal partner in the continent's matters. But the colossus to the north, because of its hegemony, will always be treated differently. Moreover, Cuba continued to stoke resentment in the region against Uncle Sam, with Venezuela as its main channel. Venezuela's petro-diplomacy was still paying some dividends.

10

The *McCHAVEZ COMBO*, TROPICAL DIET
Oil Distribution to Exert Regional Influence

Welcome to the Independent Republic of the Amazon, a country that has not yet joined the United Nations but which is completely detached from Venezuela and has already been recognized by Cuba, Bolivia, Ecuador, and other ALBA countries... This announcement is fictional. But Hugo Chávez did envision the possibility that he could suffer a defeat at the polls that he could not challenge because of a large opposition turnout on the streets and a reluctance by part of the armed forces to let the *comandante* get away with electoral fraud. For such a potential scenario, three months before the last elections he contested, Chávez signed the latest version of the Guyana Shield Plan, under which he and his followers would hunker down in the eastern and southern parts of Venezuela. Under the plan, if Chavismo were forced to strategically retreat, it would create a safe haven south of the Orinoco-Apure rivers.

This plan was predicated on a lot of romanticism on Chávez's part. The Venezuelan president was undoubtedly reminiscing about the days of his hero Simón Bolívar, who, after being defeated in his initial struggle for independence from Spain, retreated to the same region, to the town of Angostura (today named Ciudad Bolívar). He then regrouped his forces before launching his final victorious offensive. But it would have been very hard to execute the Guyana Shield Plan. In addition to the inherent difficulty of transferring rebel forces to a remote part of the country, would Chávez have really wanted to flee to the jungle? In the case of a forced retreat, the most realistic destination for the chavista leaders most likely to be sought by foreign law enforcement agencies would have been Cuba. In Cuba they could have enjoyed a serene exile. They would have been beyond the reach of foreign extradition requests and international arrest warrants as long as they did not fall out of favor with the Castros regime. But if Chávez's objective had been to prevent relinquishing power by employing military force to defy Venezuelans' democratic wishes, the plan would have made sense despite the fact that it amounted to a pipe dream.

Beyond its lack of realism, this contingency planning revealed Chavismo's inherent anti-democratic nature. Chávez ratified the update of the plan in July 2012. A month later he appointed a trusted military officer, General Clíver Alcalá Cordones, as the new head of the Guyana Integral Defense Region (REDI), where the Fifth Jungle Infantry Division was stationed. The military region encompassed the states of Amazonas, Bolívar, and Amacuro Delta, the heart of what would have become the Amazonian Republic. As a defensive garrison, the region's geostrategic advantages were undeniable. It enabled through its southwestern tip to link up with the Revolutionary Armed Forces of Colombia (FARC), thus cornering the market on drug trafficking; in the northwest, control of the Orinoco River and its flow into the Atlantic ensured a main supply route; to the south, the little-watched border with Brazil offered an escape route in case of attack.

The region did not just provide geographic advantages. There is a big hydroelectric plant on the huge Guri dam on the Caroní River, in the state of Bolívar. It is the biggest plant in Venezuela and supplies electricity to most of the country. Moreover, the region boasts significant river port facilities at Puerto Ordaz, as well as industrial infrastructure of the Guyana Venezuelan Corporation (CVG), the second-largest public company in Venezuela after PDVSA. CVG exploits the region's important mineral wealth: iron, bauxite, gold, and diamonds.

The Guyana Shield Plan took its name from the extensive mountain range that runs along the south and east of Venezuela, the three Guyanas, and the northern tip of Brazil. The plan called for the deployment of state-of-the-art anti-aircraft artillery on the Guri dam. In the bunkers built on the dam as well as the nearby hydroelectric plant of Macagua satellite and teleconferencing communication networks were set up, according to military officers who were involved in the plan. The preparations made also sure that food and weapons were stored. In addition, a landing strip was built that could accommodate Sukhoi Su-30 fighters, the Venezuelan Air Force's main combat plane.

But these actions amounted to war-games that probably nobody took very seriously. The coordination meetings convened by General Alcalá really had other purposes. At a time when Alcalá had been removed from the core group of chavista officials running narco-trafficking operations, the president had compensated the general by placing him in a posting were he could take profit from the gold mining business. Venezuela did not rank among the top producers of gold in the world (it was between the twentieth and thirtieth place in world production), but the more than ten tons of gold extracted from its mines yearly could yield handsome rewards for whomever ran the business. Moreover, gold was used as a means of laundering the profits generated by the cartel of the Suns.

Clíver Alcalá's methods enraged the indigenous peoples that inhabit the region. In February 2013, a group of Pemon Indians disarmed and held approximately forty members of the National Guard. A week later, a woman from the town of Urimán directly confronted General Alcalá and berated him publicly in an incident that went viral on You Tube in Venezuela. In a claim filed, the Pemon Indians denounced the "massive and intensified militarization" of their lands, as well as the confiscation of material they regarded as necessary for their livelihoods, and that the military deemed was employed towards the illegal extraction of gold.

Another reason for deploying the military along the banks of the Orinoco was to safeguard the trafficking of drugs. In the spring of 2013, after Nicolás Maduro became president, a summit held at Puerto Ordaz was attended by several chavista officials related to such a business. According to a witness present at the site who handled the event's logistics, Adán Chávez, brother of the deceased president and governor of Barinas state, arrived at the scene with two Colombian leaders. Tareck el Aissami, the former minister of Interior and governor of Aragua, brought Ghazi Nassereddine and another Hezbollah operative to the meeting. Military officials with sun pins on their fatigues were also present, such as General Hugo Carvajal, director of military intelligence, as well as generals Ramón Carrizales and Ramón Rodríguez Chacín. Generals Cliver Alcalá and Wilmer Barrientos, who a few weeks later was appointed to minister of the President's Office, also took part in the meeting.

At the time, the governor of Amazonas state, Liborio Guarulla, reproached the presence of more than four thousand Colombian guerrillas in his state, a fact that the Venezuelan armed forces knew. Guarulla was one of only three non-chavista governors out of a total of twenty-three in Venezuela. He complained to the press that the guerrillas had taken over control of the extraction of gold and the gasoline business, and that they had also built four runways for the small aircraft that covered the narco-trafficking routes. The indigenous people complained about being forced not to leave their homes at night so that the narco-terrorists could ship supplies of food and fuel for their flights upstream on the Orinoco towards their camps.

Geopolitics' Ironies

Any leader worth his salt has a map office in his presidential quarters. Nicolás Maduro inherited that of Hugo Chávez. At the Miraflores Palace, in a space reserved for meetings, a big panel displayed several maps. The first one showed part of the continent, cutting out the areas north of Cuba and south of Venezuela. It therefore paid special attention to the Caribbean and to Central America, and to Venezuela's relationship with this area. There were no other regional maps in the room. There were others that zoomed in on parts of Venezuela and there were also maps of the world. The Venezuelan presidency was right on target when it set its geopolitical sights towards the northeast, although it was flawed in not including at least the southern tip of Florida, as if the United States did not play any role. It was also revealing that at Miraflores there were no maps of the rest of South America hanging on the wall.

Venezuela is primarily a Caribbean country. For those Venezuelans who would like to sever ties with Cuba, the great irony is that, on paper, the most logical relations for Venezuela are the ones with the main islands of the Greater Antilles. And for those Venezuelans who covet a scenario of no U.S. influence in the region, the irony is that, due to its location, Venezuela is bound by a necessary link to the great power on the other bank of the Greater Caribbean (the area encompassed by the Gulf of Mexico and the Caribbean sea). In an ideal world where the brotherhood of nations flowed naturally, an alliance between Colombia and Venezuela would secure the leadership among the Hispanic nations in the middle of the Americas. But both countries have comparable area, population, and gross domestic product, which prompts a rivalry and prevents the priority of one over the other. It is therefore inevitable that Bogota and Caracas should not get along, thus confirming the saying that all American republics are brothers, with the exception of Colombia and Venezuela, which are first cousins.

South America's orography hinders its integration. Its physical obstacles obstruct genuine interaction between the nations that make up the subcontinent. The Andes and the Amazon divide South America in three parts. There is the northern part of South America, where Venezuela and the Guyanas are located, and whose terrestrial communications with the south are thwarted by the vast and impenetrable tropical forest and jungle. This expanse of tropical forest is akin to the Sahara desert in Africa, which splits Africa into the Maghreb in the north and sub-Saharan Africa in the south. South America has a southeastern area, made up of non-Amazonian Brazil, Paraguay, Uruguay, and Argentina. This region is the only one in South America that lends itself to the development of a close-knit community of nations. And then there is the western part of South America: there the Andes run through but don't link Chile, Peru, Ecuador, and Bolivia. Colombia, as a cornerstone that connects the Pacific area of South America with the northern one, is probably the country with the most geostrategic leverage, with the exception of Brazil.

The Amazon and the Andes force Venezuela to look to the Caribbean, and that sea belongs to the United States. Nicholas J. Spykman, one of the founders of contemporary U.S. geopolitics, asserted that the Greater Caribbean is to Washington what the Mediterranean was for Rome and the Aegean for Athens. The Greater Caribbean is the "sea in the middle" whose control the United States acquired as a necessary condition in its quest to become the Western Hemisphere's superpower. Beijing's current intent to secure sovereignty over several disputed archipelagos and islands in the East and South China Seas from its neighbors is a similar desire to consolidate its status as an emerging superpower. But the Chinese regime is up against stronger rivals, especially Japan, than the United States had to confront to control the Greater Caribbean at the end of the 19th century (Spanish-American war) and the beginning of the 20th century (the so-called banana wars). China will not be able to banish from its near abroad the United States' foreign military presence with the ease that the U.S. came to dominate the Greater Caribbean by successfully displacing Spain from Puerto Rico and Cuba.

Without another great power that can challenge it, the United States exerts a logical control over the Caribbean. In November 2013, Secretary of State John Kerry delivered at speech at the Organization of American States' headquarters in Washington. The United States' top diplomat asserted in those remarks that "the era of the Monroe doctrine is over," a line that received considerable applause. Secretary Kerry was proclaiming the end of any worry that the United States might have about a big non-American power, especially from Europe, carving out a significant sphere of influence in the Western Hemisphere. This was what the original doctrine wanted to prevent. But the European powers long ago lost the ability to rival the United States in the Americas. In his remarks, however, Kerry did not explicitly reject the enduring logic of the Monroe doctrine, namely that the United States will continue to ensure that it remains the only hegemon in the Western Hemisphere. Washington will resist rivals from projecting their power in the Caribbean, which secures its southern flank and access to the strategic Panama canal.

Another one of Spykman's axioms that we should bear in mind is that the great geographic division is not between North America and South America, but rather between the vast territory that lies north of the Amazonian jungle (from the Arctic Circle to the Equator) and the much smaller area that stretches out south of such a population vacuum. The Great Caribbean does not separate, but rather unites and permanently links the southern part of North America and the northern part of South America, in the same manner as northern Africa has historically been more intertwined with the Mediterranean region—which includes southern Europe—than with sub-Saharan Africa.

Moreover, the rivers of the Amazon basin furnish an east-west communication link, but not a north-south one. This reinforces Venezuela's Caribbean orientation. Close ties between Caracas and countries from another area—such as Bolivia or Argentina—can therefore be attributed to temporary ideological alignments but are not feasible in the long term unless their intent were to isolate a hypothetically hostile Brazil. Venezuela's membership in Mercosur is similarly not likely to be very active and enduring given that it is a regional integration scheme of an area where the Bolivarian republic does not geographically belong.

Legend of a Liberating Country

Chavista Venezuela's attitude of being the patron of an attempt to override the *Pax Americana* can be understood as a combination of two factors. On the one hand, the aspiration to play a leadership role by a country that regards itself as the guarantor of Simón Bolívar's legacy; on the other, the *castrista* Cuba's experience. "Since Bolívar's time, Venezuela has portrayed itself as a country with a historical, cultural, and popular starring role. Venezuela's legend is that of a liberating country, with a distinct and important place in history," according to Harold Trinkunas, director of the Latin American Initiative at the Brookings Institution. Trinkunas was born and grew up in Maracaibo, where his father had moved his family to from the United States in order to work in the oil industry. "I therefore know very well how history is taught in Venezuela. Ninety percent of the school year is devoted to the study of the period leading up to the battle of Carabobo," he states, referring to the decisive 1821 battle against the Kingdom of Spain's troops, "and the ensuing 150 years are glossed over as if nothing significant had happened during that period of time."

The conviction that Venezuela is called upon to be a medium-sized power with the capability of projecting its influence is ingrained in the national psyche and was part and parcel of the diplomatic policies of governments for decades. The wealth spawned by oil allowed Venezuela to make itself heard and be taken into account in the region. The San José treaty of 1980 established that Mexico and Venezuela would commit to provide crude oil to several Central American and Caribbean countries on a concessional basis. This pact enshrined Venezuela's inherent inclination towards that region. The novelty with Chávez's rise to power was that, for the first time, Venezuela's capability to project power combined with the historical aspirations of the Cuban revolution of ideological leadership in the rest of Latin America.

Cuba had the know-how. It is the only country that succeeded in resisting the tutelage of the U.S. hegemon and promoted a similar struggle by some of its neighbors. The first goal was achieved because a large power from outside of the region, the Soviet Union, was willing and able to support Cuba's defiance of the United States. The second objective was not accomplished because the USSR itself restrained its assistance, knowing that the plan was excessively audacious. The lessons learned by Fidel Castro—the hemisphere's greatest geopolitical fox of the last century—during Cuba's decades of revolution were extremely useful to Chávez. The new revolutionary leader copied Cuba's strategy of approaching big foreign powers—Russia, China, Iran—in order to keep the United States at bay. Nonetheless, Venezuela's adoption of mutual commitment strategies with anti-U.S. foreign powers was of a lesser magnitude than the Soviet-Cuban entente, which was a product of the Cold War's rival blocks.

"No other Latin American country, aside from Cuba under Fidel Castro, has taken on the United States in such an overt and persistent manner as Venezuela under Chávez," as Harold Trinkunas explains. Since it did not confront Washington with substantive hostility, chavista Venezuela was granted some leeway by the United States to foster its domestic agenda and seek to recruit allies among its neighbors' governments. Trinkunas asserts that the Chávez-Fidel international play does not make sense unless we understand that the two countries were pursuing a joint mini-max strategy as described in the theory of simultaneous games. Both countries hence took turns in permanently trying to attain a maximalist objective of creating a multipolar world where Venezuela and Cuba would be one pole, and a minimalist one that safeguarded the revolution in both nations. The play often advanced both goals: the investment in oil resources undertaken by Chavismo not only enabled the creation of alliances but also facilitated the disruption of the U.S. international order that promotes democratic standards.

After Peru's experience with the presidency of Alberto Fujimori between 1990 and 2000, the inter-American system laid down a framework to protect democracy in the continent. One of its most important tools was the Inter-American Democratic Charter, which was approved by the Organization of American States (OAS) in 2001. Such proclamations paved the way for the development of a consensus regarding how and when the international system should intervene to pre-empt or correct scenarios such as an interruption of democracy or a serious violation of the constitutional order among the countries in the Americas.

To prevent actions against Venezuela's slide into authoritarianism, Chávez "deliberately violated" the consensus, according to Trinkunas. "He exerted influence on countries to shape their policy and in others acted via lobbies so they would pressure their governments into not criticizing Venezuela. When a political crisis broke out in Venezuela, friendly countries' governments staunchly spoke out in support of Chávez, whereas those that opposed his policies barely uttered a word. Cuba also benefited from this pattern, because these public statements by Latin American governments "undermined U.S. proposals for the Western Hemisphere." These initiatives were based on the premise of North-South continental integration in the context of a negotiated agenda that addressed economic and security issues. "Cuba clearly wanted to stymie these proposals in order to make it easier for the Castros to evade the restrictions that Washington imposed on Havana." After some of Chávez's actions were criticized, the Venezuelan president announced in 2012 that his country would walk out of the Inter-American Human Rights Court and Commission, two institutions that operate within the OAS's system. Nicolás Maduro formally took Venezuela out of the two bodies in 2013 when the opposition appealed to these institutions to examine its claim of electoral fraud in the presidential elections.

The results of Chavismo's dual external influence vectors were mixed. Chávez did not manage to forge an anti-U.S. grouping within the United Nations or other global international institutions. Moreover, there were very few countries that joined the international Bolivarian project. The effectiveness of Chavismo's *positive influence* was not big. But in terms of its *negative influence*, namely shattering the consensus in favor of democratization that had emerged in Latin America at the turn of the century, Chávez did achieve his goal.

The *McChavismo Pack*

This is what the authors of *Dragon in the Tropics* refer to. "Despite these big differences," Javier Corrales and Michael Penfold write, referring to Chavismo's meager success in terms of forming an international coalition, the "rewards as pertains to secondary objectives were impressive." Although Venezuela's anti-U.S. foreign policy was unable to put together a broad and cohesive front against Washington in Latin America or within the broader South-South movement, the stance did strengthen left-wing movements within the country and internationally, which politically benefited Chávez. On the one hand, as these two experts point out, it contributed to sustain the radical national movements, which could have become disillusioned as the revolution's luster gradually faded. On the other hand, it impressed the external radicals, safeguarding "an international sector willing to overlook Chávez's excesses and the mistakes of his government," while it urged most governments in the region to "employ friendly relations with Venezuela as a way of appeasing domestic radical groups."

In addition to the anti-U.S. attitude, which the authors describe as *soft-balance*, as the confrontation was not extreme, there was the second dimension of chavista foreign policy—the oil assistance. Corrales and Penfold call it *social-power diplomacy*, and point out that it produced political benefits. "It allowed Chávez to win over opinion makers who would otherwise have been aghast at Chávez's domestic and international setbacks."

Without an abundant production of oil at a high price, Chávez would not have been able to stand out within the hemisphere. He would also have failed in this regard without Cuba's advisory role. Cuba did not only assist in shaping the chavista oil diplomacy. It also came up with the measures that turned Venezuela into an attractive model for its neighbors' leaders. Havana was responsible for developing the Bolivarian missions that provided social assistance as well as the wily logistics and IT systems that allowed the chavista regime to control the electoral process. Chávez gradually became entirely dependent on Cuba as he tasted the effectiveness of an elixir that enabled him to remain in power permanently.

Having ascertained the formula's success, Chávez focused on spreading it to the rest of the hemisphere. The Venezuelan president was offering a packaged product. He taught other leaders how to do away with a country's democratic checks and balances, curtail the independence of supreme courts and electoral authorities, suppress freedom of the media—especially that of television channels—, and extend presidential powers formally or informally while harassing the opposition. The formula for extending presidential powers featured constitutional reforms that sanctioned re-election to consecutive and even indefinite presidential terms, an alien notion for Latin America. Defined as the most hyper presidential country in the region, Venezuela was a template for a hybrid system or a competitive authoritarian one.

At a time when the number of true democracies in the world was diminishing, after a boom in the 1990s, Chávez was a model for those who, within the same cultural context, sought to remain in power in defiance of the legislation that had attempted to rid Latin America of authoritarian leaders.

The *McChavismo combo* also included three truly delicious ingredients. The first was the display of popular legitimacy—control of the electoral process. "Chávez's government is able to claim more legitimacy than many authoritarian regimes due to its success at the ballot box, even if the latter owed a lot to ingenious fraud," William J. Dobson wrote in *The Dictator's Learning Curve* (2012), a book that ranks Venezuela on a par with China and Russia in terms of democratic deficiency. The combo's second appetizing ingredient was the guarantee of social legitimacy, as Chavismo had managed to be judged positively at the international level in some quarters due to its assistance programs for the lower classes. The third ingredient, which was especially tasty, was that the combo included financing through the supply of oil on very favorable terms. This benefited the finances of associated countries and made it easier for allied political parties and their leaders to rely on unexpected funding.

McChávez came as well with undeclared additives, such as collaboration—or turning a blind eye to—to drug trafficking, narcoterrorism, and money laundering in the region. "Venezuela exported a particular kind of corruption," concludes the book *Dragon in the Tropics*.

A country's ties to Venezuela depended on how many ingredients from the combo it chose. There were many levels and types of political support provided to Venezuela by countries in the region. They ranged from a tacit acceptance of Venezuela's higher profile in the Caribbean to a complete alignment with Caracas' strategy. Thus there were countries that simply express some sympathy towards Venezuela due to the benefit of long-term contracts that postponed for many years payments for oil purchases (it was the case of the Bahamas). Other countries received assistance from Venezuela and in exchange closed ranks and defended certain Venezuelan policies in some international institutions such as the OAS (the Dominican Republic, for instance). The highest degree of commitment with the Bolivarian strategy was displayed by countries that subscribed to a premium form of consultancy, such as the ones belonging to ALBA (Bolivia was one of them).

Founding of ALBA and Petrocaribe

Hugo sold the product, but Fidel was the manufacturer. The Venezuelan government itself admitted as much. The sponsorship provided by Castro and Cuba was highlighted in a PowerPoint presentation by the Ministry of Oil and Mining in June 2012. Hugo Chávez's first participation at a Summit of the Americas as president of Venezuela was in its third edition, which was held in Canada in 2001. At the conference, Chávez underscored his opposition to the proposed Free Trade Area of the Americas (FTAA) because of its exclusion of Cuba and its alleged alignment with the United States' interests and the ones of transnational capital. "A short time later, the presidents of Cuba and Venezuela joined forces to lay the groundwork for today's ALBA," the PowerPoint presentation indicated. The design was completed by the end of 2001 and ALBA (Bolivarian Alliance for the Peoples of Our America) came into being in 2004 with a joint declaration by Castro and Chávez signed in Habana. It was ALBA's first summit. The following two editions, in 2005 and 2006, also took place in the Cuban capital. Cuba and Venezuela were the only participants in the second edition, and Bolivia joined the founding members in the third one.

The initiative, that was founded with the intention of building a broad front, had little success in terms of attracting members. Nicaragua joined in 2007; the island of Dominica did so in 2008; Ecuador and two tiny countries—Saint Vincent and the Grenadines and Antigua and Barbuda—became members in 2009. Excluding the small island states of the Caribbean, Venezuela and Cuba were only able to lure Bolivia, Ecuador, and Nicaragua into joining ALBA. The three countries' respective presidents—Evo Morales, Rafael Correa, and Daniel Ortega—had established left-wing records. Ollanta Humala's Peru toyed with membership of ALBA, but soon distanced itself. Honduras actually joined after President Manuel Zelaya's sharp swing to the left, but after his overthrow the country withdrew from the organization in January 2010. The idea for ALBA was spawned by a desire to have a partisan political tool and a strategic political league that adopted the name Bolivarian Alternative for Latin America and the Caribbean. In order to coax more countries into joining, it soon dropped the term "alternative," which had a confrontational overtone, and replaced it with "alliance." It also underscored its trade dimension and officially changed its name to Bolivarian Alliance for the Peoples of Our America-Peoples' Trade Treaty (ALBA-TCP).

Since ALBA had an excessively ideological nature, Castro and Chávez immediately designed a more broad-based and economically appealing initiative, Petrocaribe, which did not require membership in ALBA. While the latter association was able to attract only eight members, Petrocaribe was founded in 2005 with fourteen participants, and later reached eighteen: six countries from ALBA (minus Bolivia and Ecuador, which are not Caribbean), in addition to the Bahamas, Belize, Grenada, Guyana, Haiti, Honduras, Jamaica, the Dominican Republic, San Cristobal and Nieves, Saint Lucia, Suriname, and El Salvador. The latter country became a full-fledged member in 2014; Guatemala had left a year earlier.

Through its subsidiary PDV Caribe, the Venezuelan oil giant PDVSA set aside in 2012 for the aforementioned countries a quota of

130,000 daily barrels of oil and derivatives. This amount had increased in the prior years after construction of refineries and storage and distribution infrastructure at several locations in the region. There were an additional 100,000 barrels shipped to Cuba whose financing terms were even more concessional. The countries for which a higher quota was earmarked were the Dominican Republic (thirty thousand daily barrels), Nicaragua (twenty-seven thousand) and Jamaica (twenty-three thousand), although the actual deliveries did not reach the targets.

PDV Caribe had set up fourteen joint ventures in eleven countries for its operations, in most of which it owned more than 50 percent of the capital. The payment terms were very concessional. Forty percent of the total had to be paid after ninety days, and the remaining 60 percent in twenty-three years (with an additional two-year grace period) and an annual interest rate of 1 percent. Both the initial and long-term payments could be carried out in cash or by providing services, selling products or financing infrastructure projects. The financing terms could vary depending on the dollar's value.

Since the launch of Petrocaribe in 2005 until the middle of 2012, PDVSA delivered approximately 200 million barrels, according to the company's accounts. During this time period, as a payment in goods worth $1 billion, Venezuela had received 19,397 trousers, 34,522 steers, 10,129 heifers, 13,557 tons of pasta, 62,532 tons of UHT milk, 765,660 quintals of coffee and 30,443 tons of beans, among other merchandise, which also included olive oil, rice, and sugar. If Venezuela obtained through imports so many goods that it could produce nationally, why should it continue to grow or manufacture them at home?

Neocolonialism at Venezuela's Own Request

One of the main arguments against colonialism, or what was later denounced as imperialism, is that rich countries took poor countries' raw materials and sold manufactured products to them. Developing countries even were made to buy certain basic goods from rich countries, thereby slowing down the development of a local manufacturing base. This is very similar to what happened to Venezuela, with the key difference that in the case of the Bolivarian republic the wound was self-inflicted. "It is paradoxical that the policies espoused by Chávez's socialist revolution wound up becoming a source of profits for the capitalist systems he condemned," *The Wall Street Journal* judged at the time of Chávez's death. "During his fourteen years in power, he nationalized big agricultural estates, redistributed land, and instituted price controls on food products as part of his strategy." But these policies actually turned Venezuela from a net exporter to a net importer of several products, among them rice, some of it purchased from Arkansas and other U.S. states.

When Chávez was first elected president in 1998, Venezuela's non-oil exports were worth $5.2 billion; fourteen years later, in 2012, the amount had been cut in half to $2.5 billion. Imports, on the other hand, skyrocketed, rising from $14.2 billion to $47.3 billion, as Venezuela's National Statistics Agency indicated. Venezuela's imports ballooned in 2006 after the launch of ALBA and Petrocaribe. Taking Nicaragua as an example, Venezuela went from practically not purchasing anything from it to importing increasing amounts of goods, which reached a value of $415 million in 2012. Statistics underscored Venezuela's increasing dependence on foreign products, in stark contrast to its stated objective of attaining an endogenous or self-sufficient development model.

Of special symbolism, given Chávez's ideological construct, was Venezuela's trade balance with the United States. In 2012, non-oil exports to the United States had dropped by half compared to 1998, while imports had doubled. When Chávez came to power, Venezuela imported five times more goods from the United States than it exported. By the time of the Bolivarian leader's death, the ratio had spiked to twenty to one.

The deterioration of Venezuela's economy was caused in large part by the policies of nationalization, expropriation, forced creation of cooperatives, and exchange-rate and price controls. Chavismo's foreign policy also brought about economic decline. As opposed to countries that seek to augment their weight on the world scene by placing more of their goods in foreign markets, thereby developing a national industry and fostering technological process, Chávez sought to raise his regional power by doing the opposite: he promoted other countries' exports to Venezuela and sacrificed his country's, thereby inflicting great damage on the republic's economy. In order to increase his personal standing in Latin America, Chávez gave out oil through Petrocaribe and allowed his clients to pay for the bill by selling products to Venezuela. This barter frittered away PDVSA and harmed Venezuelan productive sectors, which had to cope with the inflow of foreign goods which were not necessarily of a better quality and which could have been manufactured nationally.

Punishing the national private sector was one of Chavismo's tactical aims because most of the traditional business class backed the opposition. Chávez preferred to import food products from Colombia and that other countries supplied other merchandise than to allow Venezuelan businessmen to thrive and potentially undermine his political situation. The supply shortcomings stemming from the plunge in national production also turned into a political tool for the government as it could determine which shops in which neighborhoods were stocked with products. Rationing also allowed Nicolás Maduro to install fingerprint scanners in grocery stores, which paved the way for a greater control over consumers.

In order to be able to ship crude and its derivatives to its partners in Petrocaribe, PDVSA had to cut its export quota for the United States, which was the only country that paid the entire bill in cash immediately for supplies. Stepping up deliveries to Caribbean countries entailed not only a change in client, but also fetched a lower price. Allowing Petrocaribe members to pay off more than half of the bill over more than twenty-five years at an interest of only 1 percent was akin to giving the oil away for free. When Venezuela began to face acute budget problems and its citizens had to get used to long lines and a dearth of supplies in stores, the government still continued to generously bankroll the region in order to win over peoples' hearts and minds.

Chávez justified such generosity towards his allies in sharing an asset that belonged to all Venezuelans by asserting that it was a contribution to reducing poverty in other countries of the region. "In actual fact, Venezuela's social empowerment diplomacy had very little to do with social development. Foreign governments and politicians that were the beneficiaries of the Venezuelan help were free to use the funds as they saw fit," according to the authors of *Dragon in the Tropics*. "Hence, from their standpoint, Venezuela's aid successfully competed with the traditional alternative of securing financing from international institutions. The latter funding comes with conditionality and audits. The Venezuelan assistance, on the other hand, came with no strings attached and amounted to a blank check for any type of domestic spending. Moreover, the funds did not always benefit the poor."

Fondness for Cristina

Hugo Chávez had a special soft spot for Cristina Fernández de Kirchner, a kindred spirit in many regards and whose maternal demeanor spawned a special chemistry and trust between the two leaders. The Argentinian president at times played the role of a substitute mother to Chávez's daughters, especially the second, María Gabriela. Kirchner lodged with them in La Casona, the official residence of the president's family, when she traveled to Caracas and feasted them when they vacationed in Argentina.

The relationship was forged during Néstor Kirchner's presidency. Cristina Fernández's husband presided over the country between 2003 and 2007, precisely when Chávez was implementing Bolivarianismo. At a time when ties to Iran were a priority for the Venezuelan president, nuclear matters were discussed between the three countries. Chávez intervened so that Argentina and Iran could cooperate in the realm of nuclear energy, thereby overcoming the break in bilateral contacts that followed the 1992 and 1994 bombings in Buenos Aires against Jewish institutions, attacks whose inspiration was attributed to Tehran.

When Ahmadinejad made an official visit to Caracas in 2007, the Iranian president and the Venezuelan one discussed the matters. Due to the limitations imposed by the International Atomic Energy Agency, Iran was seeking secret assistance in order to modernize installations built before the 1979 revolution by Siemens using the same technology as it did for reactors in Argentina and which had been subsequently modernized by a Korean company. Chávez knew that Néstor Kirchner was interested in taking advantage of possible Iranian progress, as at the end of 2006 the Argentinian president had again taken up the processing of uranium. Chávez was also aware of Argentina's financial straits, and therefore was eager for Iranian financing. He accordingly offered to play a mediating role between Tehran and Buenos Aires.

Chávez and Ahmadinejad quickly got down to business and agreed that a discrete visit by Iranian scientists to Argentina would ensue. In order not to raise suspicions, the team would travel to Argentina via Venezuela. At the end of the conversation, as a witness recounts, Chávez gripped the translator's arm and said: "Of everything we discussed, tell him that the most urgent item is the support to our friends. We must facilitate everything for Argentina." This secret rapprochement between Iran and Argentina could be the explanation for what in 2015, at the time of his suspicious death, Argentinian prosecutor Alberto Nisman exposed: a pact between Cristina Fernández and Iran to nullify the accusations against former Iranian officials regarding the savage terrorist attacks carried out in Buenos Aires in the early 1990s.

Iran's payments to Argentina would have been conducted through contracts of Iranian companies with PDVSA, several of which where in the housing construction sector. When the president of PDVSA once took up the matter of overpricing with the Venezuelan president, Chávez supposedly answered: "Pay the amount, this is money the Iranians will give to Argentina."

The strong alliance with Kirchner implicated Chavismo in one of the most outrageous financing scandals in South America. In August 2007, a few days before Chávez arrived on an official visit to Buenos

THE *McCHAVEZ COMBO*, TROPICAL DIET

Aires, the Venezuelan businessman Guido Antonioni Wilson was arrested in the Argentinian capital after landing on a private plane and carrying a briefcase with almost $800,000. Antonioni revealed that the money was meant to finance Cristina Fernández's electoral campaign. Although he did not disclose the funds' origin, all indications pointed to PDVSA—or maybe a payment of Iran through the Venezuelan oil company. This is what the investigation conducted by the FBI in Miami with Antonioni's collaboration concluded. As the Argentinian journalist Hugo Alconada detailed in his book *Los secretos de la valija* (2009) [The secrets of the briefcase], there was a coordinated effort by Chávez, PDVSA President Rafael Ramírez, and the leadership of the Venezuelan intelligence services to obstruct the investigations, but they were to no avail.

The briefcase was not the only monetary gift for the Kirchners. Chávez arranged in 2007 for the cancellation of Argentina's foreign debt of $1.8 billion. "I am very pleased that Venezuela helped Argentina to free itself from the International Monetary Fund," he declared at the time. By then the government of Venezuela had $6 billion in Argentinian bonds. Previously, in 2006, Caracas and Buenos Aires had teamed up to design the so-called Southern Bonds, which blended issuance of sovereign debt from both countries. This formula allowed for a slight improvement in Argentina's financing conditions, but increased the interest rate that Venezuela had to pay in international financial markets.

The strategic collaboration between Chávez and Fernández de Kirchner enabled the launch of regional economic fora that excluded the United States. From both extremes of South America, they linked up to spawn a consensus in the continent, with the contribution of the ALBA partners and the active participation of Brazil. The Union of South American Nations (UNASUR) was thus launched in 2008, and the Community of Latin American and Caribbean States (CELAC) was founded in 2010. The latter institution came into being as an alternative to the historical Organization of American States (OAS), headquartered in Washington since its creation in 1948: its members were the same, with the exclusion of the United States and Canada

337

and the inclusion of Cuba. CELAC was precisely the means that allowed Cuba to fully join the continental discussions, given its exclusion from the OAS because of its lack of respect for human rights at the behest of the United States. The OAS did not fade, but CELAC got off to a fast start. The 2013 summit was held in Havana, and many Latin American heads of state had their picture taken individually with Fidel Castro—a big triumph for the unrepentant ageing dictator.

Brazil was an important pillar in this institutional framework. It was probably the country that gained the most relative weight in the continent with the exclusion of the United States, as it became the big economic partner at the gatherings of the aforementioned institutions. This big brother role played by Brazil, however, did not prompt it to guide Chavismo towards a greater respect of democratic standards, as the Venezuelan opposition criticized. President Dilma Rousseff, for example, failed in her attempts to inject some sanity into the grotesque handling by Caracas and Havana of Chávez's health, and later barely had any moderating influence during the tough crackdown on the street protests that took place in Venezuela in 2014.

In Brazil's case, which did not need Venezuela's oil, complicity had been purchased with contracts for Odebrecht, a multinational that builds infrastructure and which former President Luiz Inácio Lula da Silva marketed around the world. Venezuela became Odebrecht's main client outside of Brazil, with projects that in 2010 amounted to 21 percent of the company's overall turnover, and 38 percent if its operations from Brazil itself were excluded.

Other maneuvers by Chávez to scuttle the Washington Consensus faced more headwinds. His announcement in 2007 that Venezuela was withdrawing from the International Monetary Fund (IMF) and the World Bank Group, both headquartered in Washington, did not prompt other allies to follow suit. This meant that Venezuela did not withdraw completely from either institution, although Chávez blocked any supervision by IMF staff. In fact, since 2004 the Venezuelan leader did not allow the IMF and World Bank staff that regularly visit member countries to meet with government and central bank officials, business leaders, labor unions, and civil society organizations and exchange information on the country's economic and financial situation (so-called Article IV consultations which are conducted annually with each IMF member state) in order to disguise the true state of the Bolivarian republic's finances and thus be in a position to deny foreign estimates. Chávez inopportunely called for a boycott of the IMF precisely at a time when the institution took on a leading role in coordinating and assisting governments in their efforts to pull the world economy out of the Great Recession.

The creation of the Bank of the South (BancoSur) in 2009, launched originally by Argentina and made up mostly of the members of Mercosur and ALBA, did not bring about the consolidation of an alternative to the IMF, the World Bank, or the Inter-American Development Bank (IDB), the regional development bank also headquartered in Washington. The Unified System for Regional Compensation (SUCRE), created in 2008 as ALBA's payments system and currency, and which sought to replace the U.S. dollar in interregional trade, also made little progress.

"Brother, Check with Nicolás"

Nicolás Maduro rose up the ranks of Chavismo's foreign-policy apparatus at the behest of Hugo Chávez himself. Named minister of Foreign Affairs in 2006, Maduro was entrusted with tightening Venezuela's bonds with the members of ALBA and Petrocaribe. In addition to his public activities, he undertook purposely secret demarches. As Foreign minister, he oversaw the issuance of visas that alleged members of Hezbollah obtained at the Venezuelan consulate in Beirut. He also met with Hezbollah's leader in Damascus to discuss its involvement in drug trafficking and was the contact person for other actors implicated in continental narco-trafficking.

A case in point is the Farabundo Martí National Liberation Front (FMLN), the former guerrilla movement turned into El Salvador's governing party. Whenever it needed any assistance from Venezuela as part of the *McChávez* combo, it directed its requests to Maduro. There is also evidence that there were specific requests from other parts of Latin America. El Salvador case is especially revealing because documents provided by a confidant who worked in the Venezuelan government brought to light Maduro's links to drug trafficking in the region.

A dispatch of March 2011 indicated that Maduro personally mediated so that the FMLN could improve its access to drug trafficking networks. "Brother!! This is a request so that you lend us a hand with the overflight permit. Commander Ramiro ask that you check with Nicolás regarding the visit to Apure. Greetings." This text discloses the measures coordinated between the office of Maduro, who was the Foreign Affairs minister at the time, and that of José Luis Merino, the FMLN's strongman, whose alias during his guerrilla days was commander Ramiro.

This very meaningful communication was sent by Erick Vega, Merino's right-hand man, to Gustavo Vizcaíno, who at the time worked with Maduro at the Foreign Affairs Ministry and then moved with his boss's election as president to Miraflores. This dispatch was meant to facilitate the trip by a drug chieftain to the Venezuelan state of Apure, which borders Colombia. There was also information regarding the jet and the passenger, Roberto Adamo, whom the FBI believed was a member of the Calabrian mafia involved in narcotrafficking. The reports sent by Vega included Adamo's passport and that of the pilot, a U.S. citizen of Iranian descent, as well as the technical information of the twin-engine executive aircraft, registered as N769M. Merino had been linked to narco-trafficking in the past because of his close ties to the Colombian guerrillas. "There is enough evidence to prove Merino was in close contact with the FARC," according to Michael Braun, an expert in the war on drugs given his prior service for the U.S. Drug Enforcement Administration. Braun recalls that Merino's name appeared in the documents found in Raúl Reyes's camp. Reyes was a leader taken out by the Colombian armed forces. In addition to a terrorist group, the   were considered the "world's biggest producer and distributor of drugs."

The messages sent by Maduro's and Merino's respective assistants, in the 2010-2012 period, highlighted the FMLN's close coordination with Chavismo. Such messages also specified the details of trips by Merino to Caracas as well as several areas of cooperation between the two governments. Although Merino was not a member of El Salvador's government, the messages reveal that the former guerrilla leader was the FMLN's strongman. Moreover, Merino was in charge of overseeing the oil assistance from Venezuela which was delivered through the company Alba Petróleos de El Salvador, where he was listed as an advisor to the board of directors. The Venezuelan oil was a major source of financing and political leverage for the FMLN.

The FMLN's leaders paid for a large part of the oil with goods, basically coffee, which was sold to Venezuela at a price that slightly exceeded its market listing, thereby laying the groundwork for possible undercover operations. The accounts of Alba Petróleos de El Salvador were very murky. The company refused to publish its earnings report, despite managing public money invested by the municipalities run by the FMLN. They managed funds which could not be legally earmarked to establish companies. The arrangement especially benefited the FMLN mayors, who could sell subsidized gasoline in their towns and thus increase their popularity.

Shortages and Lines, a Model Which Has Lost Its Appeal

The chavista leadership's main reason for extending its influence to El Salvador as well as Honduras stemmed from their location as vertebrae on the Central American spinal chord, through which the drug traffic flows to the United States. There was a time when the drugs' journey northwards turned Panama into the first chain link, with the later complicity of the Sandinista Nicaragua, which in the middle of the 1980s harbored Pablo Escobar, making an operational base available to the Medellin cartel. Escobar was given safe haven by Panama and Nicaragua, and used their territory to develop links to Cuba. The powerful narco-trafficker's stay in Nicaragua was never admitted by the Sandinista Front for National Liberation (FSLN), but it was corroborated in 2010 by disclosures made to the media, among them by the drug lord's own son—who lived with him in Nicaragua—and his right-hand man, alias Popeye. By the 1980s the United States was aware of the situation due to the work of undercover DEA agents. To pre-empt an accusation that would tarnish the Cuban regime's masquerade, Fidel Castro ordered the trial and death sentence of General Arnaldo Ochoa in July 1989. Castro turned Ochoa into the nomenklatura's scapegoat. At the end of 1989, U.S. troops invaded Panama and took its dictator, Manuel Antonio Noriega, into U.S. custody. Sandinista leaders at the time crossed their fingers and committed themselves to not dabble so openly in drug trafficking again.

This prompted a realignment of the Colombian drugs' routes, which eventually were allowed to use Venezuela as their main distribution platform and turned Honduras into an intermediary base in Central America that could reach Mexico and eventually the United States. The involvement of Honduras in this business occurred especially during the presidency of Manuel Zelaya (2006-2009). It was part of the *McChávez* combo. Midway through his term, against the wishes of part of his party, Zelaya veered to the left and decided that his country should join Petrocaribe and ALBA.

Ecuador and Bolivia had in Rafael Correa and Evo Morales, respectively, quick apprentices of Hugo Chávez's strategies. Correa was especially bent on controlling the judiciary and silencing any who used the media to criticize his policies; Morales went on a nationalization spree, taking over companies in the energy and mineral sector; both presidents sought to assert control over the national electoral body. In addition, they soon partook in the murky transactions with Iran spearheaded by Chávez. They also ramped up their trade with Venezuela, although such transactions were easy pickings for phantom companies. Ezequiel Vázquez-Ger, from the Center for Investigative Journalism in the Americas (CIJA), underscores this development. He has collected evidence on several operations, especially in Ecuador. "There are Venezuelans who register companies in Ecuador who send fake exports to Venezuela, and even used empty containers. These companies launder money and benefit from the financial engineering derived from the successive exchanges between sucres, the ALBA currency, and dollars."

After their first successful runs for the presidency—Morales in 2006 and Correa in 2007—both leaders promoted referendums to reform the Constitution, as Chávez had already done. In Honduras, Zelaya attempted to pull off the same operation. The Supreme Court ruled that a lower court's decision to block the poll was legal. The parliament, the electoral body, the attorney general, and the ombudsman all agreed with the Supreme Court's ruling. But Zelaya did not flinch and proceeded with his planned referendum. On the day when the plebiscite was supposed to take place in 2009, he was deposed by the Honduran parliament. Caracas waged an international campaign to reinstate Zelaya and then provided consulting and advisory services in 2013 for the presidential electoral campaign of Zelaya's wife, Xiomara Castro de Zelaya. But the international perception of Chavismo had begun to shift.

Zelaya's wife came up short in her presidential bid in November 2013, and the Farabundo Martí National Liberation Front, which at first had a big lead in the polls, barely managed to eke out a victory in El Salvador in March 2014. In November 2015 Mauricio Macri ended the Kirchner era by winning the Argentinian presidential elections, and in February 2016 Evo Morales lost a referendum he had called in order to allow him to again run for re-election. Internal factors obviously played a role in every country, but close ties to Chavismo were becoming an electoral liability. Venezuela was regularly in the news due to its lack of basic goods and widespread popular discontent. It was no longer a role model.

The Venezuelan economy's downward spiral, which featured a dramatic drop in reserves and shortage of currency to purchase imports, should have prompted the termination of the Petrocaribe program. Venezuela's oil and derivatives could then have been sold to whomever paid the bill fully and quickly. But given the mess in PDVSA's accounts, the quota of barrels was not one of its biggest headaches. The day when the plug on Petrocaribe would be pulled would come someday, but in the meantime Maduro maintained the shipment of tankers, although reduced in number, to continue to reap the rewards of this peculiar type of petro-diplomacy.

As street protests spread in the first months of 2014, their crackdown risked the government's international condemnation as a repressor and torturer. But Venezuela pulled off an impressive show of diplomatic force in the Organization of American States (OAS), where it resorted to its allies. Out of the OAS's total membership of thirty-four countries, twenty-two toed Caracas' line. Most of the Caribbean islands, beneficiaries of the chavista hand-outs, backed Venezuela. Eleven countries that were neither members of ALBA nor Petrocaribe voted against Caracas. The oil card also enabled Venezuela to obtain a non-permanent seat at the United Nations Security Council in October 2014. María Gabriela Chávez, the president's favorite daughter, was appointed as her country's "alternate ambassador" to the U.N. But Venezuela's impending economic collapse was curtailing its geopolitical clout, and when it did not exert enough pressure on its allies its policies were backed only by a handful of countries.

If Chávez Came Back to Life...

Chavismo could now only count on the support of the ALBA countries, and even Cuba was going rogue and negotiating with the United States. "The international expansion of Bolivarianismo has peaked and has started receding," Harold Trinkunas asserts. The expansion had been bankrolled by the constantly high price of the barrel of oil in the prior decade and, "historically, whenever the price of oil has risen, Venezuela has been more influential." Hence, neither the higher profile achieved by Chávez, who maximized playing the oil card, nor the logical reduction in Caracas's clout as oil prices plummeted was a new development.

"Chavismo's failure was its economic model," according to Douglas Farah, a researcher at the Washington-based think-tank Center for Strategic and International Studies. "What made Venezuela appealing was its social spending, but it was distributed according to electoral calculations, and it turned out to be unsustainably corrupt and partisan." Farah believes that Chavismo's last attempt to "meddle" in new countries such as El Salvador, "was no longer an expansion but a readjustment. As they await an improvement in the situation, many chavistas are looking to add to the markets where they launder money. The ideal countries are those where like-minded parties are in power, as they reckon there will be no investigations and their banks will be able to launder their money." This "readjustment" is also happening at a historical time for the FARC, who are preparing to implement the provisional peace agreement struck with the Colombian government. The FARC had begun to sell their narco-trafficking franchises to Mexican cartels and Colombian bands. "Hence the money moving around from one place to another in the region originated with the Colombian guerrillas and the Venezuelan chavistas, who are convinced that Maduro cannot remain in power for long."

Why did Chávez build an economic model with such feet of clay? "Chávez had a big ego and a strong desire to irk the United States; that is what did him in." Douglas Farah believes that the deceased Venezuelan president was unable to acknowledge that the economic model he imposed did not adapt to the real world. Its organization into economic and social communes and the gradual stifling of private enterprise wrecked the economy. Chávez was able to continue to pursue his ideological construct due to the abundant funds from PDVSA and the political wiliness engineered by the Cubans. But with the benefit of hindsight, after the economic ruin he inflicted on his country, if Chávez had had the opportunity to go back into office as president, he would have been more pragmatic, if only in order to ensure his survival.

This is what happened with Daniel Ortega. The Nicaraguan president was fully aware that his first term (1985-90) had been an economic failure, as well as a security challenge given the United States' support for the Contras. When Ortega was elected to a second presidential term in 2007, his Sandinista brand was less dogmatic. "He decided he would not take on the *gringos* nor on the big capital," as Farah explains. "He urged private companies to jointly negotiate and he set up an alliance with all of Nicaragua's big fortunes. This enabled him to avoid much opposition by the business community to the amendment of the Constitution he was pushing for in order to allow indefinite re-elections to the presidency." Ortega also gave the green light to some anti-drug cooperation with the United States. He accepted that the DEA monitored the Atlantic route, where most of the seizures occur, while he opened the door to drugs through Nicaragua's Pacific coast. For the drug trafficking, according to Farah, Ortega shunned the Mexican cartels and the maras, as these groups are very violent and complicate ties to the United States. He also eschewed payment in goods and opted for cash, thereby ensuring that only a small amount of drugs remained in the internal market and avoiding the violence it spawns.

Nicaragua's Ortega, as well as Evo Morales's Bolivia and Ecuador's Rafael Correa, who were opening up to foreign private companies—more than they did at the beginning—, liked to fancy themselves as a possible model to replace Chavismo within the Latin American left. To that effect, they emphasized their countries' good economic performance. But none of the three presidents had the capacity to generate the international alliances that Hugo Chávez's Venezuela developed.

The United States had also learned a lesson. If it wanted to restore its authority over the Caribbean, or at least avoid that someone would attract unwanted guests to the region, it had to take a page out of Venezuela's strategic book. Washington needed to help the countries in the Caribbean, especially the small islands, to ensure access to reliable supplies of energy. After years of inaction in the face of Chavismo's growing external influence, Washington began to design an international financial program to fund initiatives that would diversify the countries' sources of energy. The U.S. administration fostered alternative sustainable production of energy at the local level, one of whose aims was to reduce demand on oil. In January 2015, the Obama administration hosted the first Caribbean Energy Summit.

Its aim was straightforward: "Finish the dependency you have on one country's supplies," as the White House explained to the participants.

In May 2016, the Organization of American States activated its Democratic Charter for a possible suspension of Venezuela as punishment for its "serious disturbance of the democratic constitutional order." OAS Secretary General Luis Almagro, an Uruguayan politician from the left, denounced in his report Venezuelan government's "abuses and arbitrariness" and accused Maduro of violating the separation of powers, imposing unjustified states of emergency, controlling the judicial and electoral powers, and harassing opponents—facts that amounted to a situation of "illegitimacy." Nobody from the OAS's leadership had ever spoken so critically about Chavismo.

The Bolivarian tide was receding in the region. The steep drop in the price of oil and minerals, so important for many Latin American economies, curtailed the ability of populist leaders to maintain the allegiance of key voting groups by funding certain programs and presaged a move towards greater pragmatism. Chávez's foreign boomerang was starting to rebound.

ACKNOWLEDGEMENTS

A list of notes is not included at the end of the book. I have opted to point out the sources of information throughout the manuscript, even if this results in some repetition. This book is the result of three years of journalistic research and a substantial share of its content stems from personal sources. When we refer to accounts by persons to the media, we specifically mention their origin.

The first persons I wish to thank are those whose names are already printed on previous pages as authors of substantial contributions to certain chapters. A case in point is Harold Trinkunas, director of the Latin American Initiative at the Brookings Institution, and Douglas Farah, researcher at the Center for Strategic and International Studies, whose contributions appear in several chapters. I owe a debt of gratitude to the analyst Pedro Mario Burelli for, among other items, the information related to the ties between chavista Venezuela and the United States; to Antonio de la Cruz, executive director of Inter-American Trends, for a large part of the data relating to the oil business; and to Christopher Bello, CEO of Hethical (Ethical Hacking), for his experience as an auditor of the Venezuelan electoral system.

I also want to thank a long list of persons whose names do not appear in the book who very generously gave of their time and shared their expertise about Venezuela with me, as well as those who helped me to check information: Martín Rodil, Miguel Angel Mirabal, Leopoldo Martínez... I gratefully mention as well those who gave me good advice in the process of editing the text: Paul Coppola, Tom McDonough, Lawton King, Daniel Carr, Joseph Walker, and Jorge Rodríguez.

The English version omits a chapter from the original Spanish version which dealt with the relationship between Chávez and Spain. It detailed the close ties between Chavismo and Podemos, the left-wing populist party that burst onto the Spanish political scene in 2014. Perhaps it was too local for global audience. On the other hand, several chapters have been updated to include recent developments.

Made in the USA
Middletown, DE
18 June 2016